# THE PSYCHODYNAMICS
# OF LEADERSHIP

# The Psychodynamics of Leadership

*Edited by*

EDWARD B. KLEIN, Ph.D.
FAITH GABELNICK, Ph.D.
AND
PETER HERR, M.A.

PSYCHOSOCIAL PRESS
MADISON, CONNECTICUT

The following publisher has generously given permission to reprint on p. 161: Excerpt from "East Coker" in *Four Quartets,* copyright 1943 by T. S. Eliot and renewed 1971 by Esme Valerie Eliot, reprinted by permission of Harcourt Brace & Company.

**Library of Congress Cataloging-in-Publication Data**

The psychodynamics of leadership / edited by Edward B. Klein, Faith
   Gabelnick, and Peter Herr.
      p.      cm.
   Includes bibliographical references and index.
   ISBN 1-887841-13-X
   1. Leadership—Psychological aspects.   I. Klein, Edward B.
II. Gabelnick, F. G. (Faith G.) III. Herr, Peter.
BF637.L4P78 1998
158′.4—dc21                                                              97-17770
                                                                            CIP

Manufactured in the United States of America

*This book is dedicated to*
*Margaret Rioch and our children.*

# Contents

# Introduction

*Faith Gabelnick, Ph.D.*
*and Edward B. Klein, Ph.D.*

Everywhere in society the pace of change is accelerating. Even the currently popular word, *paradigm,* which implies a somewhat stable organizing principle, may soon be an obsolete reference to a time when we believed in model reliability. Today's organizational diagrams try to capture a process of almost continuous transformation, and perhaps the best we can do is to communicate a stance in relation to these complex transformations. In our text that stance is psychodynamic and developmental because we believe it provides the greatest opportunity for learning and work in these emerging technologies.

The chapters in this book are connected through a psychodynamic developmental perspective on organizational systems. The authors explicate the internal psychologies of self and system in relation to the so-called realities of organizations, and in so doing, offer specific cases or stories for reflection and application. The papers offer the reader an internal view of complex systems and also provide a tapestry of reflective analyses to expand our understanding of how systems work and how leaders take up their roles in them. While it is tempting to try to rationalize and systematize these chapters toward a coherent framework, their texture of complexity and open-endedness mirrors the challenges that we face in this new century.

Leaders in the twenty-first century will need to draw on their own histories and theories of organization. It is not now nor will it ever be sufficient to have moved up in the ranks of a system, because the systems themselves will become increasingly dispersed. Workers will be involved in projects or teams and may not be employed for a long time by one company. Many leaders will be temporary and temporal—hired for the skills they can deliver on a particular project. Company loyalty will become a quaint phrase, while time on task and productivity will be the guidelines for "success" and survival. Leaders will move away from the heroic, charismatic model and adapt a more collaborative and facilitative way of working. Yet, while the style of leadership is shifting toward involvement and connection, employment patterns are becoming more disconnected and depersonalized.

This climate of change and displacement is causing anxiety among today's workers, and we expect that this state will increase as predictability and stability of the work environment decreases. Leaders will thus need to lead from a more vulnerable yet learning-centered posture. Their own sense of who they are in relation to a specific task will enable them to survive, perform, and contain the regression that inevitably accompanies change and transformation.

Importantly, a psychodynamic, open systems approach to leadership supports risk and change. It may be that women and minority group members will bring a particular sensitivity to this stance because they have had to argue for and enact strategies that brought together their person and role. All leaders regardless of race, gender, class, or nationality will encounter an environment that demands openness, connection, insight, and psychological maturity.

A psychodynamic stance invites the reflection and anxiety that accompanies learning. This text may assist the readers in deepening their own visions of their work and its relatedness to person, task, and role, but it will not provide answers. The book is an invitation and an opportunity to join with others in a complex task of understanding the dynamics of leadership and change and to provide a new intellectual and psychological space for creativity and learning.

This work is intended for those in major organizational roles in private and public institutions: executives, managers, educators, and consultants and for students and teachers who will consult to those in leadership roles. It includes chapters by British, Australian, and American authors providing social systems analysis and personal experience that offer insights into the working of modern organizations. Through portrayals of challenging consultations, readers gain knowledge and understanding of psychodynamic aspects of current institutional life and its implications for visionary leadership in the twenty-first century.

To frame the chapters and engage the reader, the book is divided into two parts: theory and transformational leadership. In Part I, "Organizational Theory and Visions of Leadership," the theoretical stance used in the book is spelled out in seven chapters.

In chapter 1, Eric Miller, based on his consultations for the Tavistock Institute, suggests that during the past decade the flattening of organizations has resulted in marked distance between managers and workers. In the past, organizations encouraged dependence; leaders in today's era of change and chaos have the opportunity to promote psychological presence by fostering autonomy. David Berg next focuses on the devaluation of followership, a neglected area of study. He stresses the need for a collaborative relationship between leaders and followers that can release the vibrant follower in each of us.

In chapter 3, W. Gordon Lawrence of London uses psychoanalytic theory as a tool for cultural enquiry. He describes the unconscious pressures on leaders and the necessity of exploring meaning if we are to avoid destruction. James Krantz next notes the role of anxiety in the new order with its greater freedom, insecurity, and lack of control. He stresses the need for social defenses that help people to think and link creatively in the modern workplace.

In chapter 5 Larry Hirschhorn explores the mutual need for leaders and workers to become more partnerlike to utilize their vision so that the enterprise will succeed. Yvonne Agazarian and Berj Philibossian next illustrate a systems theory of leadership by using practical behavioral problem-solving examples to address complex issues in the workplace. In chapter 7 Marvin Skolnick details the personal and administrative costs involved in directing a community health facility for over two decades in a changing environment. He notes how we psychologically use those labeled mentally ill while ignoring deeper societal issues.

There will be a vast change in the way work is experienced in the future. Eighty-five percent of new employees between now and the year 2000 will be women and minority group members. In Part II, "Transformational Leaders: Vulnerability, Diversity, and Connection," issues of uncertainty, instability, and authentic relations within and between groups are addressed in six chapters.

Kathy Kram and Marion McCollom Hampton, in chapter 8, while discussing their own complex leadership roles, clearly use theory and experience to illustrate how the visibility of women in authority often leads to greater vulnerability. Susan Long, an Australian management consultant, next uses the Lacanian discourse to explore whether women in corporate leadership roles are the transformers or the transformed.

In chapter 10 Barbara Winderman and Margaret Sheely poignantly discuss some of the costs involved when women exercise authority in the legal profession and offer a paradigm that helps women to understand their workplace struggles. Edward Klein, Ellen Kossek, Joseph Astrachan, and Claudia Fleming next analyze how female managers' and executives' work lives are affected by women's minority group status and developmental stage.

In chapter 12 Vivian Gold describes self-authorization dilemmas that women experience as group leaders in America and Israel. Faith Gabelnick next connects "new" leadership modes with our mythic heritage. She suggests that leaders can retrieve powerful images or guides from within our world cultures to assist in dealing creatively with change and uncertainty.

Even with the aid of these richly illustrative examples, the question remains whether women and minority group members will have an advantage in this new environment. They will certainly become major players in this new era in the workplace. The second section, portraying the struggles of some of these groups to emerge and survive in traditional, heroic systems, points to a type of learning that acknowledges vulnerability and connection. Will those who have incorporated diverse life experiences bring a more durable character to the challenges of leadership in the 21st century? We cannot say. Perhaps the stories that we hear from a variety of cultures provide clues about new leadership paradigms. These pull us inward and draw us back toward essential relationships and beliefs where we authentically encounter the elemental modes of human interaction.

As the reader can see, this text offers an opportunity to engage with a variety of presentations about organizational life. The authors display a rare honesty as they uncover organizational and personal patterns that influence how people work together and how they construct their leaders and work systems. The paradox toward which this text moves is the proposition that leaders should be more connected and collaborative at the same time that work systems are becoming more diffuse and temporary. Psychodynamically we advocate a more internally complex, integrated leadership stance in the face of externally increasing chaos and instability. The ability of individuals to tolerate ambiguity and change will rely on the strength and flexibility of their psychological character. These papers provide a glimpse of how challenging that task will be.

# Contributors

**Yvonne M. Agazarian** is a Consulting Affiliate, Friends Hospital, Philadelphia, Pennsylvania.

**Joseph H. Astrachan** is Associate Professor of Management and Entrepreneurship, Kennesaw State College, Kennesaw, Georgia.

**David N. Berg** is Clinical Professor, Psychiatry Department, Yale University, New Haven, Connecticut.

**Claudia H. Fleming** is a graduate student, Psychology Department, University of Cincinnati, Cincinnati, Ohio.

**Faith Gabelnick** is President, Pacific University, Forest Grove, Oregon.

**Vivian Gold** is a psychotherapist at the Veterans Administration Hospital, University of California at Los Angeles.

**Marion McCollom Hampton** is Associate Professor, Organizational Behavior, School of Management, Boston University, Boston, Massachusetts.

**Peter Herr** is a graduate student, Psychology Department, University of Cincinnati, Cincinnati, Ohio.

**Larry Hirschhorn** is Principal, Center for Applied Research, Inc., Philadelphia, Pennsylvania.

**Edward B. Klein** is Professor of Psychology, University of Cincinnati, Cincinnati, Ohio.

**Ellen E. Kossek** is Associate Professor, School of Labor and Industrial Relations, Michigan State University, East Lansing, Michigan.

**Kathy E. Kram** is Associate Professor, Organizational Behavior, School of Management, Boston University, Boston, Massachusetts.

**James Krantz** is Principal, TRIAD Consulting Group, New York, New York.

**W. Gordon Lawrence** is Director, IMAGO East-West, London, England.

**Susan Long** is Associate Professor in Management and Director of Graduate Programs in Organisation Behaviour, Swinburne University, Melbourne, Australia.

**Eric J. Miller** is Consultant and Director, Group Relations Programme, Tavistock Institute of Human Relations, London, England.

**Berj Philibossian** is an M.B.A.

**Margaret D. Sheely** is a Family Therapist, Houston Family Institute, Baylor College of Medicine, and the University of Texas Health Science Center, Houston, Texas.

**Marvin R. Skolnick** is Professor, Training Program, Washington School of Psychiatry, Washington, DC.

**Barbara B. Winderman** is an Attorney at Law, Houston, Texas.

# Part I

## Organizational Theory and Visions of Leadership

# 1

# The Leader with the Vision

## Is Time Running Out?

*Eric J. Miller, Ph.D.*

I was working with the internal consultancy group of a major British company, with over 100,000 employees, which had just completed a substantial downsizing exercise, with the forecast of more to follow. We were trying to diagnose the "state of the organization." They described a widespread perception of a top management—and it was physically located on the top floor of the headquarters' offices—promulgating policies and decisions that people in the field saw as often irrelevant or misguided: "Up there they have no idea of what customers' real concerns are." The powerful image that emerged was of a Berlin Wall, topped with barbed wire, dividing "them" and "us," with middle management leaping back and forth, identifying first with the one

©The Tavistock Institute 1993: revised December 1996

3

side and then the other, but never bridging the two. (Given that image, I felt that bridging would have been a singularly uncomfortable experience!) It seemed to me that there was a collusion to maintain the Wall: it insulated top management from the pain of thousands of individuals whose jobs were lost or threatened; and it insulated most of the working population from the complex forces that those at the top were having to grapple with.

Now for a view from the deputy CEO of a major bank: He described the board of directors and senior management as moving the bank in a clear and appropriate direction, but the main operational system, which included the great majority of employees, seemed to have become disconnected and was proceeding on a trajectory of its own.

If we take the familiar formulation that leadership is the boundary function of a system, mediating between the internal world of the system and its external environment (Miller & Rice, 1967; Rice, 1965), one corollary is that the function is not necessarily monopolized by a single designated leader; it is likely to be distributed: a telephone operator, a receptionist, a salesperson, and a chief executive is each from their different positions representing the system to the outside world and reflecting pictures of the outside world back into the system. In both the illustrations above, the leadership at the top was plainly failing to reach and relate to much of the internal world of these enterprises, and in the second case the system had apparently produced—albeit implicitly—an alternative leadership.

The first part of this chapter explores the changing relation between leader and led. The first theme is the seemingly widespread phenomenon of the distancing of overall leadership, and of "the leader" in particular, from the employees of the enterprise: I float a hypothesis that may go some way toward explaining it. Second, there is an examination of signs of a change in the relatedness of the individual to the employing enterprise. This is followed by a discussion of changes in the configuration and boundaries of many systems: "inside" and "outside" are becoming blurred. The second part reviews some of the taken-for-granted assumptions that have to be questioned and probably abandoned, and suggests modes of thinking that have to replace them if new and effective models of leadership are to be created.

## WHERE ARE THE FOLLOWERS?

### The Changing Shape of the Pyramid

In the 1980s, one prominent theme in the management literature was the so-called flattening of the hierarchy. Two or sometimes more layers of supervision and middle management were to be removed. Some managers were shifted sideways from line to staff positions; many others lost their jobs. Except by the casualties themselves, this "delayering," as it was called, was widely seen as a positive shift. "Democratization of the workplace," which, particularly in western and northern Europe had been the flavor of the 1970s, had commonly been seen as obstructed by conservative middle managements and it had mostly foundered in the recession at the end of that decade. Now empowerment, its 1980s successor, looked as though it might be realized. The flattened pyramid seemed to promise much speedier, more direct, and more open two-way communication between the top and the bottom (Figure 1.1).

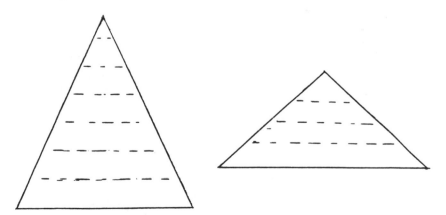

*Figure 1.1. From the steep pyramid to the flat pyramid*

By the end of the 1980s, however, we were seeing increasing evidence of a countervailing trend: the pyramid in many businesses was effectively becoming steeper. Fewer levels there might be, and the base smaller through intensive efforts to increase productivity; but the felt social distance between bottom and top was no less than it had been before, and in many cases the apex had reared higher than ever. It is no longer a pyramid but a steeply pitched pagoda, with a celestial tip which, as in our second case above, is in danger of becoming detached (Figure 1.2).

This is expressed in differentials of remuneration. Ten years ago in Britain, for example, the pay of the chief executive of a medium to large company might be 10 or 12 times the shop floor average. Now, with the increasing add-ons of stock options and performance bonuses, the differential extends to 20, 50, and even 100 times. This seems to be following the trend in the United States, where reported differentials are even higher. Moreover, wider use of 3-year rolling contracts provides generous insurance against the consequences of failing in the job. (As I write this, the newspapers report one failed CEO happily walking away with $4.5 million.) The wealthy tycoon, of course, is no new phenomenon; but this has usually been someone who has amassed the fortune by building up a business or acquiring a set of businesses

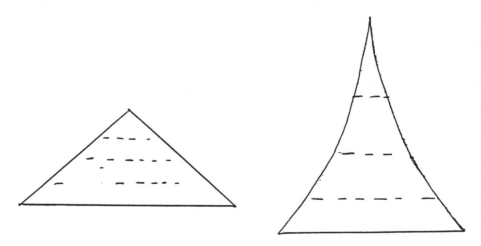

*Figure 1.2. The ideal of the flat pyramid; the reality of the pagoda*

and often putting other people in to run them. Some of these still exist, though several of them in Europe and the United States have crashed spectacularly in the last few years. The newer version is essentially a hired hand. He—this is almost an exclusively male role—has sometimes been promoted from within, though the highest remuneration goes to those who have been brought in at the top. Their photos appear regularly in the press, and not only on the financial pages. They are the leaders who rank along-side the tycoons.

The reality of the pointed pagoda is so obviously dissonant from the image of the flat hierarchy, with its rhetoric of empow-erment, that we need to understand how it has come about.

As we well know, the leader–follower relation is all too prone to become pathological. In Freud's terminology, the leader be-comes the "ego-ideal" and mobilizes in the followers primitive needs for security and certainty and "basic assumption" behavior of dependency or fight-flight (Bion, 1961). Their capacity for critical judgment—their ego functioning—is suspended. They surrender some of their own power and thereby inflate the power of the leader. Moreover, distance lends enchantment: the leader who offers a vision but is socially out of reach of the rank and file is more likely to acquire mythical status and have magical powers attributed to him (Katz & Kahn, 1978). At the same time, unconsciously, the dependency also generates rage. The success-ful leader diverts that rage from him or herself by offering an-other object for it. Thus Hitler needed first the Jews and then foreign enemies. War imagery is common in business: the leader mobilizes the troops to fight a competitor; casualties are to be expected. Applying such thinking to the pagoda model, one might postulate that anxiety about survival impinging on those at the base of the hierarchy during a period of deep recession has caused them to invest even greater power in the leader and elevate him still higher to protect them from "the enemy" and secure their salvation. That proposition would account for the distancing. However, it is quite inconsistent with the examples of disconnection in the middle between the workforce at the base and savior at the apex.

It may be therefore that we are looking for the leader–follower dynamic in the wrong place. Banks and institutional investors are nowadays the major stockholders in most large- and medium-sized businesses. Huge sums were borrowed in the 1980s for expansions that have failed to generate the expected return. Anxious the workforce may be; but so are the banks. It is these stakeholders who have the power to appoint the leader—power roughly proportional to the size of their stake and the risk to their loan. It is they who are looking for the savior with the vision. When the loan is in the billions, a remuneration in millions is relatively modest, and a sought-after candidate is in a strong bargaining position. Once the appointment is made, it is they who are the followers to be kept in a state of suspended disbelief; it is for them that the leader they have placed on the pinnacle has to offer hope.

This proposition could account for the tendency toward separation or cleavage within the enterprise: the leader is paying more attention to the followers outside than to the potential followers within. But there is a further twist. As we have seen, to maintain credibility with the followers—or, to put it more unkindly, to maintain their credulity—it is helpful if the leader can offer a common enemy. In many enterprises it is the employees—those who swallow up so much of the finances in wages and salaries—who have now themselves become the surrogate enemy. If they can be decimated, the enterprise will survive and the external stakeholders will be satisfied. Of course, the paradox is that mobilization of the internal followers would seem to be a necessary condition for survival, while at the same time their unconscious rage has become conscious and is less easily diverted away from the leader onto alternative objects. They are aware that the savings on the first hundred lost jobs simply go to pay for the salary of the new CEO. Small wonder that prospective CEOs are demanding the insurance policy of the 3-year rolling contract.

Meanwhile, certainly in Western Europe and probably elsewhere, there has been a shift in the relatedness of the individual to the employing enterprise.

## Psychological Withdrawal from "The Organization"

Organization is a process of assigning roles to activities and relating roles to each other for the performance of the task of an enterprise. Beyond this "task organization" it has long been recognized that a second form of organization is also required for the sentient system, which meets psychological needs for affiliation and identity. In some settings it is possible to combine both within a single sociotechnical system: the semiautonomous work group is the prototype. In more complex and changing situations the task and sentient needs have to be met through separate systems; thus a third form of organization is needed to relate them to each other (Miller & Rice, 1967). Use of the term *the organization* as a collective noun lumps these functions together. It is a woolly construct that may include the site, buildings, machinery, the technology, a source of employment, a set of social relations, a somewhat indefinable culture, and so on, upon which are deposited all sorts of projections, both by people working "in" "it" and also from outside (the quotation marks are intentional). Actors involved tend to take it for granted that the construct has a shared meaning and for subgroups this is largely true; but ultimately each individual's picture is unique.

What is important here is that "the organization" has been a very significant construct in the life-space of most people in employment. It has conferred identity and given meaning; it has often felt like a surrogate family; and its structures and culture have offered a vehicle for expressing quite primitive emotions and provided defenses against anxiety (Jaques, 1955; Menzies, 1960). That is hinted at by my quotation marks. As I have argued elsewhere, what the task of an enterprise requires from people is essentially their activities, their roles. It is the roles that belong inside the boundary of the enterprise, not the people who enact them.

> This implies that the appropriate perspective for examining the relationship between the enterprise and the individuals who supply roles within it—and, indeed, whose role-taking gives the enterprise its existence—is an intersystemic perspective: it is a relationship

between the enterprise as a system and individuals (or groupings
of individuals) as systems. (Miller, 1977, p. 38)

But because of what Goffman called the "encompassing tendencies" of institutions (Goffman, 1968, p. 15), the idea of the inter-
systemic relationship has been difficult to hold on to. The
prevailing assumption is that the person as well as the role is
inside, that it is a relationship between part and whole—as if the
individual were a subsystem of the enterprise as a suprasystem.

This is changing, certainly in Europe and probably much
more widely. The idea of "belonging to an organization," with
its connotations of proprietary ownership on the one side and
emotional involvement and commitment on the other, is becoming obsolescent.

Let me take Britain as an example. During the postwar period up to the mid-1970s there was a pervasive dependency culture. The state was a benign mother, unemployment was low,
unions were strong, and job security was high. This was widely
seen as a proper and permanent state of affairs; the reality that
Britain was becoming internationally less and less competitive was
largely ignored. Between 1974 and 1976 unemployment doubled
to just over 5%, which was regarded as immorally high. Between
1979 and 1983, under the first Thatcher government, a combination of recession with monetary policies intended to control
mounting inflation sent the official figure up to 13.5%, though
many economists put the true figure as nearer 18%. People felt
betrayed, both by the state and by employing institutions. Collapse of the dependency culture left them in a mode of what
some observers called "failed dependency" (Khaleelee & Miller,
1983, 1985; Miller, 1986, 1993c), characterized by psychological
retreat and withdrawal: flight into fantasy, withdrawal of psychological investment in institutions. Thatcher's identification of Ar-
gentina as the external enemy in 1982 provided only a brief
respite. For those still in employment, survival was the name of
the game; the strategies were risk-avoidance and compliance.
There was some envy of those who had made a successful transition to self-employment. Between 1985 and 1989 the economy
seemed to be on an upward trajectory again. As jobs became more

plentiful, the painful memories began to recede; some optimism reemerged. The lull was temporary; 1989 brought a new and deep recession which continued. The figures for unemployment escalated, and, as a result of delayering, downsizing, and the collapse of whole firms, now included a much higher proportion of managers and professionals than ever before. They are learning that employees at all levels are readily disposable. Psychological withdrawal from "the organization" is increasing. Behavior—of managers as well as on the shop floor—is more calculative. Compliance is a chosen, intentional response rather than a habit, and there is a good deal of overt cynicism (Miller & Stein, 1993). I recently heard the term *calculated sincerity*.

That is the British process; but the outcome is similar in many parts of the Western world. In a recent American survey of people in employment, 55% said most working people today show less loyalty to their employers than before; while 64% perceived employers as less loyal to their workers (*New York Times*, March 3, 1994, p. A14). Paid work is undoubtedly still for many people an important confirmation of worth and status; but the relationship has been becoming much less "part-whole" and more instrumental. Because "the organization" is no longer the reliable mother, it is ceasing to fulfill its function of providing social defense mechanisms. Though uncomfortable, this could be seen as a much more mature, healthy relationship than operating at a primitive level of dependency.

It is of interest here to quote from a Frenchman writing shortly after World War II:

> The day will come when the masses will understand that these chiefs who have risen pathologically from their midst are all, in spite of their prestige in another age, abnormal people, barbarians thrown up regressively in the course of the progressive development and liberation of society. (Hesnard, 1946, p. 92)

Quoting this passage, another French writer commented:

> I believe that these regressions are caused by the existence in one part of the population of a more or less repressed need for dependence and in another part the need for domination, which can

be satisfied only by identification with a leader. They show how recent and fragile, even among the civilized, are the liberation and reconstruction of the personality on experimental, democratic foundations. (Mannoni, 1955, p. 194)

The latter writer also postulated that "the only animals which can be truly tamed are those species whose young are for a time dependent. . . . The rest can only be trained. . . . Taming is simply the artificial prolongation of the childhood bonds of dependence . . ." (p. 205).

Psychological withdrawal implies that many employees have become untamed. For some, the leader and top management have become objects of rage, for others contemptible or disregarded; and whilst some pockets of the more basic dependency remain they are getting smaller. We have not reached the golden age of liberation predicted by Hesnard and Mannoni. Indeed, I have suggested elsewhere that the loss of credibility of established institutions and their leaders has left potentially dependent followerships seeking other, sometimes bizarre alternatives (Miller, 1993b). But in the meantime the leaders of business and other employing enterprises need to recognize that familiar assumptions about their followerships may no longer be valid.

## Boundary Changes

I referred earlier to the common parlance of "belonging to the organization," which has connotations of surrendering one's individuality and being owned. That is certainly becoming a less appropriate phrase. Moreover, to have a sense of belonging to a group or institution it is necessary to have a reasonably clear and agreed sense of the boundary between inside and outside. Notwithstanding the variation in meanings attached to an organization as a construct, until recently there has tended to be a reasonable consensus about the location of its membership boundary, marked by shared employment status. It might be that in a subsidiary company of a larger group the most senior managers were more identified with and actually on the payroll of the group, rather than of the subsidiary (which posed problems of its own), but such cases were unusual.

Over the last decade a number of factors have combined to make the boundaries much more fuzzy in many enterprises. One is the trend toward outsourcing: many jobs previously done by employees have been contracted out. For example, a company may decide that its internal printing department does not fit with its core activities and may then support the staff of the department in leaving and setting up their own business—for which the company then continues to be the main customer. Sometimes jobs such as office cleaning or computer programing continue to be done on the premises by the same people, but they are now self-employed contractors or work on behalf of an agency. In the wards of some British hospitals employed nurses are outnumbered by quasi-permanent agency nurses. In cases such as these the identification with the workplace—the boundary around "we"—becomes quite problematic. At the same time in many countries the ratio of part-time to full-time employees is steadily increasing. Part-time workers are much cheaper to employ and more easily disposable—and correspondingly likely to be less committed.

Another international trend is the blurring of the supplier–customer boundary. For example, suppliers tied to big supermarket chains find that they are subject not only to strict quality control but to firm advice, sometimes through imposed consultancy, on organizational and management arrangements. In the manufacturing sector, engineers from the supplier are drawn right inside the customer's design, development, and marketing functions. All this makes for more effective business processes, but, to take the manufacturing example, what organization do these engineers "belong" to?

This blurring of the boundary between inside and outside is problematic not only for the nurses or engineers but for the leaders of the two systems they are linked to, the suppliers and the hosts. Which leaders, if indeed any, are these professionals willing to follow?

## CHALLENGES FOR POSTMODERN LEADERSHIP

The obvious challenge, of course, is the rapidly changing environment in which enterprises operate. This has become such a familiar theme that it requires only token mention here. Chaos theory features in most management texts, and every manager knows, intellectually at least, that the interaction of environmental forces will generate unforeseeable futures over which the enterprise can have minimal control. However, two points arising from it are important to underline. First, it is the speed of change in the external environment that receives most of the attention; but, as the first part of this chapter has shown, the internal environment of the enterprise is shifting just as quickly and perhaps as unpredictably. Second, there is often a big gap between managers' intellectual understanding of chaos theory and their grasp of its implications.

I was hesitant about using the term *postmodern* in the heading above, because what began as a critique of contemporary assumptions has become postmodern*ism*, a movement whose adherents have developed an increasingly esoteric language of their own, which more ordinary mortals find difficult to penetrate. I am using the term in a simpler sense. Current—modern—theories-in-use in the field of management and organization are becoming demonstrably unserviceable. Conventional wisdom has to be questioned and possibly turned on its head if we are to develop paradigms appropriate to the next decade. We cannot know what the world will be like 10 years from now, but perhaps we can develop a mind-set that will help us to engage with it. A good way to start is by examining what is happening today against what we would like to believe is happening. I am looking at this under two related headings: leadership and motivation, and leadership and change.

### Leadership and Motivation

We may start by considering managerial responses to the phenomenon of psychological withdrawal. One response is to deny its existence. In the company referred to at the beginning of this chapter a senior personnel manager talked to me about the effects of downsizing on employees, including managers at her level who still remained. She described them as anxious about their own futures, with many just waiting for the age—in that company, 45—when they could leave with a minimally reasonable payoff. But "they," she said, meaning top management, assumed that motivation was unaffected.

Other companies have treated it as a problem of commitment. There has been a surge of so-called training programs, which would be more accurately described as attempts at reindoctrination. A "winners' program" is designed to make people feel valued members of the organization. A follow-up of one such event revealed that it had actually increased the disenchantment of employees, who saw it as "fraudulent" and "two-faced"—an attempt to "brainwash" them into becoming "company persons." Other devices—company videos, mission statements, total quality movements—also not only fail to reverse psychological withdrawal but often reinforce it. "Indeed, those companies that try hardest to eliminate negative or ambivalent feelings may instead stimulate the most resentment, mistrust and suspicion" (Miller & Stein, 1993, p. 36). To attempt to mobilize "employee loyalty" to a company and management which have been profoundly disloyal to hundreds of employees by declaring them redundant is rightly perceived as laughable.

These two types of responses to psychological withdrawal—denial and attempts to indoctrinate—express two different mental models of the employees held by managers. In the first they are interchangeable mechanisms—programed robots that can be switched on and off—without feelings. In the second they are infants, who will believe what their parents tell them. (These may be versions of Mannoni's training and taming respectively.) The one is a noncaring leadership, indeed, nonleadership; the other is a leadership that assumes that it can be the ego-ideal, a kind of magnet for human iron-filings.

Many managements are understandably concerned about psychological withdrawal from the organization. Because of the combination of technological advances and enhanced productivity a growing proportion of the jobs that remain are more complex and more demanding and have a more direct effect on business performance. What they require is even greater "psychological presence" (Kahn, 1992): being wholly there, giving total attention, putting all of oneself into the role. But for that requirement, it might be tenable to accept as the reality the instrumental relationship of the employee and act accordingly: monitor performance closely, pay well for a job well done, attend to Herzberg's "hygiene factors" (Herzberg, Mausner, & Synderman, 1957), and do not expect commitment. So now the natural question for managers to ask is: "How do we procure psychological presence?" And in the very formulation of that question lies the nub of the problem.

With a few honorable exceptions, the mass of the literature on motivation is about how X can get Y to do what X wants done (which probably Y doesn't want to do). *"Managers believe they are the cause of subordinates' behaviour* [while] at the same time they believe in equality and democracy as a principle of life in society" (Dickson, 1981, p. 927; emphasis added). The whole apparatus of motivation theory rests on this dubious assumption. Techniques have of course become more sophisticated. "Participation" ostensibly espouses the egalitarian principle; in practice it is often used as a way of trying to mobilize support for decisions already made. "Empowerment" sounds better, but genuine power cannot be given, only taken, and again in practice firm boundaries are usually drawn around the zone in which exercise of the power so given is permissible. I share Dickson's proposition that the belief that managers cause subordinates' behavior is no more than a comforting myth. Consequently most motivation theory has to be discarded.

I start from a different assumption:

Every individual employee may be conceived as being a "manager" in two senses. First, there is management of the boundary between person and role; the individual determines what skills, attitudes, feelings, etc., he will devote to the role and what he will withhold. Secondly, there is management of activities within the role and of transactions with other role-holders. These two elements are included in the term, "managing oneself in role." In practice, therefore, the individual will act as a manager in these two senses: the issue is whether room will be made for him to do this in the service of the task of the organization or alternatively, perhaps, to its detriment. (Miller, 1977, p. 59)

(Writing today, I would have included "she" as well as "he," but that is the only change I would make). Kahn, in his exposition of psychological presence, makes a similar assumption. Individuals vary in their ability to be "present," and there may be distractions inside or outside the workplace that inhibit such presence, but there has to be room made for it to become available. The work elements—tasks, roles, interactions—have to be meaningful, and the social system has to be experienced as safe (Kahn, 1992). A key element of safety that I would emphasize is safety to use one's own authority to speak out, knowing that one will be heard. But these conditions do not procure psychological presence; they only make it possible for the individual to choose to give it.

Some companies, whether intentionally or intuitively, are recognizing the importance of choice by subsidizing employees in training and development that they themselves want, irrespective of its relevance to the job, and that may indeed qualify them to move elsewhere. Paradoxically, this seems a more effective counter to psychological withdrawal than the active attempts to restore commitment. The individual who has transferable skills, who has the choice of staying or leaving and who chooses to stay, is much freer to be psychologically present.

Psychological withdrawal from "the organization," in terms of structures of power and authority and an attendant culture, is not inherently inconsistent with psychological presence in the role. If the task itself is challenging but realizable, its achievement can be a significant source of personal satisfaction. In a 1992 U.S. survey of people in employment, by far the most frequently mentioned personal measure of success in work life was satisfaction from doing a good job (Galinsky, Bond, & Friedman, 1993): "making a good income" was well down the list. But given the condition that there has to be room to exercise real authority in the role (and that same survey confirmed the high value attached to "open communications" and "control over job content"), one wonders how far this can be acceptable to current senior managers. Authority based on competence in the task is always a threat to a hierarchy based on status. Writing in the early 1980s about the prospects for realizing Maslow's related concept of self-actualization, Schwartz (1983) was pessimistic: "One might even hypothesize that those organizations that most require persons at the self-actualized level are least likely to tolerate them, since organizations whose myths are in danger of collapsing, who most need clear perception and creativity, are likely to feel most threatened by it" (p. 452).

I believe that the value of psychological presence, and, indeed, its necessity for survival of the enterprise, are gaining recognition and that there is the beginning of a search for the alternative paradigm of leadership that would make it possible. But it is one that overturns a great many taken-for-granted assumptions about the world of work.

The notion of distributed leadership is not new, but set alongside full recognition of the autonomous, choice-making individual it takes a much more radical form. One way of expressing it is to say that it does away with followers: organization becomes a process of negotiation between leaders, each recognizing the competence of the other—or being open about perceived incompetence. In their day-to-day roles each is managing and operating on the boundary of a system of activities, ranging from a tiny one-person subsystem to the macrosystem of the enterprise. The enterprise is defined by its activities and outputs, though as noted earlier, these boundaries may not fully correspond to the boundaries of employment affiliation. Hierarchy (which, given its original Greek meaning of "rule by priests," has never been an appropriate term), gives way to a mode of relatedness that is closer to a network. Business process reengineering, which was adopted in a variety of businesses (and often fiercely resisted by middle managers), implied a more horizontal organization: from division of labor to integration of labor.

Additionally, distributed leadership involves explicit recognition that it is not only through their day-to-day roles that people

relate to the task of the enterprise. Through those roles themselves they are relating to other subsystems and to parts of the
environment of the enterprise. As people with other roles outside
work they are also elements of that environment. Through all
these links they collectively acquire a mass of information about
the internal and external worlds of the enterprise. And they are
concerned, for example, about the new computer system that is
not going to work, but no-one dares tell management, or management does not want to hear; or about reports of customer dissatisfaction with the product. Usually, however, this information is
shared informally in small groups: data that could be potentially
important to the enterprise are not tapped. Recognition of the
"citizen of the enterprise" as another role, institutionalized
through regular meetings of cross-departmental and cross-level
groupings, is not new (Miller, 1977, 1993a, 1993c), but it is still
uncommon. In the postmodern paradigm it is taken for granted.
Internal whistle-blowers are not a threat but an asset.

These are the consequences of taking psychological presence
seriously. Many managers would see this as a route to anarchy.
In fact it is *polyarchy*—another, and more appropriate, Greek term
for distributed leadership. It certainly does not fit with current
ideas of control. Curiously, the anxiety is never about how managers themselves might respond to such a régime; the anxiety is
about the irresponsibility of the lower orders. It is tempting to
quote again from Mannoni: "There is a sociological law which
admits of no exception that all peoples, even the most ignorant
and backward, are capable of governing and administering themselves, provided, of course, that they are left to choose their own
methods" (Mannoni, 1956, p. 174).

If that is too uncomfortable to swallow, there is another compelling consideration. There was an old Tavistock adage: it needs
a group to understand a group. I would postulate that an enterprise needing to engage with unpredictable variety and complexity in its external environment will be better able to do so if it
can make full use of the variety and complexity within. The need
for overall leadership does not varnish; but it is a leadership that
promotes autonomy and eschews dependency.

This last point raises one of the questions that may be properly asked about the viability of the model sketched out here. If dependency on the leader is a threat to the task, what happens to dependency needs in the workplace? We lack evidence to give a firm answer. To some extent, at least, these needs should be adequately met through horizontal relationships and groupings, Beyond that, it is not unlikely that the next generation will be socialized into having quite different expectations about the pattern of social systems that meet their needs for defenses against anxiety.

A second valid question is how far distributed leadership could be applicable to large systems. I would argue that it is certainly relevant to the workplace—be it factory, hospital, or government agency—and probably extendable to a multisite enterprise operating within a common socioeconomic system. Currently, however, global businesses, which are largely outside the control of national governments (Miller, 1993b), are able to act arbitrarily in withdrawing investment in one country and transferring it to another. There are nevertheless signs that a few multinationals are becoming more like federations of self-contained components which, for example, through management buyouts, can be and sometimes are floated off as independent businesses. In these, distributed leadership is certainly possible. Whether this is the beginning of a more pervasive trend is of course unforeseeable. And this brings us to the next section.

## Leadership and Change

Visiting manufacturing companies in Britain it is far from uncommon to find that a major restructuring, commenced perhaps 2 years ago and still not fully implemented, is being superseded by a new change program. The vision and strategic plan that had seemed robust have been punctured by factors such as new global competition in quality, an unexpected shortening of a product's life cycle, or a technological breakthrough. Meanwhile, every year brings a new crop of management literature on how to manage change. Cultural change has received increasing attention: There are debates about incremental versus transformational change and almost every consultancy group offers its own recipe.

Underlying nearly all this theoretical and practical activity are several assumptions which are largely implicit: that leaders can identify and define a desired future state or stance for the enterprise; that this will be a better fit to the future environment; that it will ensure competitive advantage; that it is achievable; that their job is to manage change and overcome resistance, whether by persuasion or force; and, perhaps an unacknowledged wish, that this will be the change to end changes. There are a few more cautious voices: for example, one writer on the implications of chaos theory says:

> From what seems to be today's most popular perspective, strategic thinking is the process of applying some general prescriptive framework, derived from best practice, to each new specific strategic situation encountered. . . . The notion is that successful people think and decide what is to be achieved before they act. . . . In turbulent times, when we are faced with a rapidly changing world, a succession of ambiguous situations, and actions with unknowable consequences that generate continuing conflict, it becomes impossible to think before we act. Strategic thinking then becomes reflecting *while* we act. (Stacey, 1993, p. 11)

This echoes Schön's term, *reflection-in-action* (1987). It is an ordinary and familiar experience for all of us. For example, if I am driving on a freeway, see that the traffic ahead is slowing to a standstill, and also notice that I am just approaching a side turning, I may make a snap decision, almost intuitive, and begin to reflect on its implications: if I have turned, on finding an alternative route; if I have stayed on the freeway, on how to deal with being late. This is also an example of what has been called an "emergent strategy" (Mintzberg & Waters, 1985).

All the assumptions listed above are suspect, except perhaps the first: it *is* possible to *envision* a desired future state. The others reflect a wish to control the uncontrollable. The leader on the pinnacle sets himself up or is set up collusively by his followers to believe that he can do just that. No wonder some of the more prominent examples have a short life-cycle. By contrast it is noticeable in some of the large British or Anglo-Dutch companies with a long-term record of success—ICI, Unilever, Shell—only occasionally has the leader been a public figure. More usually it is someone with long service in the company who operates less as an autocrat than as *primus inter pares;* and in none of these three cases does he have an inflated pay package.

The proposition that in the postmodern world change in the external environment of the enterprise is unmanageable—that it can only be engaged with, or ridden—calls for a rethinking of assumptions about managing change within the enterprise itself. Top-down change is certainly possible, and the management texts are generous with their formulae, ranging from the directive through the indoctrinative to the conciliatory. The question is whether it will enable the enterprise to engage more effectively with its unpredictable environment. Outcomes almost invariably fall short of expectations. Moreover, and this is an increasingly crucial consideration, imposed change is inherently antithetical to psychological presence.

Paradoxically, the way forward lies not in generating a vision of a desired future form of the enterprise but in a full appreciation of what it is and how it works at present. In the case of one major corporation, only after it implemented a decision to "delayer" its first-line supervisory level did it discover that half the workforce was illiterate in English. The role of the supervisor as interpreter had not been recognized. Proposals for change often ignore, at their cost, other functions that the existing system fulfills. Thus there is the sense of being part of a surrogate family. Also (common parlance 40 years ago but much less heard today) there is the "informal organization": that network of relationships that transcends, sometimes subverts, and often complements, and compensates for gaps in, the formal organization. Beyond that again is the operation of the social system referred to earlier, as a defense for its members against quite primitive unconscious anxieties. Of course, that existing system is not optimal; of course, it includes many elements that are inefficient and costly; but much resistance to change is a rational protest against nonrecognition of the more hidden and positive attributes. Attempts to demolish and replace the current system are not unnaturally felt as discrediting those positive features and the commitment and loyalty that they have represented.

It is this examination of the existing organization—the needs that it meets, the processes that produce the current outcomes—that is the appropriate beginning of "the learning organization," about which there is a growing literature (e.g., Argyris, 1990; Senge, 1990; Stacey, 1993). It is a task in which everyone can share. Too often, of course, those at the top act as if they had no need to learn: they know. In the postmodern enterprise it is taken for granted that ignorance of the future too is shared by everyone—the designated leader does not have a crystal ball—and that learning is therefore a communal process. The leadership that is critical for the postmodern enterprise is leadership of the learning process, while at the same time being part of it. It involves cyclical processes of taking actions, studying the effects, intended and unintended, and using the data to inform the next set of actions; and also, through this process, constantly questioning and modifying one's assumptions or mental models—the double-loop learning described by Argyris (1990). New ways of doing things are a natural consequence of evolving new mental models and using and testing them in engagement with the changing environment. Change just happens.

In the postmodern world the successful leader (and probably the successful consultant) is the one who identifies a change that is ready to happen and is given the credit for it.

## REFERENCES

Argyris, C. (1990). *Overcoming organizational defenses: Facilitating organizational learning.* Englewood Cliffs, NJ: Prentice-Hall.

Bion, W. R. (1961). *Experiences in groups.* London: Tavistock.

Dickson, J. W. (1981). Beliefs about work and rationales for participation. *Human Relations, 36,* 911–931.

Galinsky, E., Bond, J. T., & Friedman, D. E. (1993). *The changing workforce: Highlights of the national study.* New York: Families and Work Institute.

Goffman, E. (1968). *Asylums: Essays on the social situation of mental patients and other inmates.* Harmondsworth, U.K.: Penguin.

Herzberg, F., Mausner, B., & Snyderman, B. (1957). *Job attitudes: Review of research and opinion.* Pittsburgh, PA: Psychological Services.

Hesnard, A. (1946). *Freud dans la Société d'après Guerre.* Geneva: Editions de Mont Blanc.

Jaques, E. (1955). Social systems as a defense against persecutory and depressive anxiety. In: M. Klein, P. Heimann, & R. E. Money-Kyrle (Eds.), *New directions in psychoanalysis* (pp. 478–498). London: Tavistock.

Kahn, W. A. (1992). To be fully there: Psychological presence at work. *Human Relations, 45,* 321–350.

Katz, D., & Kahn, R. (1978). *The social psychology of organizations.* New York: Wiley.

Khaleelee, O., & Miller, E. J. (1983). *Making the post-dependent society.* Unpublished paper.

Khaleelee, O., & Miller, E. J. (1985). Beyond the small group: Society as an intelligible field of study. In: Pines, M. (Ed.), *Bion and group psychotherapy* (pp. 353–383). London: Routledge & Kegan Paul.

Mannoni, O. (1956). *Prospero and Caliban: A study of the psychology of colonization.* (Translated from French). London: Methuen.

Menzies, I. E. P. (1960). A case-study in the functioning of social systems as a defense against anxiety: A report on a study of the nursing service of a general hospital. *Human Relations, 13,* 95–121.

Miller, E. J. (1977). Organizational development and industrial democracy: A current case-study. In: Cooper, C. (Ed.), *Organizational development in the UK and USA: A joint evaluation* (pp. 31–63). London: Macmillan.

Miller, E. J. (1986). Making room for individual autonomy. In: Srivastra, S., & Associates (Eds.), *Executive power* (pp. 257–288). San Francisco & London: Jossey-Bass.

Miller, E. J. (1993a). The human dynamic. In: R. Stacey (Ed.), *Strategic thinking and the management of change: International perspectives on organizational dynamics* (pp. 98–116). London: Kogan Page.

Miller, E. J. (1993b). The vicissitudes of identity: Opening address to the International Group Relations Conference, Exploring Global Dynamics (Victoria, Australia). (Doc. No. 2T 670). Tavistock Institute, London.

Miller, E. J. (1993c). *From dependency to autonomy: Studies in organization and change.* London: Free Association.

Miller, E. J., & Rice, A. K. (1967). *Systems of organization: Task and sentient systems and their boundary control.* London: Tavistock.

Miller, E. J., & Stein, M. (1993). Individual and organization in the 1990s: Time for a rethink? *The Tavistock Institute Review, 1992–93*, 35–37.

Mintzburg, H., & Waters, J. A. (1985). Of strategies deliberate and emergent. *Strategic Management Journal, 6*, 257–272.

Rice, A. K. (1965). *Learning for leadership*. London: Tavistock.

Schön, D. A. (1987). *Educating the reflective practitioner*. San Francisco: Jossey-Bass.

Schwartz, H. S. (1983). Maslow and the hierarchical enactment of organizational reality. *Human Relations, 36*, 933–956.

Senge, P. (1990). *The fifth discipline*. London: Century Business.

Stacey, R. (Ed.). (1993). Preface: Learning organizations and emergent strategy. In: *Strategic thinking and the management of change: International perspectives on organizational dynamics* (pp. 11–14; 77–97). London: Kogan Page.

# 2

# Resurrecting the Muse

## Followership in Organizations

### David N. Berg, Ph.D.

What are the psychological consequences for organizational members of the current focus on leadership? What have we been asking of organizational members and how has it affected their ability to work? When we promote leadership, what exactly are we trying to change about people's relationship to work? Are we being successful? What is the connection between leadership and followership? What are the ways in which these apparent opposites are similar? What have we been denying about *each* that has left the other impoverished and hollow? Is it desirable from the individual or organizational point of view to change the way we think and feel about followership and leadership? Is it possible?

*Acknowledgments.* I would like to thank Clayton Alderfer, Marshall Edelson, MaryLou Phillips, Elana Ponet, and James Ponet for thoughtful contributions to this chapter.

Much is made of leadership these days. In the political arena especially, when the frustrations and failures in the public sector involve a breakdown in hierarchical *relationships* as much as the insufficiencies of an individual at the top, the call goes out for better leaders. In corporations and schools, the overwhelming emphasis is on developing leadership skills, for it is on these skills that the future of our competitiveness as a nation rests. Followership, on the hand, is rarely brought up when leadership is being discussed, in spite of its obvious importance in the grand leadership plan (Kelley, 1988). The proliferation of university courses and organizational training sessions that have leadership in the title is not matched by complementary attempts to teach and learn about followership.

This is a troubling state of affairs. It raises a number of questions that I would like to explore in this paper. Why have we created an emphasis on leadership, an emphasis which makes it difficult to include an examination of followership? Does this emphasis compensate for something in our culture or our organizations that fills us with an exaggerated need to promote leadership and to silence whatever haunts us about the notion of followership? These questions and answers to them have not yet become part of our conversation about influence and authority in organizations.

Throughout this paper, in an attempt to address these questions, I will refer to my experience in 10 short workshops on the topic of followership and leadership in which I asked participants to explore what these terms mean. I began these workshops a few years ago in my early forties. It occurs to me now that my growing interest in the historically neglected topic of followership may have been an expression of a parallel theme in midlife: a return to aspects of the self neglected or left behind in early adulthood (Levinson, Darrow, Klein, Levinson, & McKee, 1978). The participants in these workshops were all managers, mostly, though not exclusively, white and male, from a variety of countries. Many of the participants are also at midlife. My goal in these workshops has not been to convey information about leadership, but instead to give participants the opportunity for serious reflection about followership, an opportunity along with me, to revisit a neglected topic.

## FOLLOWERSHIP

The first thing I do in the workshop is ask people to write down two or three words that come to mind when they hear the word *follower*. Most of the class members have little trouble doing the task, though a review of this apparently simple assignment reveals that there is some difficulty reporting uncensored thoughts and feelings. After all, the request to write down one's associations to the word *follower* signals that this session on "Leadership and Followership" is going to start at the "bottom." In the vast majority of organizational settings in which I have asked for such associations, the initial reactions are negative and demeaning: "sheep," "passive," "obedient," "serf," "lemming." Subsequent comments seek, in my opinion, to rejuvenate the image of a follower: "implementer," "cooperative," "team player," "learner." This collective effort to resuscitate the notion of followership is only partially successful.

To the extent that the participants engage in this associative exercise, I think they have passed through a variety of stages in their relationship to the role of follower, a role each of them plays in their organization. First, the participants articulate the negative reactions associated with a role that has, for the most part, been demeaned by the institutions and the society in which they function. The frequency with which certain words are reported suggests that these are cultural or collective images that have been accepted by individuals.

Second, the vast majority of the participants have split off the follower role in the face of the organization's devaluation of it. Who wants to acknowledge being a follower when the role is so organizationally and psychologically devalued? To make matters worse, all of these participants consciously believe they have come to this class because of their "leadership" qualities. They have come to enhance their leadership, sent by organizations increasingly calling for employees to be (transformational) leaders (not managers and certainly not followers). In such a group, the question, "How many of you want your reputation to be that of a superb follower?" elicits only a handful of affirmative responses. Yet most were probably selected as much for their unarticulated followership qualities than for any other attributes.

Finally, I think the members of the class begin to realize that they often find themselves in follower roles and more important, all of them supervise people who might legitimately be considered "followers" in some sense. The desire to rejuvenate the concept of followership may reflect the group's effort to create a positive image of follower as they begin to reclaim it. As they begin to describe followership in positive, valued terms it becomes easier to acknowledge and to claim their own followership. By the end of this part of the class, someone asserts that good leaders are really good followers and vice versa. Followership, transformed into leadership, can now be accepted. But what kind of follower has been "taken in"? In the context of current organizational life, what does it mean to be a team player, or an implementer or a cooperative employee? What kinds of followers have we allowed inside our organizations and why? What kinds of leaders do they require?

## LEADERSHIP IN ORGANIZATIONS: A COMPENSATION?

Research on leadership in the social sciences has paralleled society's interest. Researchers have studied charisma, leadership styles and decision making, leadership traits, the functions of leadership, autocratic and democratic leadership, leadership and authority, and of course, the personality of leaders. But the last decade has seen this interest mushroom. It was said in the 1970s that all biological research needed to be presented as cancer related in order to have a chance of being funded. Leadership is, excuse the analogy, the cancer of the behavioral sciences in the 1990s. Not only does the topic attract research dollars, it has also lent its name to an increasing number of chaired professorships, executive development courses, journal articles, and position descriptions within academe.

Outside the university, the development of leaders has replaced management, participation, strategic planning, and organizational change as the single most important issue facing modern institutions. It is the leader who provides vision and inspires commitment within organizations. Global thinking, customer focus, continuous improvement, and cutting edge technology are some of the *tools* needed to maintain competitive productivity and service, but it is leadership that makes it all come together.

The organizations of the 1950s and 1960s had done a very good job of creating loyal, obedient, hard-working employees. In the United States, the psychological employment contract that emerged after the Second World War promised security in exchange for loyalty and the willingness to follow direction. Leaders, those at the top of the organization chart, set the course, and the rest of the organization followed. Managers made things happen as efficiently as possible. Large private corporations became famous for voluminous job descriptions that provided detailed outlines of each job's duties and responsibilities (AT&T), for "management training" programs that taught employees the latest methods for improving production and quality (General Electric), and for consistent standards of behavior that were reliably observable throughout the organization (IBM). The Second World War also placed the United States in the driver's seat of the world's economy.

In conceptual terms, one could argue that the economic dominance of the United States had allowed leaders in this country to ignore the relational aspect of leadership. It was as if the follower did not exist as anything or anyone other than the object of leadership. The decades immediately after the Second World War gave rise to a psychologically impoverished notion of follower. In the movie *Twelve Angry Men* (1961), for example, a "working man" is asked to "suppose" that the apparently guilty defendant is innocent. His response, "I'm not good at supposing, my boss does the supposing, but I'll try one. . . ." This meager view of followership was all that leadership in the United States needed from its followers. Why complicate the leader–follower relationship when a simple one will suffice? Why ask more of leaders and followers when less will do? Why examine the leader–follower relationship, when focusing exclusively on the leader appears to yield the desired results?

When competition from both home and abroad began to put pressure on organizations in the United States the status quo no longer had the same appeal. "Leaders" began to realize that in training obedient "followers" they had created a workforce that was ill-equipped to take initiative, envision problems, or opportunities and act upon them, and perhaps most important, collaborate with those above them. They began to complain about employees who retreated from organizational problems by contending that solving such problems was "not my job." These same leaders began to notice that their employees had been taught methods for handling relatively stable economic conditions but were unable to manage in "turbulent," changing work environments. It became increasingly clear that the behavioral norms intended to ensure consistency and conformity had worked too well. Independence and creativity were in short supply. Everyone seemed to complain about the people *below* them. No one seemed to realize that someone was complaining about them.

There arose a "progressive" call to harness the expertise that existed at all levels in the organization, to free the voices and the wisdom that had been locked up inside most employees by formal, rigid hierarchies. Now, all of a sudden, those at the top wanted their followers to speak up, to offer new ideas, to criticize if such criticism could improve organizational performance. The whole notion of management came under attack from academics and corporate leaders. The consummate manager was now inadequate for the task. Organizations needed leaders at all levels, people with initiative and vision, *not just people who followed directions.* Those aspects of most people's jobs which had just recently been rewarded were, over the course of a decade or so, devalued. What had been a limited but valued concept of followership was replaced by the notion that organizations didn't need followers at all, they needed more leaders.

When the story is told this way, the current emphasis on leadership in organizations can be interpreted as compensation for the limitations of the followership model created and nurtured in America during the 1950s and 1960s. The contemporary value placed on leadership is the organization's attempt to adjust to defects or inadequacies in the hierarchical relationships it has fostered. The defects in the leader–follower relationship have not been addressed directly, rather they are being compensated for by a renewed emphasis on one side of the relationship, the leader. This conscious emphasis seems to suggest that if the follower were more like a leader, the organization would be better able to face and solve its problems. The focus remains on the subordinate rather than on the leader–follower relationship and the implicit devaluing of followership is now total and complete. The ideal organization is populated exclusively with leaders who, paradoxically think and act in accord with *the* leader at the top of the hierarchy.

To anyone familiar with organizational life, small-group dynamics, or collective endeavor of any kind, the idea of a group or organization filled with leaders and only leaders is not an appealing one. Task-driven systems cannot function without responsible followership, so what can it mean when current conventional wisdom exhorts *everyone* to be a leader? My answer to this question is that the new emphasis is what Smith (1984) would call a "morphostatic" shift. The lexicon has changed but the underlying structure of the leader–follower relationship remains the same. The responsibility for making the leader–follower relationship work remains with the "follower." In the past the follower was asked to sign on, get with the program, follow orders, and support the boss. More recently, this same follower is asked to be a leader, to have a vision, inspire others, solve problems, think long term, and be prepared to move on when opportunity (better offer) or circumstance ("downsizing") arise. In both the old and the new version the leader–follower relationship stays the same. The underlying paradigm of obedience remains, and the demands on the person in the "leader" role remain unexamined.

The defects or limitations of this relationship, the unchanging request for obedience, will continue to give rise to various forms of compensation unless they are examined and altered.

What would it mean to expand the meaning of responsible follow-ership? What would such a follower be like?

## EXEMPLARY FOLLOWERSHIP: RECLAIMING WHAT WE KNOW

In the second part of the workshop I ask the participants to think about an exemplary follower, someone they would like to have working for them. I ask them to consider followers from litera-ture, mythology, life, movies, and television. The purpose of the exercise is to see what images are in their minds about "good" followers and then to examine what it is about these followers that makes them exemplary. Usually, I ask the participants to discuss their images in small clusters and then we list them and analyze the "nominations" in the large group.

The examples that are generated by this exercise are wide ranging, from Oliver North of Iran–Contra fame to the President of South Africa, Nelson Mandela, and Mother Teresa, world fa-mous for her work with the poor in Calcutta. But there appear to be some underlying "types": Spock (from the original "Star Trek" television series), Radar (from the "MASH" television se-ries), and George Bush (during his years as Ronald Reagan's Vice President) illustrate the *Second-in-Command* follower. These fol-lowers have a clear, military-style, subordinate relationship with the leader. Most people, in describing why George Bush qualified as an exemplary leader, talked about his loyalty and his willing-ness to subordinate his own views in the face of his leader's goals and policies. This description makes it clear that people saw George Bush as having had his own opinions, different from Ron-ald Reagan's, and that he suppressed these in public for the sake of the leader. Radar, the slightly goofy assistant to the colonel who commanded the mobile surgical unit on "MASH", is cited as a follower because he always seemed to be able to bail the colonel out of difficult situations by attending to things that the colonel ignored or could not handle. Radar was always there to clean things up in ways that almost always turned out all right.

Spock is the most complex of this group. He is literally the second-in-command of the *Enterprise*, Captain Kirk's First Officer. Spock is seen as an exemplary follower because he is loyal, smart, competent, dependable, and possessed of a set of skills that complement his captain's. Like Radar, Spock sometimes rescues Kirk, but his contribution to Kirk is located as much in the relationship between the two as in Spock's personal qualities. Where Kirk is emotional, instinctive, psychological, Spock is rational, analytic, and behavioral. Interesting too, is the fact that Kirk is human, and his First Officer is part human and part Vulcan. Spock is literally from another planet.

There is another "type" that resembles the second-in-command, but feels distinct because the hierarchical relationship between the leader and the follower is not a formal, organizational one. These followers are *sidekicks*, assistants who usually accompany the leader, performing an important function but without an institutional role. Tonto (the "Indian" friend of the Lone Ranger from the radio and television series), Watson (Sherlock Holmes' physician companion), and Lassie (the dog!) are illustrations of this follower. Tonto is described as a loyal sidekick who, like Spock, has a set of skills complementary to those of the Lone Ranger and is often able to help his leader because of his relative invisibility ("no one pays attention to the Indian"), especially when contrasted with the Lone Ranger's imposing and distinctive persona. Also like Spock, Tonto belongs to a different "group" from the Lone Ranger and many of his contributions (tracking, information, stealth) derive from his membership in this group. Finally, it is clear from the description of Tonto that the Lone Ranger trusts him implicitly.

Watson is to Sherlock Holmes what Tonto is to the Lone Ranger. Watson, too, has a unique set of skills that complement those of the Great Detective. Where Holmes's mind is always racing ahead, Watson is left to tie things up, gather information, attend to details. Holmes notices everything, Watson appears to notice almost nothing. Yet it is to Watson to whom Holmes turns for important research and information. Here again it is interesting to notice that Watson belongs to a different "group," he is a physician, what today we might call a medical examiner, whose skills enhance those of his leader, detective Holmes. Unlike the second-in-command, these sidekicks are intimately connected to their leaders ("My dear Watson") in ways that make it almost impossible to imagine one without the other. Bush went on to be President, Radar served at least two colonels on the "MASH" series, and Spock became a towering "Star Trek" figure in his own right. But, it is hard to imagine Tonto without the Lone Ranger or Watson without Holmes.

The final sidekick is unusual. Lassie is not only from a different group, but from a different species altogether! Yet the themes remain. It is precisely Lassie's difference that enables her to perform invaluable functions for her master. Time after time, Lassie saves the boy by being able to escape, to track, to retrace steps, to intimidate intruders, and incite other animals as only a dog could. At other times, and in an oddly psychoanalytic way, Lassie's inability to speak English allows the boy to express and explore feelings that might otherwise be impossible. And of course, Lassie is dependable, loyal, skilled, and competent.

The third type of exemplary follower is the *Partner*. In my experience with this exercise, partners are most often female just as second-in-command and sidekick examples tend to be male. This is undoubtedly an artifact of the social roles that have been available and assigned to men and women in literature, movies, government, and mythology. It may also be the way we interpret the roles that women have played in the leader–follower relationship. It is also interesting to note that some might not even consider a partner to be a follower, and yet these relationships involve mutual contributions across a hierarchy, though a hierarchy that is societal rather than organizational and informal rather than formal.

Alice B. Toklas began a lifelong partnership with Gertrude Stein in the early 1900s. To the outside world, Gertrude Stein, born to wealth and endowed with a lively, poetic creative spirit was the artistic talent. Alice B. Toklas was her companion and lover, whose support and management made Gertrude Stein's contributions possible. Gertrude was the genius, Alice took care of managing this genius in public. The relationship was more complex and textured than this simple story line. Alice took care of the details, the shopping, cooking, scheduling, and finances, and these "chores" enabled Gertrude Stein to devote herself to writing. Alice took to her work with the same energy and vitality that Gertrude brought to hers. Both acknowledged that Gertrude's career could not have unfolded the way it did without Alice's many faceted support.

One could also say that Alice was Gertrude's muse, the partner whose presence, intellect, love, and companionship provided the necessary stimulus for Gertrude's literary talent. Was Alice the leader and Gertrude the follower? It seems clear that Alice could not write the way Gertrude could. It also seems clear that Gertrude might not have been able to write, and certainly would not have been as successful at publishing, had it not been for the role Alice played in her life (Souhami, 1991). Did one "serve" the other? It would seem so, but it remains a matter of frame to decipher who was the master and who was the servant in the various domains of their life together. (Some have even argued that Gertrude wasn't a great literary talent at all, but that Alice's management made her so. Who's the genius now?)

Marie Sklodowska was born in Warsaw, Poland and denied entry into the University there because she was a woman. Early in her adult life she tutored the children of rich families to earn a living. When she went to Paris, finally, to study physics, her life changed. There she met Pierre Curie, a professor of physics, and together, first as student and teacher, then as wife and husband, the two discovered radium, won a Nobel prize (she won two), and pioneered a field that influenced everything from cancer treatment to atomic energy. So why does Marie Curie's name come up when some people (men and women) are asked to think of exemplary followers?

To some extent the answer to this question is rooted in gender stereotypes, the historical diminishing of a woman's role in the domains of work traditionally dominated by men (like science), and the inevitable attempts by those who witness a collaboration to pick apart the contributions in order to answer the insidious question, "Which of the two was really the genius?" When I look at the relationship between Marie and Pierre, embedded as it was in a world which had straitjacket expectations for both men and women (Marie Curie became the first female professor at the Sorbonne in its 650-year history only after the death of her husband), I notice two things that are strikingly similar to the relationship between Gertrude Stein and Alice B. Toklas and therefore might explain a piece of the perception of Marie as a follower.

First, as was traditional in her time, Marie Curie took care of all the household responsibilities (including raising two children) *in addition* to her scientific work. In this sense, the division of her energies enabled her husband (the older and academically more senior "partner") to devote his full energies to work. Second, in dividing up the work on radium into the various investigations that needed to take place, Marie, in spite of her superior training and experience with radium, took the more tedious, mechanical work giving Pierre the more stimulating experimental tasks (Curie, 1937; Giroud, 1986). In both circumstances the "choice" may have been overdetermined by the society as well as by contemporary marital arrangements. As a consequence of these choices, Marie Curie not only did her own scientific work, but supported her husband's as well.

Eleanor Roosevelt too emerges in some discussions of exemplary followers, especially when both men and women participants are prompted to think about women in followership roles. Again (and this is striking) the context for a leader–follower partnership is (at least initially) a love relationship, and again, the perception of the woman's follower role is likely to be heavily influenced by the construction of women's roles in society. Eleanor Roosevelt was given a platform for the expression of her intellectual gifts, her vision for America, and the world, and her moral voice, as a result of her husband's election to the Presidency of the United States. But her interests had been developed through long and sustained commitments and they were different from her husband's.

Though a leader in her own right after Franklin Roosevelt died, Eleanor Roosevelt used her relationship to the President to advance her concerns (e.g., The United Nations Declaration of Human Rights). There is a way in which Franklin Roosevelt's leadership was enhanced, both during his life and after his death, by the independent actions and causes of his wife. Especially after the deterioration of their romantic relationship, the "marriage" was held together, in part, because each of them needed the other (Lash, 1971). Franklin needed Eleanor for political reasons; Eleanor needed the resources her association with Franklin could generate in order to develop her own projects.

Finally, the request for exemplary followers has elicited a fourth type, *Groups*. There were many fewer examples of this type, in part because the instructions suggested an individual follower. The apostles of Jesus Christ are often mentioned. This group of men carried on the work of their prophet, spreading his teachings throughout the Western world, and eventually founded a Church in his name. The initial discussion of the Apostles emphasizes loyalty and commitment to the vision of the leader as the defining characteristics of their followership. A second look reveals that most of them struggled with betrayal and doubt (Peter denied Jesus twice, Judas Iscariot betrayed him, and Thomas has lent his name to the expression "doubting Thomas") during their followership. Some raised questions of Christ all along the way. Others, in the face of danger and persecution, found it hard to acknowledge their allegiance publicly. Still others fled the responsibility of discipleship when the leader died. The story of the Apostles' followership is an account of both loyalty and betrayal; obedience, fidelity, and doubt. It is a particularly valuable example of followership not only because it involves a group, but also because it testifies to the difficulties inherent in the most devoted of leader–follower relationship.

Japanese Kabuki theater also provides an interesting example of a group of followers. In addition to the actors, Kabuki theater includes two other roles present on stage during the performance. One of these, kurago, refers to helpers who provide the actors with the props they need. These helpers are dressed in black (like the background of the theater) and become "invisible" to the audience, though present on the stage, throughout the play. The kurago are a necessary and integral part of the presentation, but their function is to supply the actors with what they need and thereby promote the action and flow of the story.

The third example of a group of followers also comes from Asia. There are many versions of the story of the famous leader Liu Pei, but all of them describe his relationship with three followers (Mercatante, 1988). Liu Pei was a great, charismatic leader whose leadership appeared effortless, and he had had three followers. Chang Fei was as strong as a bull but witless. He was a loyal, obedient follower whose strength protected Liu Pei and all that he stood for. If Chang Fei was a foot soldier, Kwan Kong was Liu Pei's General, an army chief whose combination of military leadership and worldly wisdom made him a valuable counselor. Kong Wing was the clever assistant, strategic in his thinking and expert in charting a course through the political waters of Liu Pei's domain. The story of Liu Pei's followers is often summed up: "Every hero needs three to help."

## THEMES IN THE DATA

The richness of the examples generated in these workshops surprised me. In light of the initial reactions that participants had to the notion of a follower, I expected their examples to be flat and forced. I imagined the participants would draw the picture of a follower in muted tones, browns, grays, beige, to match the psychological image they carried around with them. Instead, the exemplary followers were extremely interesting characters. All of them were bold and colorful, the kind of people (and a dog) you would like to meet and get to know.

In almost all of the examples presented here, the follower is described as loyal and supportive. Only in the case of the Apostles was there evidence of disloyalty and this was the unexpressed, "shadowy" side of a relationship that was offered as an archetype of discipleship. Eleanor Roosevelt struggled with her commitment to Franklin Roosevelt in the aftermath of his infidelity, but she remained in the marriage and supported the president in the service of her individual and their shared goals. In every other example, loyalty and support appear to be the bedrock of the leader–follower relationship.

Yet in most cases, the words *loyalty and support,* while accurate, do not capture the emotional connection between the leader and this "exemplary" follower. In most of these examples there is more. Affection, and in many cases love, is also present in these relationships. Not only is it present where one might expect it, in the partners, it is also present in the military examples (the mutual affection between Spock and Kirk is itself the subject of a number of the show's episodes; Radar's relationship with the Colonel is warmly familial), in the sidekick examples (Tonto, Watson, and Lassie), as well as the follower groups (most notably the Apostles).

It is difficult to know whether affection and love are necessary conditions for an exemplary leader–follower relationship or whether it is a by-product of such a relationship. The presence of these emotions suggests that, whatever their cause, they play an important role. Perhaps the affection reassures both the leader and follower during those times when each must show his or her limits and weaknesses to the other. Love might serve as an antidote to fears of exploitation, allowing for the expression of vulnerability and increasing the chances of meaningful collaboration. Mutual affection might enable the follower to express both competence and strength, contributions that might be suppressed in the face of a less accepting emotional relationship. It is also possible that a leader–follower relationship that includes affection and love is better able to survive the strains such a relationship inevitably faces: conflict, disagreement, betrayal, tension, incapacity, and danger.

Another theme in these examples is that the follower seems to have his or her own distinct voice. The follower's voice can be heard alongside the leader. It is as if one is listening to music, a duet, or in some cases an ensemble. Each voice is distinct and contributes an element to the overall sound of the piece. In some of the examples, the actual voice is a concrete representation of this metaphor. Spock, for example speaks in deep measured tones. Lassie barks, Tonto speaks with the accent of a native American who has learned the language of the white man, Radar has the timing and cadence of a Vaudevillian comic, and Watson persists in posing questions. One can also imagine Marie Curie's

French spoken with a Polish accent. In a more metaphorical way, Liu Pei's followers each had his own voice, each sang a different tune, each consistently played a distinctive theme.

In most of these examples not only do *we* hear the voice of the follower, it is also apparent that the leader hears this voice as well. The ideas, concerns, special perspective, and even conflicting views of the follower do not go unheeded. Alice B. Toklas succeeded in supporting and developing Gertrude Stein's career because the latter was willing to listen and be influenced by the former. The Lone Ranger respected and relied upon Tonto's special abilities and skills. He often wondered out loud about events that mystified him, thereby soliciting Tonto's thoughts. Often Tonto's ideas became a catalyst for a plan or course of action. In a similar way, Captain Kirk relied on Spock to provide information, perspective, and insight. Like Gertrude Stein, the Lone Ranger and Kirk treated their "exemplary follower" not merely as a helper or source of information, but as a muse, a person who inspired their own thinking, their own creativity.

Many of the followers identified by participants were somewhat invisible to the outside world, they "labored in the shadow" of the leader. The leader is the main character of the story, the elected official, the actor, the prophet, the colonel or the captain, the writer or detective. The spotlight is usually on the main character and as a result the follower works in relative obscurity, off stage or behind the scenes. Tonto is sent off to scout things out, Spock to do an analysis, Toklas to take care of the arrangements, Watson to provide materials and back up. The kurago in Kabuki theater are dressed in black to match the darkened background so as to be literally invisible as they perform their function. And, in the United States, Vice Presidents are known for disappearing right after the election for approximately $3^1/2$ years. In some cases, these followers emerge from this relative obscurity upon the death or retirement of the leader (Curie, Bush, some of the Apostles). In other cases, public visibility is never a part of their lives (Toklas, Watson, Tonto).

The phrase "laboring in the shadow" of the leader also has a psychological meaning, however. This meaning helps explain the lack of public prominence as well. In Jungian terms, the shadow includes those aspects of the personality that we want to hide or disown. Often (though not always) it is that which we feel is inferior, weak, worthless, horrid or otherwise unacceptable. The psychological work of becoming whole involves a kind of reconciliation with the shadowy aspects of our personality. From this perspective, the follower works on those issues that the leader, for whatever reason, keeps hidden and cannot engage directly. The follower may be invisible precisely because of the leader's unconscious desire to keep these shadowy issues from being exposed.

Spock, for example, represents pure rationality, a Vulcan trademark, while Captain Kirk symbolizes uncanny intuition and the importance of emotional connection. Spock is thinking, rational and conscious. Kirk is feeling, irrational and unconscious. While Spock is fascinated with the existence and function of emotion in human beings, Kirk *struggles* against Spock's rationality, a quality that Kirk too must have in great quantity because of the training and selection required of a twenty-fourth century starship captain. Spock's work is in Kirk's psychological shadow and Kirk's work is to maintain a meaningful conversation with Spock.

Tonto, in a similar way, can be seen as representing those aspects of the Lone Ranger that, especially in the Texas Ranger culture of that era, were deemed inferior and unacceptable. Tonto was an "Indian," a Native American deeply connected to the land, essentially nonviolent—and nonwhite. He was an outsider to the culture, imperiled because of his identity. The Lone Ranger, white from head to toe seemed to *struggle* with violence. He carried two guns, was dedicated to bringing criminals to justice and to avenging wrongdoing, yet he always aimed to disarm or disable his attackers, never to kill them. And, of course, his identity was a major source of struggle. The masked man wore a mask because disclosure of his identity placed him in danger.

Alice B. Toklas took care of all those details that Gertrude Stein couldn't and didn't want to handle. Perhaps most interesting, Alice managed Gertrude's career and made sure that Gertrude had the notoriety and exposure that she loved and enjoyed while at the same time sparing Gertrude from having to attend to such things. Alice labored in those shadowy aspects of Gertrude's personality that Gertrude may have considered beneath her at worst and unappealing at best, but Gertrude knew how important this work was to ensure her satisfaction with life. She maintained a loving and sustained relationship with Alice and through Alice with these mundane and ambitious aspects of herself.

This discussion of the shadow suggests that the role of muse has both personal and extrapersonal dimensions to it. In addition to the ways in which a follower's different views, identity characteristics, group memberships, and experience can stimulate or inspire the thought or action of the leader, the follower can also allow the leader to develop a relationship with the leader's own unconscious, the hidden, shadowy issues that are simultaneously a source of struggle and creativity. The follower can "help" in this way only if he or she can express these shadowy issues with some integrity and only if the leader is able to not only tolerate but engage them.

Finally, all of the examples describe a *special* leader–follower relationship which is collaborative and complementary. The followers are not merely clones of the leader, each complements the leader in one or more ways; skills, views, commitments, experience, background, identity, group memberships, or emotional makeup. As the picture of the follower is developed more fully it becomes clear that the leader could not have succeeded without this complementarity. The relationship, rather than the individual (leader or follower), emerges as a unit that was able to accomplish what neither could have done alone. The collaboration between leader and follower is a creative connection across one or more dimensions of difference. It is the differences that make the creativity possible. In some of the examples described above the differences involved organizational role, position in a formal hierarchy or authority in the wider world. In other cases the leader and follower came from different worlds, both literally and figuratively, deriving their individual perspectives from the cultures in which they were raised. In still other cases, background and training provided the complementary difference. In all of the cases, the leader–follower relationship was far more than the obedient, faceless, voiceless image that most of us initially associate with "follower." In its exemplary form, the leader–follower relationship is a collaboration.

## IMPLICATIONS

A collaborative relationship between leader and follower, like any collaborative relationship places a number of demands on both parties. But unlike a collaboration between peers, the leader–follower collaboration is a hierarchical one involving differences in authority and status. Such a collaboration makes special demands on the leader, the follower, and the relationship that binds them.

## Demands on the Leader

Perhaps most important for the leader who seeks to create a relationship that enables the follower to contribute his or her skills, perspective and "wholeness" to the work is an acceptance by the leader of his or her own weaknesses and limits. Most of us subscribe to the notion that all humans have weaknesses and limits, but many fewer of us are comfortable with the personal consequences of this notion. It is difficult to take an intensive, systematic, and public look at our weaknesses, and the entire process of being reminded of our limits can be distressing. Leaders in organizations face an additional hazard in acknowledging weakness and limitation: organization members tend to admire perfection in their leaders, thereby putting pressure on them to hide or cover up their shortcomings (Kaplan, Kofodimos, & Drath, 1987). As a result, the natural inclination away from scrutinizing weakness, combined with the organizational press for perfect leaders, conspires to rob leaders of some significant self-understanding and followers of a chance to form a collaborative relationship.

In one recent workshop the participants were describing a valuable follower as a person who can save the leader when he or she gets into trouble. Someone used the metaphor of "pulling the leader out of a burning house." In our discussion of this metaphor, it became clear that the leader had to allow him or herself to be rescued. The leader needed to accept help, to acknowledge his or her inability to survive alone. In the extreme, leaders who could not accept their limitations (or the limitations imposed on them by a situation) would tell the rescuing follower to get out of the burning house shouting, "I can handle the situation just fine, thank you." Such leaders would perish.

An acceptance by the leader of his or her imperfections and limits allows followers the opportunity to contribute valued competencies. I use the word *acceptance* because the challenge for the leader is not merely an intellectual understanding of the concept of strengths and weaknesses prevalent in the general population, but a personal understanding that allows weakness and limitation to coexist with strength and expanding potential. Winnicott's (1965) concept of the "good-enough mother" would seem to be applicable to the leader–follower relationship as well. The good-enough leader is someone who provides enough direction, guidance, skill, and influence to enable the follower to make their own contribution to the work but is not someone who conveys that he or she is able to know and do everything (better than anyone else). The perfect leader leaves no room for the contributions of the follower. Fortunately, there is no need for a leader to manufacture areas of weakness; the struggle is often to allow ourselves to acknowledge and accept them.

Hierarchical differences, formal and informal, between leaders and followers also raise another critical issue. For those *with* authority the issue is how they respond to rebellion, and for those who feel *without* authority the issue is how to initiate and conduct rebellion. In many cases the act of rebellion is how followers make the relationship with leaders and institutions their own, how they develop an investment in something they may not have created but of which they have become a part. I believe such a feeling comes, in part, out of a successful rebellion, successfully handled.

The leader–follower relationship must be established and then developed. Since this relationship involves different levels of authority or power, one question confronting the relationship is how much influence each will have on the other. Rebellion is sometimes the follower's expression of this question. How that rebellion is handled is the authority figure's answer. In its simplest form, a rebellion is handled successfully by a leader when he or she is able to convey that disagreement, even strong disagreement is a part of any leader–follower relationship and is often necessary for the *relationship* to succeed in its work. This, of course, requires the leader to have a substantial level of comfort in the face of being challenged. At the same time, the leader must convey that the expression of strong disagreement is part of a continuing relationship and is therefore different from an effort to destroy it, for such an intention, if recognized should be dealt with on its own terms. This requires that the follower launch his or her rebellion from a platform of some significant commitment to the leader.

A final thought regarding the demands on the leader who chooses to move toward a collaborative relationship with a follower. Striving for creative connections across intergroup differences (e.g., race, gender, ethnicity, social class) brings with it two kinds of struggles, ones that we have glimpsed in the examples discussed in this paper. The connection across identity group boundaries always takes place in the context of both the historical and current relationship between the two groups (Alderfer & Smith, 1982). Kirk's relationship with Spock therefore occurs against the backdrop of Earth–Vulcan history as well as the current relationship between the two planets. The Lone Ranger's relationship with Tonto is formed and maintained in the face of the historical and contemporaneous relationship between the white man and the Indian in America. Similarly, relationships across an organizational hierarchy (e.g., the army) are formed and sustained in light of the way those levels have interacted in the past as well as the present. If, for example, senior management has a history of exploiting middle management and has recently hired new senior level executives from outside the company instead of hiring from within, any leader–follower relationship will struggle with both of these contextual influences.

For the leader this means managing (1) their relationship with the group or groups to which the follower belongs, and (2) their own group's reactions to a leader–follower relationship that spans two different groups. In the first case, the leader may have to cope with stereotypes, family experiences, cultural prejudices, ignorance and fear in order to make a relationship with a follower. The fire chief who hires a female firefighter into a historically all-male department, and the white store owner who hires a

Hispanic clerk for the first time, face the legacy of their own group memberships as they reach across culture and identity to initiate this kind of new relationship. Branch Rickey, the white owner of the Brooklyn Dodgers faced not only his own prejudice, but the wrath of baseball's other white owners when he signed Jackie Robinson as the first black player in baseball's major leagues (Polner, 1982).

But these leaders also face another struggle, as potent if not more potent than the first. They must manage their relationship with their own group's reactions to the followers they have chosen or recruited. The fire chief is likely to encounter significant anger and hostility from the male firefighters who not only resent the presence of women in the firehouse but now view the chief as a traitor. The white store owner may have to face jokes and innuendo from other store owners. And Branch Rickey suffered the taunts and castigation of fans, players, and owners alike for breaking the color barrier in baseball. A leader–follower relationship that has the potential for collaboration across individual differences also demands that both the leader and the follower contend with the groups to which each belong.

## Demands on the Follower

This paper contends that the follower depends on the leader for many of the conditions that foster effective followership. But a collaborative leader–follower relationship also places certain demands on the follower. The follower must find his or her own voice and the willingness to use it. The follower's voice is the vehicle by which he or she expresses an idea, a solution, a critical perspective, an opinion or a feeling. Finding this voice means developing a way of communicating with the leader that allows for direct and relatively uncensored exchange. Finding the willingness to use one's voice means developing the capacity to take the risks necessary to say what one actually thinks and feels, an especially difficult undertaking in a hierarchical relationship.

This last requirement points out that followers need a certain amount of plain courage to play their role. The strength to persevere when confronted with fear or difficulty is often crucial to the development of a collaborative leader–follower relationship. While it is true that the leader, too, may be fearful at times, the followers themselves bear most of this burden. Speaking up to or against someone with more power and authority always entails the risk of losing one's job, being demeaned, feeling inadequate, or being attacked. The hierarchical character of the leader–follower collaboration heightens the follower's need for courage. As the relationship develops, the need for courageous acts might decline, but in a hierarchical world, it never disappears.

## Demands on the Relationship

The leader–follower relationship is an entity all its own. The stance taken by both the leader and the follower toward their relationship influences the degree of candor, conflict, support, and trust that develops between them. In addition, there are many forces acting upon this relationship. How the relationship manages these forces shapes the nature of the leader–follower collaboration.

In most organizations, for example, evaluation and promotion practices are part of the context in which leaders and followers are asked to work together. In a world in which followers are competing for the jobs of those above them, it is difficult to expect leader–follower relationships to discuss the limits of each other's skills. If such a conversation were to take place, it is difficult to imagine that it could be free of concerns about the misuse of information in the highly charged promotional sweepstakes always at play. On the other hand, this same environment raises concerns about exploitation, for the leader too is engaged in finding a place further up the hierarchy and may be tempted to present collaborative work as individually conceived. These are just two examples of the potentially corrosive effects of "standard" organizational practices on a collaborative leader–follower relationship. Although there are no simple remedies for these circumstances, a relationship that denies such forces exist or somehow reinforces in the leader and follower a belief that these forces will not affect them, is crippling itself.

A collaborative relationship may also face the effects of shifting subordination. Unlike a leader–follower relationship in which the leader's opinions and decisions always dominate, a collaborative relationship, by its very character, involves periodic shifts of influence. The complementary strengths and weaknesses require the leader to follow (at times) and the follower to lead (at other times). Can the relationship tolerate the leader being "down" or the follower being "up?" Does this shifting subordinacy threaten to undermine the authority differential that is part of the leader–follower relationship? How does this shifting subordination look to the world surrounding the leader–follower relationship?

This last question points to still other forces pressing on the leader–follower relationship. Among the many groups leaders and followers belong to are their peer groups within the organization in which they work. Other "leaders" may be subtle or bold in the ways they communicate their reactions to a leader in a collaborative relationship. When, for example, a Board of Education president invites public participation at a Board meeting, he may hear from his colleagues (in Executive Session!) about the need to be firmly in control at all times or he may receive a suggestion to limit comments by "visitors" to the final item on the meeting's agenda. Followers, too, receive messages from other "followers" about how they should or should not relate to leaders (e.g., union members who have a stake in the status of leader–follower relationships throughout an organization). As is the case with other "external" forces, the leader–follower relationship must provide a setting in which these messages can be discussed and in which both leader and follower can explore ways of managing them. If the relationship cannot function in this way, the relationship runs the risk of being swamped by intergroup pressures or cut off from them, in either case limiting its viability in the organization.

Finally, the Latin roots of the word *collaboration* trace back to *both* colabor (to work together) and colapsis (to fall apart). The emotional reality expressed in these apparent opposites describes the possibility as well as the hazard of collaborative work. A leader–follower relationship must struggle with the inevitable strain of holding together a creative undertaking that is founded on nurturing difference as well as commonality. To nurture difference is to cultivate precisely that which has the potential to divide, to separate, to inflame while simultaneously revealing connection and illuminating new possibilities. Differences are at the heart of relational creativity (much like divergent thinking is at the heart of individual creativity), but these differences demand that a collaboration survive periods of conflict, disagreement and separation.

## CONCLUSION

The increasing preoccupation with leadership runs the risk of relegating followership to the dim, grey often shameful back alleys of organizational life. Paradoxically, the more we praise the virtues of leadership, the more we disparage the notion of followership; the more we encourage people to lead, the more we dissuade people from following. It is the connection between leadership and followership that needs our collective attention. If we create a *relationship* between leaders and followers that can enable and contain a full collaboration, perhaps we can release the vibrant, colorful follower present in each of us.

## REFERENCES

Alderfer, C. P., & Smith, K. K. (1982). Studying intergroup relations embedded in organizations. *Administrative Science Quarterly, 27,* 35–65.

Curie, E. (1937). *Madame Curie: A biography.* Garden City, NY: Doubleday, Doran.

Fonda, H. (Producer), & Lumet, S. (Director). (1957). *Twelve angry men* [Film].

Giroud, F. (1986). *Marie Curie: A life.* New York: Holmes & Meier.

Kaplan, R. E., Kofodimos, J. R., & Drath, W. H. (1987). Development at the top: A review and prospect. In: W. Pasmore, & R. Woodman (Eds.), *Research in organizational changes and development.* Greenwich, CT: JAI Press.

Kelley, R. E. (1988). In praise of followership. *Harvard Business Review,*
     *66,* 142–148.
Lash, J. P. (1971). *Eleanor and Franklin.* New York: Norton.
Levinson, D. J., with Darrow, C. N., Klein, E. B., Levinson, M. H., &
     McKee, B. (1978). *The seasons of a man's life.* New York: Knopf.
Mercatante, A. S. (1988). *The Facts on File encyclopedia of mythology and
     legend.* New York: Oxford.
Polner, M. (1982). *Branch Rickey: A biography.* New York: Atheneum.
Souhami, D. (1991). *Gertrude and Alice.* London: Pandora Press.
Smith, K. K. (1984). Rabbits, lynxes and organizational transitions. In:
     J. R. Kimberly, & R. E. Quinn (Eds.), *New futures: The challenge of
     managing corporate transitions.* Homewood, IL: Dow Jones-Irwin.
Winnicott, D. W. (1965), *The maturational processes and the facilitating
     environment: Studies in the theory of emotional development.* New York:
     International Universities Press. London: Hogarth Press.

# 3

# Unconscious Social Pressures on Leaders

## *W. Gordon Lawrence, (Doctor rerum oeconomicus)*

> *We are at the beginning of a new era, characterised by great insecurity, permanent crisis and the absence of any kind of status quo. . . .*
> —(M. Sturmer quoted in Hobsbawm, 1994)

## THE PRESENCE OF PSYCHOTIC ANXIETIES IN INSTITUTIONS

The use of psychoanalysis as a tool of cultural enquiry and criticism allows us to see what is taking place at an unconscious level in all the groups and institutions in which we participate but only if we make ourselves mentally available to give attention to this social phenomenon. This heuristic perspective was first pioneered by the early scientific workers at the Tavistock Clinic before

World War II and after it by the founding members of the Tavistock Institute.

The startling discovery they made was that much of the unconscious social arrangements human beings make to organize
their social life is designed to defend themselves against psychotic
anxieties. In this context "psychotic" means the fear of annihilation, the fear of being made a nothing, the fear of not being able
to make sense of what realities may be, the fear of disorder and
chaos, the fear of disintegration, the fear of loss, ending, and
death. These fears are acutely present in the individual's psychic
life during earliest infancy and can be reactivated at any time in
subsequent adult life when persecutory circumstances trigger
them.

Psychotic anxieties suffuse our institutional lives in contemporary societies. Robert Young makes the point succinctly: "much
if not most of our group behaviour and institutional arrangements are quite specifically and exquisitely designed to avoid consciously experiencing psychotic anxiety. Moreover the psychotic
processes are in danger of breaking through from moment to
moment" (Young, 1994, p. 156).

Understanding the fear of psychosis which is present in institutional life allows us to understand something of what I call the
"rational madness," which can permeate the social configurations that human beings coconstruct collectively. By this I mean
that the human desire to have order, say, in an industrial organization, often masks a profound "madness," which can never be
looked at because that might lead to a deconstruction of the
order. Role holders in the organizations of institutions will subscribe to bureaucratic administrative procedures, for instance, or
collude with processes of bullying in the workplace, for example,
when they know these are dysfunctional but find themselves
caught up unthinkingly in the processes.

One of the problems of using psychoanalysis as a tool of
cultural enquiry and criticism is that the original insights come
from working with patients and analysands. It is for this reason
that we should prefix whatever clinical term we are borrowing
with the adjective *social:* hence, social psychosis, social depression,
and social anxiety. Here, I want to emphasize that the psychosis

does not necessarily belong to the individual per se but is, in fact, socially induced unconsciously. Example: In 1975 I used the term *socially depressed* when working with managers in companies which were likely to fail commercially. Most managers were denying this probability but a few were depressed. To be sure, the latter had a propensity to be depressed as characters and so were available for feelings of depression which their colleagues were denying, but, in this context, they were much more in touch with realities than their insouciant colleagues. They could anticipate what the future of the company would be if current policies were pursued (Lawrence et al., 1975).

As it was, they were not heard, indeed were disregarded, by their colleagues who continued to manage as they had always done, believing that matters would work out for the best in the end. A number of these companies became bankrupt because their managers, all honorable men (there were no women), could not understand that the world of commerce and business was changing. British Steel, at the time (1975), was losing a million pounds a day but the managers continued to construe their roles and functions as before.

It is because of the heuristic perspective which recognizes the powerful influence of psychotic anxieties that I discern as being an increasingly salient dynamic in contemporary institutions that has to be continually guarded against. To put this another way: despite beliefs in the "democratic way of life," desires to have, what Popper (1966) called, the "open society," and valuing the fact that individuals manage themselves in their roles (Lawrence, 1979), there is always a tendency in institutions, and in the larger containing society, to regress to simple, hierarchical models of authority as a way of preserving a sense of security and stability.

## THE WORKING HYPOTHESIS

The working hypothesis I wish to explore is this: As the environment is experienced as becoming more uncertain—and there is reality to this—the management of institutions become more anxious (stressed, in their terms) as they interpret their experiences of the events and happenings which occur in their institutions as these relate to their environment. This evokes and activates dormant, unconscious psychotic anxieties because their fantasy world comes more to the fore than the conscious, ratiocinating qualities of their minds. So there is a pressure on managers of institutions to bring into being organizational forms and structures which offer themselves and the other role holders a feeling of certainty which in fantasy will withstand the environmental uncertainty and banish the psychotic anxieties. In this social arrangement the majority of the role holders in the institution mutually collude. Consequently, they collectively bring into being consciously and unconsciously, authoritarian organizations which generate a totalitarian, possibly fascist, state of mind in the participants in the institution.

The collary is this: Such an organizational culture diminishes the capacity for thought and thinking and so role holders at all levels become less able to relate to the external environment which is perceived as being in a state of flux. They become entrapped in the inner, political world and life of the institution, in a life of action and reaction, doing not being. The preoccupation is with personal survival which is essentially narcissistic. This frame of mind does not allow them to anticipate the future in any way other than in individual terms. And so crises, particularly financial ones, repeat themselves until they reach such a magnitude that the institution as an enterprise fails. This is because the role holders of the institution are less able to use those aspects of their "ego," their psyche, to transact between the inner and outer world of their institution.

Throughout this essay I use the term *totalitarianism* as a metaphor, conveying the sense of control over the totality of social life. Institutions I see as being social units which are deliberately constructed and reconstructed to seek specific goals. Corporations, armies, hospitals, churches, and prisons would be included.

## THE UNCERTAIN ENVIRONMENT

The predominant experiences of life which people report in the closing years before the millennium is of their lives being discontinuous, a series of events for which they can find no shape. The well-known, taken-for-granted armatures to a life, such as life-long employment, which were installed by capitalism and industrialization have melted in the postmodern heat of the electronic epoch. Their images of the future are distressed and the millennium, once hailed by futurologists, is anticipated with concern. This is because of the rapid pace of changes occurring in the past decade. There are the following identifiable reasons for the environment being characterized by uncertainty and flux.

## Destructive Capitalism

We live in an age of hyperuncertainty. One reason for this is the acceleration of, what Joseph Schumpeter called, "destructive capitalism." By this is meant that capitalist institutions are continually destroying and making redundant their former structures and methods. This is because competition continually causes them to change to match their competitors' performance. This is taking place throughout the industrialized world. The acceleration of this new version of capitalism has been fueled by a disillusionment with socialism in all its forms because policies of public ownership, central planning by the state, and centralized administrative direction as regulatory controls have been seen to have failed because their rigidities hinder innovation, structural change, and economic growth.

## Globalization

What is now described as globalization also is causing lasting structural change. Globalization comes about through:

> Ever freer movement of final goods and services from optimal production locations to optimum markets. Vanishing exchange controls over outward movements of capital from the richer economies. Liberalising inward trade and investment policies in the "developing" world. Specifically political transformations in China and India, having the potential long term effect of adding to the world's labour supply hundreds of millions of people sufficiently

literate and disciplined to be eligible for highly skilled jobs in the world market. (Jay, 1994)

## Changing Production Locations

One result of globalization is that the institutions of the established capitalist countries cannot compete against the low production costs of, say, the Pacific Rim or India—wages in the East can be as low as 4% of those in France, for instance. Consequently, so-called "smart" institutions are running down their organizations in the northern hemisphere (*downsizing* is the word in vogue). We now speak of "deconstruction" or, more bluntly as the Australians do, of "slash and burn." And I could go on adding details of how institutions in the northern hemisphere are undergoing radical change.

Production has to take place somewhere in the world. What is happening now is that managers in the northern hemisphere are learning to bring into being "virtual" factories, or "factories in the mind" in the southern hemisphere. Because managers are now computer literate it is possible to produce elements in different parts of the world, assemble the product in another country, and sell it in the richer northern hemisphere where the company is based.

## The Spread of the Capitalist Model

Increasingly, in traditional industrial societies the public sector services are being privatized. Capitalist thinking has taken over the running of hospitals, prisons, and public utilities. The same criteria believed to be useful in running businesses such as biscuit making factories, are now applied to all institutions, including universities. Consequently, role holders in such institutions are having similar experiences to those in conventional business enterprises.

This model of organizing institutions relies on the workings of market forces which, in turn, reifies "the" economy. This is a questionable assumption. The picture of a predictable economy does not fit reality. In fact any economy seems to be on the edge of time, rushing forward, coalescing, decaying or deconstructing, certainly changing and making novel configurations which have no single optimal outcome.

## Unemployment

While it is exciting to learn of such new trends and understand the commercial possibilities of shifting capital from the northern to the southern hemisphere, for instance, the major result is the growth of unemployment in the northern hemisphere. In Britain, for example, we have seen the virtual disappearance of coal miners and those who are now employed in the private sector are working for less money than they received when the industry was nationalized. Other heavy industry occupations are experiencing the same conditions.

## Le Casino des Incertitudes

A recent seminar for managing directors of a group of companies, all which I have just tried to describe, was summarized in the phrase *le casino des incertitudes* which was coined to describe how it feels to be a manager now. Managers are, if you will, experiencing Chaos Theory at first hand. They have to live with paradox and have to find entrepreneurial creativity in the face of unpredictability and an unknowable future. All that can be done is to try and discern the shadows which the future casts before it. It is this living with uncertainty that is the defining feature of contemporary life.

## UNCONSCIOUS SOCIAL PRESSURES ON LEADERSHIP

Being in business now is experienced as being risky and it causes anxiety for owners, shareholders, and employees at all levels. Essentially, in the first instance, it is managers who carry the anxiety of the persecution engendered by being in a risky commercial situation. Managers have to respond to the protean environment which is forever in flux. Because of their roles they are always managing the boundary between the inner and outer worlds of their enterprise. The survival of institutions relies on how well or badly senior managers "interpret" the inner and external realities of the institution. This relies on how they make use of their minds and so, what can be called, the "mental disposition" of managers is critical in this interpretation of realities. By the term *mental disposition* I mean the inner landscape or *inscape*, to use Gerald Manley Hopkins's word, that is brought to bear on all that is perceived to be in the environment of the perceiving individual.

Managers being human come to their roles with their personal psychic history. My hypothesis is that given the nature of the changing, turbulent, global, commercial environment which generates anxiety and fear, managers are often pressed into only being able to interpret reality from the paranoid–schizoid position. This, if you will, is the mental disposition which is mobilized. The paranoid schizoid position is one in which

> anxieties of a primitive nature threaten the immature ego and lead to a mobilisation of primitive defences. Splitting, idealisation and projective identification operate to create rudimentary structures made up of idealised good objects kept far apart from the persecutory bad ones. The individual's impulses are similarly split and he directs all his love towards the good object and all his hatred against the bad one. (Steiner, 1987, pp. 69–70)

I fully accept that some managers will have a valency for this psychic position and will fall more readily into it than others would do. At the same time, however, I am also postulating that managers can be driven into this position by other role holders who are "followers" in the institution. The managers interpret from the paranoid–schizoid position because they are given the sanction, albeit unconscious, from whatever groups in which they make their interpretations and decisions. This is because role holders in institutions use those role holders who are in boundary management positions, i.e., managers, as "containers," receptacles, for their feelings, even though none of the parties involved may recognize this.

Why are these managers placed in the paranoid–schizoid position? The reason I am suggesting partly lies in the mental disposition of those who are subject to the managers. Elliot Jaques, using Kleinian ideas in the context of his action research in industry during the Glacier Metal project, hypothesized that institutions are used by their individual members to reinforce individual mechanisms of defence against anxieties. Through the processes of projective and introjective identification individuals become linked behaviorally with their social institutions. Consequently, "one of the primary cohesive elements binding individuals into institutionalised human associations is that of defence against psychotic anxiety" (Jaques, 1955, pp. 478–479). This basic insight was elaborated by Bion (1970) when he wrote that the central dynamics of institutions cohered around the participants' primitive psychic impulses which were based on the paranoid–schizoid and depressive positions.

In contemporary institutions the participant's persecutory fears about the state and conditions of the external environment trigger psychotic anxieties and places them more in the paranoid–schizoid position than any other. This is a repetition, but on a larger scale, of what Menzies (1960) found when working in hospitals. There she showed that the unconscious psychotic anxieties and the actual structures of the organization of the institution come to be woven together in such a way that they constitute "a social system of defence against anxiety." In hospitals nurses have to confront illness, death, and dying which provokes psychotic anxieties of annihilation. In order to defend against this the managerial systems of hospitals come to be disciplined and rigid in order to minimize risks of causing injury of any kind, such as an overdosage of drugs. This all becomes tied together conceptually and emotionally as a method of containing the psychotic anxieties.

Similarly, in Western traditional capitalist economies managers and all the other role holders are continually being faced with the ending of their institution, which will result in redundancy and unemployment for all the role holders, for the reasons I have tried to indicate. Managers and others, I repeat, are faced with real fears which are not products of fantasy. There is, then, a collusive process taking place in institutions. Managers are driven into interpreting the realities of the environment from a para-noid–schizoid position and they are held in that position by the other role holders who need them to be in it so that they can avoid experiencing their psychotic anxieties. Thus a "social system of defense" comes into existence.

The wish for psychic and political security by the majority of role holders is realized by projecting into the management, particularly the "top" ones, the feelings that they are omnipo-tent, omniscient, and capable of satisfying all desires for depen-dency. The price which has to be paid for this unconscious projection is a rigid, authoritarian organization with its associated culture of dependency. It is for this primary reason that a totalitar-ian state of mind comes to be acceptable to the majority of the role holders and also because it offers the fantasy of security.

In turn, the management—the "leaders," if you will—have to introject these feelings. They in time, as a result, become more narcissistic or, a better word in this context, *hubristic*. The evi-dence for this comes from what seems to be a particularly British phenomenon which is the belief that all progress, particularly in a commercial company, comes from the top director. This is be-cause in Britain we value "expressive individualism" and laud the "outsider-acquisitor" who is "driving, clever, dynamic, blunt, and tenacious while unafraid of hard work" (Hampden-Turner & Trompenaars, 1994, p. 305). Such people, once they are in role reward themselves enormously, such as the head of British Gas or British Telecom or the water and electricity utilities.

Such role holders come to idealize themselves. They see themselves as good objects and keep themselves far apart from bad persecutory ones which are made to be located in the exter-nal environment. So any competition comes to be seen as an "enemy" which has to be killed off. This has the further function of giving other role holders in the enterprise a bad object into which they can project their unwanted feelings of hostility. Hence, we have aggressive advertising campaigns which aim to destroy any competition. Such a campaign was mounted by British Airways against Virgin Atlantic Airways.

But always we have the nagging questions: why are such people selected for their roles and why are they sustained in them, at least for a time? I am continually amazed as to how such hubristic leaders receive sanction for what they do. All of them are surrounded by role holders in the institution, often they have advisers and nonexecutive directors, if it is a commercial company, and always accountants, analysts, and bankers. They too, in my view, are implicated in the rise of narcissistic leaders and, in a sense, feed the paranoid–schizoid interpretation of the business situation.

The answer lies partly in the selection process itself. Old style British generals, for example, were selected because they were "authoritarian personalities." The army, then, with its rigid and tightly controlled structure, grounded in architectonic beliefs in obedience and command hierarchies, offered them safety "in the ambiguous world of emotions and relationships" (Dixon, 1994). Any self-doubts they had were absorbed in the rigidities and rituals of the armed services. Such characters were anxious to avoid failure and, so, preserve their fragile self-esteem. This fitted the selectors' profile of the ideal general; i.e., they wanted to have people who would offer clear-cut, decisive leadership.

In some measure history is repeating itself, but now in the nonmilitary sphere. Selectors reflect the predominant state of mind of their enterprise and choose people for roles in it to fit the culture. They cannot afford to take risks by selecting candidates outside of the mold and so choose to fulfill the unconscious wishes of other role holders in the institution by selecting those whom they think will be decisive with the consequences I am trying to illumine.

To summarize: the uncertain, global environment causes employees at all levels fear of unemployment, at the very least, which, in turn, provokes their primitive, psychotic anxieties. Consequently, managers are driven into interpreting realities from a paranoid–schizoid position. For those who have a valency for this position anyway their narcissistic, or hubristic, qualities are given free reign because the collusive process which the majority of role holders have collectively constructed in their minds and behaviorally act out gives their leaders unconscious sanction to be so. Leaders come to symbolize the purpose and reason for existence of the enterprise. The resultant totalitarian state of mind of the organizational culture is subscribed to because it offers relief temporarily from psychotic anxieties.

## Psychic and Cultural Consequences of the Totalitarian State of Mind

There are, at the very least, three consequences in terms of how individuals relate to realities as they so construct them. One, in a culture which is based on a totalitarian state of mind, there is only room for, what Winnicott called, the "false" self to be deployed in relationships because the "true" self has to be kept a secret. Sebek, a psychoanalyst in Prague, writes:

> The false self in a totalitarian society defended and protected the true self that could be expressed only in a limited, relatively "safe" space, for example, in a family, with a spouse. . . . In the totalitarian system as prescribed by communists, conditions were especially ripe for the creation of the false self. This false self was usually on the surface of personality and supplanted the true self . . . the false self adapted to the requirements of the totalitarian power—in terms of subjugation, passivity, resignation and obedience. (Sebek, 1993, p. 2)

In institutions the same process occurs. Role holders only deploy selected aspects of their available personality. They can only be calculative, goal oriented, rational—in short, essentially schizoid. And they are in the paranoid state because this is the only way to survive in a politically hostile environment.

Two, all this has consequences in terms of thinking, as I indicate in the corollary to my principal working hypothesis. When a totalitarian state of mind is salient in an institution thought and the capacity for thinking becomes diminished. I think this is how it takes place: The unconscious preoccupation is with projective identification with the hubristic leader for the reasons of defending from psychotic anxieties. The price that has to be paid is a rigid, authoritarian structure with its associated culture. The culture only rewards, and so reinforces, thinking which is sure-fire and certain, which is logical, which is convergent, because the overarching fear is of making mistakes. The fear of mistakes is such that it becomes dangerous to have thoughts which are different from the majority. Hence, there are attacks on linking which reinforces the psychosis.

Three, in such a culture, where role holders can only proceed in their thinking from certainty to certainty, from the known to the known, they cannot anticipate the unexpected. When crisis and uncertainty are experienced by them they search for a source of salvation which is consistent with the dependency culture that a totalitarian state of mind spawns. Such institutions project into their top role holders omnipotence and omniscience, and when they search for understanding of any kind they look for the same in anyone who may come to help them with their current problems and issues. The promise of the narcissistic–hubristic leader is that, messiahlike, he will save the institution and miraculously will carry them forward to a glorious future.

This wish is often projected into management consultants because any intervention into the life of the institution has to fit this mood. So experts are called in to reengineer the organization, or the banks are called on to provide, what they call, a "rescue package." These are examples of intervention which are grounded in, what I call, the "politics of salvation" (Casemore, et al., 1994) using the term *politics* to refer to methods of influence. The management of such institutions with such a state of mind become trapped by the idea that they can survive by a quick painless intervention, a magical new idea promising a "millenarian" or utopian future.

But such tactics, inspired by the politics of salvation, are never grounded in an honest, searching appreciation of the situation, never the product of lateral or divergent thinking, and so the institution continues with its culture based on its collective totalitarian state of mind.

As I outline these social processes I want to make it as clear as possible that they are, for the most part, collusively produced. To be sure, there will be occasions when they are brought about through the use of naked power. But even in so-called "open" societies there are always wishes to defend against psychotic anxieties, and so the form of civilization is always pressed toward that of a closed society.

## TOWARDS AN ALTERNATIVE MANAGERIAL MENTAL DISPOSITION

How do we find alternatives to the complex configuration of emotions which are unconsciously coconstructed in order to defend against psychotic anxiety which generate versions of the totalitarian state of mind within institutions? More particularly, how can mental dispositions be mobilized in both leaders and followers which will free them from interpreting their perception of the realities of their environment exclusively from a paranoid–schizoid position?

### The Politics of Revelation

I have argued that totalitarian states of mind are nurtured by the politics of salvation which, by their nature, preempt divergent thinking. By contrast, the politics of revelation are more a state of being than doing. I mean by revelation the work of being available for experiences whether psychoticlike or not, generating working hypotheses on these experiences, and making interpretations on the meaning and significance of the experiences. Individuals who are committed to the politics of revelation are always striving towards, what Bion (1970) termed $O$ which signifies the original "thing in itself" of an experience. $O$ represents absolute truth which can never be known by any human being but it is the journey to attain a version of it which makes us preeminently human. $O$ is more possible to attain if we can find a sense of and respect for the unconscious, for otherness, for mystery and death

(Weatherill, 1994), which are present in our lives no matter how hard we try to make them absent.

It is through the politics of revelation that individuals come to recognize the nature of their experiences. They begin, as Bion put it, to experience their experiences. Such people are those in institutions who have minds and thoughts and are capable of thinking and having dreams. They question to find the skull beneath the skin of contemporary life.

## The Depressive Position

The gateway to being able to engage in revelation starts from the experiences of the depressive position. When leaders enter this state they can start to interpret the events and happenings in their environment in a way that enhances the quality for their reality testing. The depressive position is an important developmental advance in that it allows for objects in the environment to be recognized as whole objects, containing both good and bad aspects. This shift is possible because there starts to be concern for the object, the other. This position is one of integration, of responsibility for conflicting emotions and parts of the individual in relation to objects (Harris, 1988, p. 158), i.e., whatever constitutes the other.

The recognition of whole objects comes about because of

> . . . an increased capacity to integrate experiences and lead to a shift in primary concern from the survival of the self to a concern for the object upon which the individual depends. Destructive feelings lead to feelings of loss and guilt which can be more fully experienced and which consequently enable mourning to take place. The consequences include a development of symbolic function and the emergence of reparative capacities which become possible when thinking no longer has to remain concrete. (Steiner, 1987, pp. 69–70)

In terms of institutional managers as leaders, the depressive position is the one from which market and commercial realities can begin to be put into perspective. The depressive position allows the manager to begin to have concern for the other employees in the institution, for the nature of relationships with customers and with suppliers. The field of vision, so to speak, of the manager becomes larger and he or she is able to see it in its totality without taking refuge in simplistic splitting. It is the position from which the complex, changing realities of an environment can start to be made sense of—even though it goes against accepted logic.

## Accepting Complexity

Among the reasons why leaders are held in the paranoid–schizoid position and cannot move to the depressive one is that organizations have come to be construed in terms of accountancy models. This is because the advance of "destructive" capitalism has been such that the primary tasks of institutions have changed over the last few years. The primary task is the reason for existence, or the work of the institution. As it is, the belief in market forces and capitalism has caused managers to think of their institutions as only having the purpose of making or saving money. This primary task has supplanted the idea that any enterprise exists to perform work orientated tasks. For an automobile company, say, this would be to research, develop, manufacture, and sell cars for sufficient financial return to maintain the company. The pressure to make and save money presses managers and other role holders into the paranoid–schizoid position, whereas a work oriented task holds them in the depressive one because the totality of activities are regarded as a complex whole having meaning which transcends the simplicity of economics. In the northern hemisphere we are caught in a commercial drama of our own making. This drama is around having the "bottom line" in the black. Consequently, time and time again I encounter the social phenomena I have been trying to describe. All these keep in place social systems of defense against psychotic anxieties which appear to be a feature of contemporary organizations in postmodern civilization.

This trend toward the simplification of reality is congruent with an avoidance of the depressive position which allows for the complexity of ambivalent feelings about phenomena in the environment to be entertained. Reality is kept noncomplex because the fantasy is that it will be easier to control. This inevitably presses the psyche of the individual to hold the paranoid–schizoid position with all its propensities for splitting.

There are conscious reasons why the unconscious phenomena I have been trying to isolate come into being. Life in organizations is also structured by the conceptualizations of "organizations" —and all the associated terms like *management, quality control, employee, job descriptions*—which are held in the conscious mind of the role holders in the particular enterprise. These are the terms by which individuals give meaning to their life in the work place. None of these terms are problematic because their denotations and associations are known and are taken for granted. They constitute a body of knowledge as to why organizations exist, what their purposes are, and which routines are deemed to be the most effective for fulfilling the work of the enterprise.

This consciously defined, cognitive construction of reality is brought into being through thinking by processes of ratiocination using the intellect. Thought in this sense has a creative function. All the cities, buildings we see around us, and all the science and technology we know, was created from thought "and almost everything we call nature. Farmland was produced by thought, by people thinking what they're going to do with the land and then doing it" (Bohm & Edwards, 1991, p. 8). What we think of as natural landscape is the work of the mind as Simon Schama brilliantly analyzes in his *Landscape and Memory* (1995).

Much of the thinking and thought which has created all the features and artifacts of our Western cultures have been the products of the scientific revolution which began in the 17th century. What was formulated then, and has continued through to the present day, was a method of scientific enquiry which has brought into being or constructed what is deemed to be the nature of reality. This method of scientific enquiry was postulated on the assumption that there is an objective universe whose features it is possible to observe and quantify objectively by using scientific instruments. The invention of the telescope, for example, revolutionized how the universe was seen and perceived. Such inventions of instruments for looking at the natural world reinforced the assumption that only that which is physically observable is real. These two related assumptions—the objectivist and the positivist—were linked with a third which is reductionism. This last assumption enshrined the belief that complex phenomena could be explained scientifically by analyzing them in terms of their components, elemental parts, and constituent events; nature was codified by taxonomies; causes and effects could be identified through isolating sequences of events, for example. The scientific endeavor continued to be informed by this scientific method until the beginnings of this century.

These ontological and epistemological assumptions have not only directed the way that scientific enquiry has been conducted, but have structured how other areas of social life have come to be constructed and defined. The theory and practice of management has been no exception. At the beginning of this century F. W. Tayor was formulating his ideas on "scientific management." Through time and motion studies Taylor was able to impose order on the production system in factories and gave management of the time the tools of control. Taylorism has been remarkably persistent throughout this century despite the pioneering work of early workers at the Tavistock Institute, particularly Trist and Bamforth (1951). They successfully introduced new methods of working in mines at a time when Taylorist ideas were resulting in absenteeism and industrial conflict. The emergence of the thinking on work being organized by the workers through the use of semiautonomous work groups to allow the workers to manage themselves in their roles has, however, been slow to gain credence in the minds of managers. The tendency for most managers is to go back to what they know—the models of organization and management they were brought up with—and when faced with the new ideas they can always justify their rejection of them with the phrase *the bottom line.*

Some managers have embraced and initiated new ideas, to be sure, but at this point in history the majority struggle with trying to make sense of their old, inherited models in relation to an environment which is changing rapidly. And there are, as yet, no robust, tried, and tested, fully articulated models to allow managers to give meaning to their practice in the face of environmental circumstances. Consequently, managers and other role holders in organizations become embedded in the unconscious social dynamics I have outlined.

New models of management, which will replace the basic model of scientific management, will emerge from our new understanding of science, which is changing because of a revolution in thinking about the nature of reality. This revolution came about through the development of quantum mechanics. This new understanding of reality has emerged because the old methods and assumptions of scientific enquiry were seen to be wanting in the face of what particular scientists were experiencing. There was a radical change in the epistemological assumption of scientific investigation. The new assumption was that we make contact with reality not only by using physical sense data but also by recognizing that we, human beings as "observers," are inextricably bound up with what we observe. We belong, so to speak, to the same oneness. This strikes down the classical division between observer and observed by recognizing that we participate in the construction of reality. "Participate," here means both taking part in and partaking of realities at the same time.

There is, pressing this idea of participation further, an interdependence between the reality of the universe as a whole and a second partner to which the first is inextricably conjoined. The second partner "is alive, but is not any particular organism. It is not even an entire species. Rather the second partner is all organisms—life itself" (Greenstein, 1988, p. 198). Greenstein's proposition is that the cosmos brought forth in order to exist and for it to exist even a single particle of it must be observed participatively. Only a conscious mind is capable of such an observation (p. 223). And it is the subsequent thinking by the conscious mind that brings reality into being. It is for this reason that Greenstein postulates that we live in a symbiotic universe of oneness and wholeness in which there is an interconnectedness of everything that exists. In the 1920s there occurred the Copenhagen Debates where the scientists taking part established that particles, no matter how separated over vast distances, could behave coherently. This questioned the previous assumption that they were totally separate and interdependent. So it is an illusion to think of, what we call conventionally, natural reality as being composed of separate phenomenal entities.

The corporate environment too is changing in its nature but it is not knowable with the management techniques which are embedded in the tradition of scientific management. Only part of the reality can be known in this way and managers who cannot understand that the corporate environment is an unfolding reality are left in a state of not-knowing, caught in the perceptual trap of scientific management which is based on epistemological and ontological assumptions that are now redundant.

The emerging realities in which business is being conducted are chaos, complexity, and discontinuous change—*le casino des incertitudes*. In a chaotic system none of the factors are ever stable as I have tried to illustrate earlier in this paper. What has to be looked for are the *resonances* between these factors in order to find a new coherence as to how they are related. As it is, in the face of this chaotic environment managers are driven into trying to rescue the situation by "reengineering," for instance, by searching for "strategic plans," and hoping it will all make sense and be coherent through exercising "vision." In short, managers, and all the other associated role holders in the business, are using a Newtonian version of scientific methodology because they believe that it is the way to avoid the disorder of the chaotic environment. Hence, for example, they put their faith in long-term planning which is a constructed story, a plausible fiction, about the future, which is based on extrapolations of perceptions of past success. It is difficult to replace this with a scenario approach (P. Schwartz, 1991) which postulates a range of futures based on working hypotheses on emerging social and business realities. Scenarios allow for chaos to be anticipated because the hypotheses can be modified and actions initiated on the light of changing circumstances in the environment.

As it is we are living within dissipative systems. By this I mean that every system, and business is no exception, is subject to limits to its own growth; i.e., structures of mass fall apart. The Law of Limits recognizes that chaotic systems are transient configurations of energy which will encounter their limits and so dissipate.

The energy which the system had once held captive will be released back into the environment.

W. B. Yeats's oft quoted phrase that things fall apart and that the center cannot hold was a poetic prognostication of what has now come to pass. The point at which the system reaches its limits by being on the edge of chaos is a moment when the human beings in the system face a choice. They can either make a leap by leading the processes of transformation to a higher order of complexity or they can let the system fall. They let it fall by not letting go of their belief in certainty and control and by trying to impose managerial order to bring the system back to the status quo as they knew it by using salvationist strategies.

Leadership into the processes of transformation which will bring a higher order of complexity is possible if the chaotic nature of business systems are understood and it is recognized that what looks chaotic will have an implicate order that has to be sought for and for which there are no precedents. The nature of reality continually has to be revealed.

As it is, for the reasons I have given, institutions, such as business enterprises, are driven to embrace the totalitarian state of mind because the role holders unconsciously believe that this will save their common enterprise. And it does for a while but always the Law of Limits approaches until such times as the phenomenon of dissipation cannot be avoided. For leadership in the 21st century to be credible there is an urgent task to be addressed now. This is the task of thinking and enhancing the capacity for thought by role holders in business and other enterprises. This thinking will have its roots in what have come to be called the new sciences and their methodologies. But first we have to understand the unconscious dynamics that the old paradigms of science and models of management generate. These have brought us rational madness and social psychosis. The forging of a new mental disposition that searches for revelation may yet bring substance to "the dream of modernism, the dream of progress" (J. Schwartz, 1992, pp. 201–202).

# REFERENCES

Bion, W. R. (1970). *Attention and interpretation*. London: Tavistock.

Bohm, D., & Edwards, M. (1991). *Changing consciousness*. San Francisco: Harper.

Casemore, R., Dyos, G., Eden, A., Kellner, R., McAnley, J., & Moss, S. (Eds.). (1994). *What makes consultancy work—Understanding the dynamics*. London: South Bank University Press.

Dixon, N. (1994). *On the psychology of military incompetence*. London: Pimlico.

Greenstein, G. (1988). *The symbiotic universe*. New York: Morrow.

Hampden-Turner, C., & Trompenaars, F. (1994). *The seven cultures of capitalism* (2nd ed.). London: Piatkus.

Harris, M. (1988). Depression and the depressive position in an adolescent boy. In E. B. Spillius (Ed.), *Melanie Klein today*. London: Routledge.

Hobsbawn, E. (1994). *Age of extremes* (p. 558). London: Michael Joseph.

Jaques, E. (1955). Social systems as a defense against persecutory and depressive anxiety. In M. Klein, P. Heimann, & R. E. Money-Kyrle (Eds.), *New directions in psychoanalysis* (pp. 478–498). London: Tavistock.

Jay, P. (1994). In the grip of an age of fear. London: *The Times*.

Lawrence, W. G. (1979). A concept for today: The management of self in role. In W. G. Lawrence (Ed.), *Exploring individual and organizational boundaries*. Chichester, U.K.: John Wiley.

Lawrence, W. G., Barham, P., Bell, G., Jones, P., Mant, A., & Miller, E. J. (1975). *Towards managerial development for tomorrow*. London: Tavistock Institute of Human Relations, No. 1119.

Menzies, I. E. P. (1960). A case-study in the functioning of social systems as a defense against anxiety. *Human Relations, 13*, 95–121.

Popper, K. (1966). *The open society and its enemies* (2 vols.). London: Routledge.

Schama, S. (1995). *Landscape and Memory*. New York: Knopf.

Schwartz, P. (1991). *The art of the long view*. London: Century Business.

Schwartz, J. (1992). *The creative moment*. London: Jonathan Cape.

Sebek, M. (1993). *Aggression in society and on the couch*. London: Imago East-West.

Steiner, J. (1987). The interplay between pathological organisation and the paranoid–schizoid and depressive positions. *International Journal of Psycho-Analysis, 68*, 69–80.

Symington, N. (1986). *The analytic experience*. New York: St. Martin's.

Trist, E. L., and Bamforth, K. W. (1951). Some social and psychological consequences of the Longwall Method of Coal Getting. *Human Relations, 4,* 3–38.
Weatherill, R. (1994). *Cultural collapse.* London: Free Association.
Young, R. (1994). *Mental space.* London: Process.

# 4

# Anxiety and the New Order

*James Krantz, Ph.D.*

We are reminded daily that we're heading—or perhaps careening—into the New Order where former approaches to organizing and getting work done are obsolete. Change is constant and unpredictable; markets are unstable; technological innovation is explosive and on a dramatically steep gradient; hierarchies change into networks, bosses to coaches, and jobs into ever changing bundles of shifting task assignments. The established psychological contracts between employees and their organizations are evaporating. Because change is pervasive, choice is ever present and learning is at a premium.

Wrenching change has become a fact of life, even though the institutions most of us work for exist in a kind of transitional, intermediate state between the older forms of bureaucratic organization and the new, cutting-edge arrangements. No matter how far along on the path to the New Order they are, organizations everywhere, buffeted by these turbulent forces, are under immense pressure to alter or dismantle deeply held patterns and cherished cultural arrangements. For many the losses of familiarity and safety are profoundly disorienting (Shapiro & Carr, 1991).

Organizations are adapting along lines that have coalesced into a fairly consistent and common set of overarching themes: a sharply disciplined focus on customer satisfaction; replacing "command and control" methods with ones that elicit greater employee commitment; emphasizing the ability to learn and adapt as new challenges and opportunities emerge; and addressing competitive issues through cross-functional collaboration rather than via the functional "silos" characteristic of former, more segmented, organizational structures.

Perhaps the most pervasive theme is the recognition that in order to thrive in the intensely competitive, technologically unstable, and rapidly shifting markets, organizations must create highly participative environments in which people at all levels take, and feel, personal responsibility for collective output and in which they are emotionally invested. The conforming, loyal "organization man" of the 1950s and 1960s (Whyte, 1956) has given way to the authorized, risk-taking, "enterprising" employee of the 1990s. By freeing people of the bureaucratic encumbrances and "empowering" them to take action, New Order organizations aim to promote success through more sophisticated collaboration, through teams whose members represent and integrate different specialities, and through the heightened interpersonal competence which arises as people fill their roles more passionately.

Just as organizations are expected to be leaner, meaner, smarter, more efficient and innovative, so are the people comprising them. In the words of the CEO of a major corporation: "Decision-making cycles tighten, feedback loops are shorter, and there's less room for error. The risks go up because you can get left behind a lot more quickly" (Garvin, 1995). The disciplined focus on customers forces organizations to link activities and functions that have been historically segmented. In turn, practices that emphasize the interdependence among different specialties and functional areas draw upon the ability of members representing these diverse specialties, functional areas, levels of hierarchy, and geographic regions to work together in an ever more sophisticated fashion.

Paradoxically, the very conditions that put such a premium on the ability to work together in ever more sophisticated fashion also pose serious challenges to achieving this kind of collaboration. While the loss of familiar structures, for example, may require developing new, more fluid approaches to collaboration, the loss of stable structures also stimulates great anxiety and creates pressure to mobilize exactly the kind of defensive responses that impede the required collaboration. Heightened expectations for high commitment, increased sophistication, and greater competence by members of the new organizations are accompanied by a dramatic increase in people's vulnerability. While the most obvious sources of vulnerability are the cutbacks, downsizing, and the frequency with which even senior executives are dismissed, the New Order brings with it many other ways in which psychic vulnerability is heightened, ways that are perhaps less obvious but no less challenging.

My basic argument builds upon the idea that those conditions enabling people to operate at high levels of sophistication and fully engaged collaboration must be considered a competitive advantage. Recent works highlighting the competitive significance of the workforce, and its role in creating significant strategic advantage (e.g., Pfeffer, 1994, 1995; Quinn, 1992) underscore this connection. According to Jeffrey Pfeffer's recent research (1994), for example, what distinguishes the top performing firms over the last 20 years is not the conventional strategic criteria (i.e., Porter, 1985) but rather what the firms have in common is that they rely "not on technology, patents, or strategic position, but on how they manage their workforces" (1995, p. 56).

My intention is to extend the idea that people create strategic advantages into the unconscious realm by arguing that the success of New Order organizations is deeply connected to the ways they develop to contain anxiety. The focus here is not with the part of the equation that involves basic skills or substantive knowledge, as is that of Pfeffer and others focusing on the strategic importance of human resources, but rather on the ways in which emotional experience effects the ability of people in organizations to think and collaborate. My hypothesis is that the ways in which organizations support or erode peoples' ability to maintain an integrated, realistic psychological connection to the people and events around them should be considered a competitive advantage (or disadvantage) in today's world.

The starting point for exploring this hypothesis is on the seam where psyche and system come together, where I use social defense theory to discuss the impact of organizational arrangements on people's ability to think and work effectively. Then, by threading that discussion through a consideration of several cardinal features of the New Order, I will delve more deeply into questions of how the anxieties of people working in emerging organizations are being managed. Finally, the leadership challenges for the New Order will be considered in light of these issues.

## COMPETENCE AND THE DEPRESSIVE POSITION

The two modes of psychological functioning first described by Melanie Klein (1940, 1946) provide a useful framework for thinking about the impact of anxiety, and the way it is managed, on organizational performance. Klein described two states of mind, established in very early infancy, that form the basis of how we experience the world throughout life. In one mode, grimly labeled paranoid–schizoid, people cope with intense anxieties and threatening fears by relying on the more rudimentary, primitive end of the defensive spectrum, employing principally splitting, projective identification, and idealization. This, in turn, leads to patterns of thought and experience characterized by blame, scapegoating, idealization, persecution, and other distorted perceptions. When operating from this mode, the ability to engage in interpersonal relations is seriously compromised, and concrete thinking leads to rigidity and loss of creativity (Segal, 1957). At the other end of the spectrum is what she called the depressive position, reflecting the mode in which we can experience ourselves and others as fully integrated people. This mode of experience leaves people with an increased ability to integrate experiences, to think, and to collaborate meaningfully out of concerns that extend beyond survival and self-protection.

In adult life, when people are operating in the paranoid–schizoid mode the organization is at risk since the capacity for problem solving and genuine thought are possible only when depressive anxieties and modes of managing them dominate. Operating from the more primitive paranoid–schizoid end of the spectrum brings out the grandiosity, persecution, and inflexible thinking. Laurent Lapierre (1989) has written insightfully on the effects of these two positions on leaders in their attempts to exercise power. When functioning primarily in the paranoid–schizoid mode, their exercise of power tends to be shaped by grandiose, unrealistic ideas that culminate in ineffective efforts. On the other hand, while aspirations and dreams shaped by the depressive mode of functioning may be less grand, they lead to what he calls "relative potence," as the exercise of power is more realistically connected to the external world.

From the "depressive" end of the spectrum people are more in contact with the full texture of inner and outer reality. In the words of Vega Roberts, "In the depressive position, omnipotent fantasy, obsessional ritual and paranoid blaming can give way to thinking: one can seek to know, to learn from experience and to solve problems" (1994, p. 118). When people are functioning from a depressive position they are able to mobilize their resources to confront the reality of complex tasks and challenges in sophisticated fashion. They are able to think and to collaborate as whole people with whole people. When managing our experiences in this more integrated frame of mind, we are able to tolerate complexity, assess reality from multiple perspectives, and understand realistic opportunities. It also allows us to take responsibility for our actions, rather than to externalize our unwanted parts and create "persecutors" in our environment.

This tradition of inquiry holds great promise in light of the New Order because it is the very qualities of the so-called depressive position that are so necessary in the emerging settings—necessary for individuals to succeed and necessary if the organizations themselves are to thrive. Organizations in the era of bureaucratic approaches could contain and tolerate much more behavior and functioning arising out of the paranoid–schizoid stance, along with the resulting organizational drift and dysfunction, in the less competitive world. These organizations were, to a much greater degree, able to buffer their members from confronting troubling realities and challenges of their work by absorbing a much higher incidence of splitting, denial, projection, and other self-consoling attitudes without creating the same risk of organizational failure that these same modes of psychological operation pose today. There is simply less room for error, less "play in the wheel" operationally, and much less forgiveness for thoughtlessness in today's marketplace. Now the intensely competitive marketplaces and critical speed by which organizations must continually adapt leave far less margin for error, especially the kinds of error produced by people operating in the paranoid–schizoid mode (Obholzer, 1995). While technological change and intense global competition create the conditions that foster anxious regression to paranoid–schizoid states, they equally create conditions in which doing so is extremely dangerous.

The central themes that emerge in relation to the New Order all point to the importance of enabling people to operate from the depressive position: to be able to learn from experience, to be vulnerable without feeling persecuted so that one can learn from experience, to be curious about, rather than fearful of, the unknown, to be able to link with others across important differences, and to be realistically connected to the genuine opportunities and challenges they face. From the paranoid–schizoid position it is impossible to handle the emotional and cognitive complexity of the roles that people find themselves in today. While these more primitive defensive approaches enable people to avoid the experience of anxiety and complexity, they disable people from being able to confront situations realistically and competently.

## SOCIAL DEFENSES
## AND ORGANIZATIONAL PERFORMANCE

Whether people operate out of the depressive or paranoid–schizoid mode is not simply a matter of individual functioning alone—the surrounding environment has an impact upon how people tend to function on this unconscious continuum. Social defense theory provides a way to see how impersonal organizational arrangements, such as structures, procedures, and technologies, influence the ability of people to function from the depressive position rather than operating in a paranoid–schizoid mode, or vice versa.

First developed by Elliott Jaques (1955) and Isabel Menzies (1960), social defense theory looks at the interplay between the individual's psychic defenses and organizational arrangements. It explores the ways in which the impersonal features of organizational life support the individual's defenses against the painful anxieties and emotions stimulated by participation in work organizations. Built on a Kleinian framework, social defense theory focuses on the ongoing process of projection and introjection between the individual and the organization.

People "map" their unconscious images, derived from early experience and shaped by their unconscious fantasies onto the organization and then reinternalize these meaning filled experiences, which in turn have been altered in some way by external reality. How these two realms interact—the subjective internal fantasy world of the individual and the organizational arrangements that serve both as container for projection and as a source of introjected experience—forms the basis of this theory.

Because the reality that people experience inevitably expresses some pattern in their own unconscious world of fantasy, organizational life resonates with and stirs up deep, primitive anxieties that are rooted in our earliest experiences and creates pressure to handle the resulting feelings by using equally primitive defenses—chiefly denial, splitting, and projective identification. Organizational life can either confirm and reinforce this mode of managing experiences or can help people reintegrate their experiences and operate in the more coherent mode, the depressive position.

Jaques and Menzies first saw how the building blocks of organizational life take on the extra function of helping modify, foster, or support the pattern of defenses used by members to cope with their experience. Those aspects of the organization—cultures, structures, procedures, policies, etc.—that interact with and shape the way individuals handle their emotional experiences make up the social defense system.

In joining an organization, one internalizes its splits, projective patterns, and its characteristic ways of expressing and managing irrationality. If the organization operates in such a way as to keep important elements of work disintegrated, if it fosters cross-unit projection and blame, or supports destructive or infantalizing authority relations, then more primitive, paranoid–schizoid potential of members will be supported. Alternatively, if complexity is confronted, if emotion-laden questions are addressed openly and honestly, and if challenging issues are linked and integrated rather than fragmented and split apart, then individuals will tend to employ reciprocal defensive strategies—those that involve managing experience more coherently. When the social defense system promotes this more mature functioning, those who cannot tolerate the complexity of experience will tend to leave the organization and seek out settings that are more compatible.

Menzies' seminal study (1960) clearly illustrates the meaning of social defenses. She traced the emergence of dysfunctional elements in the structure and culture of a nursing service back to the deep and primitive anxieties that were stimulated in nurses as a result of their close, often physical, contact with people who are ill. In addition to facing the distressing reality of suffering and death, nurses must also confront challenging emotional experiences arising from their work: "Intimate physical contact with patients arouses libidinal and erotic wishes that may be difficult to control. The work arouses strong and conflicting feelings: pity, compassion and love; guilt and anxiety; hatred and resentment of the patients who arouse these feelings; envy of the care they receive" (p. 96).

The nursing service shaped its organization to support an approach to work in which nurses were buffered from the kinds of fully personal contact and caregiving that would most stimulate the painful feelings. The unconscious aim of these organizational arrangements (i.e., social defense system) was to help the nurses defend themselves against the painful feelings stirred up by their work. The ways in which the organization came to be used to help nurses manage the considerable discomfort associated with their roles included structures developed and elaborated that split up the nurse–patient relationship; patients who were depersonalized; feelings that were detached and denied; accountable decision making that was replaced by ritualized routines; and the way in which responsibility for decision making was reduced by the maintenance of numerous checks and counterchecks. Finally, there was a collusive social distribution of responsibility and irresponsibility such that the "seniors" came to embody all that was competent while the "juniors" came to embody irresponsibility and incompetence.

While these features of the organization ("social defenses") may have helped the nurses shore up their own psychic defenses against the primitive anxieties stirred by nursing work, they also had destructive consequences. Most prominent was the compromise in nursing care offered to the patients which, in turn, had negative secondary effects in terms of the morale of nurses, their work satisfaction, the quality of learning opportunities available to them, and their sense of professional identity. The arrangements contributed to turnover, alienation, and withdrawal of the potential leaders who were least comfortable with the range of experience made possible by the social defense system.

## SOCIAL DEFENSES IN THE POSTINDUSTRIAL ORDER

The pioneering work of Menzies and Jaques, and those working in this tradition, have focused primarily on the receding types of organizations. While several recent works have illustrated the relevance of social defense theory to postindustrial conditions (Hirschhorn, 1988, 1990; Shapiro and Carr, 1991), I believe that this theory is not only well suited to the New Order, but is more apt than ever.

The reasons for this are twofold. One, as discussed above— the challenge of operating in today's environment—demands the kind of awareness and performance that arises when people are operating from the depressive position. Whatever ways we have of understanding how to influence this becomes all the more important. While the kinds of structures and methods that organizations have relied on to help contain and modify members' anxieties are changing as the New Order emerges, there is no reason to doubt that the same psychodynamic forces will be active. What features of the New Organizational life will come to modify or amplify peoples' primitive anxieties, and what kinds of arrangements will help them maintain an integrated stance, is the question I wish to crystallize in this article.

Second, the new world of work and organizations, if anything, elicits more deep and disorganizing anxieties, and resonates with ever more primitive mental fantasy situations. The profound uncertainty and turbulence that characterizes the world in which all of this work occurs can only compound the parallels between external reality and the inner world of fantasy. This is in keeping with Harold Bridger's (private communication, 1995) observation that today's environment actually mirrors unconscious processes much more closely than in the past because of its often contradictory, unpredictable, multilayered, and nonrational qualities.

More specifically, the great vulnerability and insecurity characteristic of today's environments are likely to resonate with the very primitive fear of annihilation and terrifying potential for psychological disintegration that many analysts have found in the primitive recesses of their patients. The enormous dislocation, job loss at all levels, loss of familiar contexts, and disorientation is likely to stimulate the fears associated with these very early, and terrifying, fears of annihilation and dissolution.

One might even speculate that this is related to the disappointing results in so many organizations that have downsized. The emerging evidence (e.g., McKinley, Sanchez, & Schick, 1995) questions the bottom-line wisdom of downsizing. Many studies point to the negative consequences of downsizing in terms of morale, commitment, and the enduring work of the "survivors." Considering these experiences in the light of psychoanalysis and social defense theory would lead one to ask whether the experience of downsizing and layoffs has left people regressed and immobilized in the face of the primitive anxieties elicited by the experience without the benefit of social defense systems that enable them to metabolize and modify the experience.

## CONTAINMENT AND THE CAPACITY TO THINK

These days the word *bureaucracy* is often used as a derogatory term, signaling the structures, roles, reporting relationships, and designs that prevent the kind of innovation, flexibility, creativity, and responsiveness required to compete in today's world. "Bureaucracy" in this vein refers to the rigid chains of command, clear hierarchical differentiation, and fine gradations in decision authority that defined the Old Order.

In line with this shift, the employment guarantees and economic security that people had come to expect from their organizations earlier in this century have been revoked. As the common cliché goes, organizations can no longer guarantee employment, only "resumable" experience that will strengthen one's hand in the labor market. Khaleelee and Miller (1985) have written about a large shift in which the caretaking and dependency meeting functions of society and its institutions have been devalued, superseded by a greater emphasis on the fight–flight features characteristic of highly competitive market environments.

Bureaucracies and their structures flourished when change was slower, more deliberate. People were often more buffered from the harsh judgments of market forces since competition was less acute and less intense. Nor did the rate of technological transformation produce a constantly shifting and unpredictable ground. People found elements of these organizations to shore up their own defenses against the painful experiences of working together to confront challenging tasks. Some organizations did a better job of fostering the higher level functioning, others lower down on the social defense "food chain" promoted more use of the paranoid–schizoid type defenses. As the former structures are dismantled, the containing function of the arrangements is also sacrificed. Many anxieties, formerly contained, become "dislodged," others are stimulated by the fact of change, and still more are elicited by the frightening and unknown conditions we often face.

As this transitional phase unfolds, new social defense systems will emerge that are suited to the new conditions. The key element in enabling people to operate from the depressive position is *containment*—in the sense that contexts must exist which can sustain the presence of potentially crippling anxieties, intense psychic pain, and disorienting confusion without themselves either confirming these experiences or collapsing in the face of them. In the Old Order, structure and bureaucracy were primarily relied upon to provide this containment, sometimes effectively and sometimes in ways that promoted individual functioning from the more paranoid–schizoid end of the spectrum. Just as organizations are searching for effective means of control without bureaucracy, they must also search for effective means of containment without bureaucracy.

## THE EMERGENCE OF TEAMS AS AN ENABLING CONTAINER

One element of organizations that serves socially defensive functions and bridges the New and Old Orders is the small team. One of the most important and lasting contributions of early Tavistock researchers (e.g., Trist, 1977; Trist and Emery, 1965) was in recognizing how the forms of organization that had grown in response to early 20th century problems had become a barrier to the kind of high performance systems required in the 1960s and 1970s. Specifically, they realized that organizations had institutionalized a splitting process in which labor and thought were split apart and "lodged" in different levels. As an approach to work design this had many problems, one of which was that it functioned as a social defense system in such a way as to promote the use of primitive defenses on the part of employees.

These researchers saw how bureaucracies based on principles of Taylorism had produced dysfunctional situations in the coal fields, factories, weaving sheds, and assembly plants. By organizing on the assumption that managers think and workers do, structures, policies, and procedures were built up that created horrific work lives for an increasingly educated workforce, engendered ongoing labor relations problems, and tremendously diminished competence "on the line," or "in the field," or wherever work occurred, without the expectation that those working could and would think, solve problems, confront complex issues, grapple with challenging tasks, and collaborate to improve work situations.

This research was on the intellectual forefront of a massive change in industrial organization, one that came to recognize the intellectual competence and creativity of workers, and embrace the essential role of collaboration across key boundaries. The chief design imperative of this work was moving organizations in the direction of self-managing teams of people who took responsibility for managing a subunit of some production process. Between the traditional, shaming work design of the assembly line and the fully self-managing work groups were all manner of employee involvement schemes that have now become de rigeur, but were quite revolutionary back then.

Technology and market instability spurred these changes along by altering the competitive equation in such a way that organizations had to improve on both quality and cost simultaneously in order to compete in the newly emergent global marketplace. And they had to know how to adapt rapidly and accurately in the turbulent environment. Putting problem-solving and decision-making capability at the boundary of the organization, close to where the problems actually occur, enabled organizations to adapt effectively. Leaving the decision making centralized ensured turgid, disjointed, and ineffective responses to the changing marketplace.

Returning problem-solving responsibility to workers, and reintegrating thinking and doing, produced remarkable outcomes, including a heightened presence of "depressivity" on the shop floor. As this experiment worked its way through our organizations, a great deal about the group and its potential value as a social defense has been learned. Well-functioning groups, it turns

out, enable their members to work at very high levels of performance by providing the essential conditions for thought: containment and coherence of experience.

In teams people create the web of relationships that enable
them to contain their experience, and by bundling the formerly
discrete bits back up into meaningful "chunks," experience
gained a coherence. The result, while no panacea, elicits a much
more mature, dedicated, competent, and sophisticated approach
to work. That is unless it creates chaos.

The move toward self-managing teams foreshadowed a trend
that would shape organizations at all levels as postindustrialism
washed over the organizational landscape. Corresponding to this
change in the shop floor, and in other blue collar settings, the
emergence of the New Order created a set of conditions that
required sophisticated teamwork on the part of engineers, techni-
cians, line managers, and the myriad types of knowledge worker
that appeared with the advent of the New Order. Now, the "functional silos" that characterized the hated bureaucratic order and
kept people who held different aspects of the same problem segmented off from one another, were dismantled. They were increasingly replaced by the cross-functional team, composed of
people from the various specialized disciplines that were required
to work together to solve problems, produce products, and address important issues.

The social technologies of team development that were
crafted for the shop floor have been elaborated and adapted to
the entire range of pink and white collar settings as well. The
basic problems addressed by using team structures have, in many
ways, become the sacred tenets of the postindustrial order: cross-
functional teamwork, decentralized problem solving, sophisticated collaboration based on shared tasks and negotiated authority, flattened hierarchy. To my mind, the self-managing teams on
the shop floor were, conceptually and historically, a key link from
the culmination of the industrial organization to the emergence
of the postindustrial setting.

Today we can see a great continuing emphasis on teams as
a key structure for enabling high performance—but primarily at

the top and lower levels of organizations. Executive team development is pervasive as the belief in the transformative effect of the charismatic, heroic leader is being supplanted by a recognition of the role of the executive constellation. Executive teams go on retreats, reflect on their experience, work with McKinsey consultants to develop themselves from mere "groups" into real "teams," and often devote themselves to learning how to work together effectively (Katzenbach & Smith, 1994). Similarly, cross-functional teams are the order of the day, handling everything from developing new products to solving problems and ensuring quality. They have become the productive backbone of modern organizations.

## KNOWLEDGE WORK AND THE INTERACTIONAL CONTEXT OF COMPETENCE

Those who have worked in systems paradigms recognize that competent work is the result of a multitude of interactions. Authorization is reciprocal—leaders need followers and followers need leaders in order to work; teachers and students rely on each other to produce learning; marketing and production depend upon each other to get the right products to market; and so on. This mutual interdependence that underpins any social system establishes the process of authorization, delegation, leadership, and interpersonal collaboration that produces work.

The importance of this perspective is heightened by the increasing reliance on knowledge and knowledge work to achieve success. Value is increasingly added through knowledge and the capacity to leverage it. As a result, managers must focus on the information needed to produce and the different kinds of relationships needed to do the work. To find creative solutions and fresh approaches, New Organizations depend increasingly on the pooling and integrating of knowledge and experience. And, as with so many other features of the New Order, such effort puts a premium on being able to mobilize the higher order defenses that enable people to think together, to bring curiosity to the task, and to link ideas together in pursuit of a shared purpose.

Yet this type of collaborative work comes at the cost of disturbing anxieties that are linked to the challenge of learning in public. When problem solving, innovation, and development depend on the linking of experience, people must be able to openly address experience without fear of reprisal, and equally to draw on the help of others to put their own thoughts and feelings into an organizational context. This, in turn, entails the capacity to tolerate the shame and frustration of not knowing, living with the vulnerability required to learn from others, and coping with the public experience of being wrong. As these experiences resonate with early life experiences, they can elicit primitive fantasies and pressure to defend against them with equally primitive defensive postures.

Similarly complex, creative, passionate, interdependent collaboration means that the subjective as well as objective, the irrational as well as analytic, the unconscious as well as conscious dimensions of experience will emerge and, ultimately, be available for deepening work. It also means that both the creative and destructive aspects of unconscious irrationality will emerge.

For example, the manager's experience of anxiety-in-role can usefully be understood (Bion, 1967) as the "shadow of the future," if people can find a way to think about and put their experiences into an organizational perspective. The anxieties that are stirred deep within managers may be one of the most sensitive scanning and early warning systems available. Yet, these capabilities can only work if the subjective, irrational dimension of experience is valued, allowed to emerge, and put into a task-related perspective.

Yet the emergence of irrationality and primary process is often anxiously avoided for a wide variety of ostensible reasons, including the kinds of efforts to avoid either offending or exposing one's prejudice that often get subsumed under the concept of "political correctness." No doubt the exposure of primary process and one's irrational experience is frightening. When the proponents of "political correctness" are unable to distinguish between destructive attribution and the exploration of irrationality or unconscious material, perhaps they are being used to defensively attack the capacity in organizations to learn from the irrational dimension of experience.

Since careful attention to the interactional context of work requires recognition of irrationality, group emotional life, and subjectivity, it also requires people to bear with the associated anxieties. Defensive flight from recognition of the interactional context of competence can be observed in a variety of defensive postures. One is the tendency to make the individual sacrosanct in knowledge-based organizations and to develop cultural practices built on this heroic notion of knowledge. Another is the creation of numerous programs and gimmicks that are ostensibly introduced to create teamwork, collaboration, positive diversity, etc., but often appear to do more to destroy true learning contexts than to foster them. I would suggest that these programs—and the magical thinking invested in them—are used to defend against the shame, dependency, and vulnerability required to achieve true collaboration and creative interaction. Finally, I would like to touch on the way that issues of diversity are at times transformed into identity group politics, and in so doing get disconnected from task. This type of flight substitutes a focus on the wider social and political issues for careful attention to how issues of diversity affect the ability to collaborate on work tasks, or vice versa, transforming collaborative challenges into identity group politics. In terms of enabling people to keep the interactional context of work in mind, this has the same obliterating effect as does radical individualism, only by moving the focus away from the organizational context, though in the opposite direction.

Can organizations find ways of containing these processes in order to harness them productively to work tasks? What social defenses will evolve to help people maintain themselves in a depressive positive while having these vulnerable experiences? Creating an appreciation of the interactional context of competence, and seeing knowledge as collectively developed, will require structures and methods that can contain the primitive anxieties and irrational emotions that are inevitably stirred when people are able to expose their experiences, link them with others, and be vulnerable enough to learn in public.

Of late, the essential role of organizational learning, and the systems view of organizations in order to function, has become a leading fad through the idea of the "learning organization." Yet

by turning these ideas into a cultlike movement complete with
its own cliches and rituals amounts to a defensive neutralization
of these potentially disruptive and anxiety producing ideas. At
the same time, the growth of a movement around the "learning
organization" clearly speaks to a desperately felt need to get access to the kinds of understanding and knowledge that reside at
the level of context rather than at the individual or even small-
group levels.

System-level learning requires an integrated capacity to link
one's own experience with that of others and the willingness to
test perceptions against other kinds of data. The paranoid–schizoid position is unwilling to tolerate this kind of stance, since when
operating from this psychological position troubling feelings and
attitudes must be projected elsewhere, perceptions become
calcified and concretely adhered, and ideas that threaten to dis-
confirm this rigidly split apart worldview must be defeated.

## THE CULTURE OF SERVICE AND ITS PERSONAL TOLL

In the New Order, the customer is all. Satisfying the requirements
of the customer, doing it better, quicker, and more effectively is
the route to survival. Many bureaucratic procedures that existed
to enhance regulation and stability also, it turns out, diminish
responsiveness across the customer boundary. They are being
removed—people are now "empowered" to meet customer
needs. However, the expectation to "satisfy" customers creates a
sense of emotional vulnerability and exposure that was before
ameliorated by the various buffering features of bureaucratic organization. Whereas before an employee could pair with a disappointed customer to blame the system for its unresponsiveness,
now the employee is likely to be accountable. Authority is thus
shifted from the "system," with its procedures and rules, to the
customer and his or her experience. The organization becomes
a world in which satisfying customers' demands and desires is the
driving criterion for decision making.

The model of the service provider appears increasingly to
be the dominant metaphor by which organizations shape their

internal worlds as well. Many organizations are replacing management hierarchies with simulated internal markets: divisions, units, etc., become profit or cost centers, cost accounting systems create simulated systems of exchange, and transactions between various subunits are expected to emulate customer, supplier, or even competitor relations that mirror the external world.

Alastair Bain (1994) speaks about one of the interesting dilemmas that this approach can create. By replacing other understandings of role relations with a kind of pervasive "provider–customer" relationship, people often lose contact with the deeper meanings, and hence sources of satisfaction and purpose, connected to their work. This is perhaps easiest to see in the public and nonprofit arenas where, for example, blood becomes another product line for the Red Cross, or the economics of "case-mix" dominate hospital planning. Du Gay and Salman (1992) explore the impact of these shifts in images of organizational life in a fascinating article entitled "The Cult(ure) of the Customer" which discusses the emergence of the "enterprising" individual as the new model of citizenship and participation. By eliminating restrictive bureaucratic control and liberating the entrepreneurial drive, the New Order will produce simultaneous innovation and improvement throughout a firm. A key element in this frame of reference is reducing the now despised dependency, which is seen as the source of inhibition in acting authoritatively to address issues.

The approaches to reducing what is regarded as this bureaucracy-induced dependency and lethargy are many: removing layers of organization, cross-functional teams, fostering individual accountability through peer review and appraisal schemes. This emphasis is on the activation of the "self-fulfilling impulses of all the organization's members" in order to "empower" all members to "add value" through their own initiative (Du Gay & Salman, 1992).

Because this picture of organizational life is inherently personality centered it tends to overlook the impact of social context, human relatedness, and group forces on performance. What happens to the social context when organizations are comprised of "enterprising individuals?" Often one can see the destructive irrationality getting projected into it and then the social context (or "system," as it may be regarded) becomes the hated, persecuting object.

Another interesting feature of this service-intensive market focus was illustrated by a film shown at a sales training event held for a large multinational firm. *The Remains of the Day* was used to illustrate what the leaders of this sales organization felt embodied the perfect "sales attitude": a complete subordination of one's own needs, constant attention to the wishes and desires of those one is serving, locating full authority in their needs. What remained from the day, or life, was a depressed, disconnected individual who was only able to live vicariously.

## SOCIAL DEFENSES IN THE NEW ORDER

With the decline of the bureaucratic order, the two key dimensions of organizational life that were used in socially defensive fashion are diminishing: stable structures and authority that is embedded in structure. To be sure, organizations operating in the Old Order provided structures and authority relations that covered the entire continuum of social defenses, from those that supported mature functioning to those that supported splitting, projection, and the whole gamut of dysfunctional relationships. Nevertheless, they provided means by which people could help to manage the painful anxieties and emotions associated with working in organizations.

Stable structures provide containers for experience—people could project aspects of themselves into these structures and then reintegrate their experience in either coherent or fragmented form. But the structures were there to offer containment. Being embedded in structures, authority was conferred from top down and authority relations in organizations served as mirrors of people's internal fantasy life in relation to authority figures. The experience of interacting with fictive family dynamics might be reparative or confirm the worst, depending on the organization, but this approach to authority nevertheless provided means of managing authority issues.

How social defense systems evolve, and which organizational practices will "take on" these additional dynamic functions, remains to be seen as we pass through the current transitional phase. Since authority that is embedded in structure produces the kind of "command and control" environment that interferes with the "empowerment" of the enterprising individual, a new form of authority relation is emerging that is based on negotiated agreement. Given this much more reciprocal approach to authorization, using authority relations as containers and metabolizers of primitive experience is increasingly dysfunctional because it contaminates the essential process of negotiation.

We can see so many variations on the theme of abdication of authority in this more complex arrangement. While "coaching," "cheerleading," "consulting," "facilitating," and "serving" have a role to play, they can never substitute for the reality of authority relations and the cycle of anxiety and defense that come along with it. New and effective social defense systems will include approaches to authority relations that do not try to evade or conceal the irrationality and aggression involved in differentiating authority and yet still embrace approaches to authorization based more on negotiation than command and control.

## "THE REMAINS OF THE DAY" IN NEW ORGANIZATIONS

The defenses that people employ when operating from the paranoid–schizoid position are, inevitably, fragmenting. Unwanted bits of experience, painful feelings, despised parts of the self are split off and evacuated elsewhere when splitting, projection, and projective identification are relied upon to manage at that end of the spectrum of defenses. The legacy of the paranoid–schizoid process is scapegoating; stalemated organizational splits; emotionally and intellectually disabled people; restricted collaborative ability across important boundaries; hateful, abusive, and paranoid authority relations; and an inability to understand immediate tasks in ways that allow people to link them to wider purposes.

Since the residue of ineffective social defense systems can be seen in the disowned split-off aspects of organizational life, the toxicity in organizations today creates an interesting window through which to observe the growing pains of new social defense systems. One example is the paradoxical and confusing ways in which responsibility and accountability are delegated in the decentralizing process. People are expected to "take responsibility," are held accountable for "self-management," and expected to respond to dictates that require inner motivation. The ways in which these messages are communicated today can be seen in much of the stilted language, fervent ideologies, and faddish practices (e.g., reengineering and learning organizations often seem to be transformed into superficial, ritualistic practices rather than thoughtful frameworks) that seems to gloss over and hide many of the contradictory imperatives that many seem to be struggling with. More important, the ambiguity that remains to be worked out in this area of required self-motivation leaves people confused and often overwhelmed. I also believe the disowned bits and residue of paranoid–schizoid functioning can be seen in the anger and bitterness of so many who feel exploited and devalued by their organizations and in the thoughtless accidents and slipups that often have devastating consequences (Obholzer, 1995).

## THE CHAOTIC MIDDLE

Recently, however, as I hear the disorienting experiences of middle managers through my consultancy work, I have been coming to regard the unconscious use of that strata as one place where unintegrated toxicity seems to land frequently. While teams hold out the possibility of providing containment, the so-called teams for the middles seem so much more amorphous and confusing than for the lowers and uppers. Instead of maintaining membership in consistent, clearly charged and coherently organized teams, middle managers seem to be bobbing around in a sea of ever changing arrangements. Middles live in a world that is more

like that of the large-group experience: tendencies toward deper-
sonalization, threats to a sense of identity and clear purpose, and
disorientation (Turquet, 1974).

Never sure what their reporting structures are any more, or
to whom they are accountable, middle managers seem to be shuf-
fled around and maintained in a permanent state of amorphous
role relations. Moreover, they seem to be doing at least two jobs
now: fulfilling the requirements, as vague as they are, of their
position, while devoting tremendous amounts of time and energy
to the latest program on quality, or excellence, or reengineering,
or learning organizations. Increasingly, these efforts become internal sources of chaos and disarray, often experienced as persecutory, holding dubious promise to them either personally or
organizationally.

As a social defense, the team structure can effectively support
members struggling to maintain their ability to think and act
competently in the midst of modern environments. However,
without the same degree of stable team structures that benefit
the top and bottom levels of organizations, I believe that the
middle suffers from the absence of a sense of embeddedness and
task to the degree that the other groups enjoy.

I do not wish to imply that the uppers and lowers exist within
a calm, stable setting in contrast to the disarray and flux of that
in which the middles exist. The basic turbulence and fluctuation
that characterize organizational life today pervade all aspects of
the organization. What is different is that structures have been
institutionalized often at the top and lower levels enabling people
to cope with the shifting realities of modern competitive environments more thoughtfully and competently than those that I see
developed for the middles.

Reasoning along these lines inevitably raises questions about
whether there is a kind of "unconscious conspiracy" to use middle management as a receptacle for the most unbearable disarray
and chaos in our New Organizations. I have wondered whether
the manifestation of the experience of dislocation is left either in
middle management or with those whose employment has been
terminated as a kind of unconscious strategy, in its own right,

to enable work to continue at the top and bottom levels of the organization.

## LEADERSHIP IN THE NEW ORDER

Much has been written about the requirements of leadership in the emerging organizations. How today's executives must negotiate and sell ideas, how leadership is intimately bound up with working across boundaries, and why leaders must rely on instilling excitement about mission and purpose rather than depend on former carrot-and-stick methods, have all been extensively discussed elsewhere. Here, I want to touch upon aspects of leadership in contemporary settings that are geared to helping people manage the complex emotional realities they face.

The shape of social defense systems that are adapted to new marketplace realities remains to be discovered. The following is a rudimentary list of principles that, in my experience, guide leaders and managers who are most successful at helping people contain their work related anxieties in ways that foster high-level functioning from the depressive end of the defense spectrum and helps avoid either the grandiosity or superficiality that so often accompanies efforts to develop systems today. This is the beginning of a set of ideas that I intend to carry forward in future writing:

### 1. Managing Change

One often encounters a sense of disorientation and depression in settings that are undergoing a seemingly endless chain of reorganization, merger, layoffs, reengineering, etc. People often seem to defend against the emotional effects of change and loss with frenetic activity. Change and the prospect of impending change often surfaces all kinds of unrealistic attitudes and behaviors and elicits primitive defenses.

Increasingly, one task of effective management is to know how to help people confront the emotional aspects of change.

As the issues of mourning and sadness, anger, denial, unrealistic fantasy, etc., that attend dramatic change become more prevalent, managers must learn how to contain the emotional process and respond effectively.

## 2. Promoting Learning

The sort of learning that genuinely enhances organizational capability is extremely difficult to achieve and comes at the cost of individuals having to relinquish important aspects of their self-idealizations. In order to create genuine learning environments people must learn in public and must expose both their experience (with all of its irrational subjectivity) and their areas of ignorance. This is what Bion (1961) meant when he discussed the "hatred of learning from experience."

Providing the leadership for this type of learning entails not only vulnerability on the part of the leader but also being able to publicly tolerate the frustration of not knowing and of sustaining the unknown question in the face of pressure to gain closure with quick answers. As Bion (1967) described, the capacity for thought arises from the ability to tolerate frustration, a state in which one can then "mate conception and realizations" and thus be able to "learn from experience." By embodying this capacity, leaders can provide the containment for others to tolerate their frustrations as well and thereby help develop this capacity for themselves. Without the ability to bear our frustrations and uncertainties in the service of productive thought, we end up projecting them into others and then undermining the precious capacity to collaborate. Heroic conceptions of leadership are inconsistent with the need to develop this capacity either oneself or in one's followers.

## 3. Preserving the Sense of Social Context

So many of the forces that shape today's organizations tend to obscure the relevance, and even existence of, the social context that has such a powerful impact on our experience and behavior. When knowledge-based organizations, for example, tend to make the individual sacrosanct, the critical interactional context required for getting knowledge used and leveraged is often forgotten. Similarly, the increasingly "virtuality" of organization can obscure the dynamic forces that link and shape people's experiences even if they are geographically dispersed. Charles Handy (1995) offers a perceptive analysis of the heightened role of trust in virtual organizations. He highlights many elements of the social context that must be created in order to build an environment shaped by trust: existence of boundaries, a predisposition to learning, an emphasis on bonding, and a sense of clear accountability.

In the New Organizations, effective leadership requires both fighting the atomizing tendencies and keeping the impact and coherence of the social context in mind. This can be accomplished by continually examining the impact of interdependency, clarifying and defining the boundaries within which the enterprising individual is free to achieve, and continuously articulating a meaningful mission to help people ground their individual experiences in collective meaning.

One great problem with "empowerment" is that it tends to create the individual as the locus of understanding. The "enterprising" individual is often regarded as an individual performer—a concept that obliterates the crucial web of enabling or disabling relationships. Mal O'Conner (private communication, 1995) developed the idea of "enrollment" as an alternative, and far superior in my view, concept. By helping people see themselves in role and understand their roles, no matter how protean or unstable they are, leaders can help people link their authority to that of others and bring their interdependent experiences into focus.

## 4. Preserve Reflective Space

We are told that successful organizations have a predisposition to action. I do believe this to be true. Yet I often see organizations with an aversion to pausing long enough to reflect on experience. Alastair Bain (1994) has hypothesized the strong defenses within organizations that are mobilized against the fantasized dangers of uncertainty, fear of loss of control, and fears of new ideas that arise from the kind of group wisdom that can emerge from authentically reflective space. Without reflective space, the learning organization becomes yet another empty gimmick.

## 5. Fostering Boundary Awareness

The role of boundary awareness in maintaining a sense of identity is key. In the Old Order the principal boundaries that people relied upon were structural. It is often erroneously assumed that because structures have become fluid that boundaries no longer exist. Many do and, if clearly developed and focused upon, can serve many of the same functions as structural boundaries. Gilmore and Hirschhorn (1992) have written about the critical role of authority, task, identity, and political boundaries in contemporary organizations. Many processes can be understood from the perspective of boundaries. For example, while sharp awareness about organizational strategies, about aligned goals, and about decision processes have important organizational benefits, it also serves to foster a greater awareness of existing boundaries. In the same vein, the varied competencies required to collaborate and negotiate across these different boundaries become an increasingly important skill in the New Order.

## THE NEW STANCE OF LEADERSHIP

Along with the changes discussed in this paper, and the entire range of sea changes that seem to be transforming our society and world into an as-yet-to-be-decoded New Order, shifts in the meaning of leadership and authority have a deep impact on our ability to understand New Order organizations. Beyond the specific management challenges detailed above, I want to also offer some speculations about the shifting *stance* of leadership required for New Order organizations.

On one dimension, I believe we are seeing a shift in the kind of *person* that is expected to appear in the role of leader or manager. Most importantly, the *person* is expected to be more visible in the role. In becoming a person again, leaders are called upon to be someone who not only represents an analysis or approach, but someone who can be seen to represent the reality of the experiences of other people as well. The new leaders are people who make their own subjective synthesis of "objective" data apparent and who can be seen to take their own feelings, their personal thoughts, and perhaps their own irrationality into account. The postmodern face of leadership is one that recognizes the inherent limitations of any ideological, scientific, or technical standpoint.

In fact, I believe that the New Leadership will be one in which the interior realm of the leader is much more visible and, in fact, the leader's own recognition of an interior realm will become an essential criterion for genuine authorization and committed followership. The 1996 presidential election in the United States offers, in my view, an interesting example of this shift in what people are expecting of their leaders.

Much was made of Bill Clinton's "character" problems—the events and behaviors that seemed to suggest that he was at times impaired by moral conflict, guilty of changing positions too readily, weak at the core, etc. Yet, in the end, these qualities of Clinton and the great focus on them throughout his first term, did nothing to dissuade the electorate from returning him to office. I actually believe that these lapses, flaws, and failings, rather than threatening his viability as a politician, were a source of electoral strength. I believe that, increasingly, people want leaders who are *human,* and leaders whose humanity is clearly available to themselves as well. Since we live in a world of such enormous complexity and uncertainty, the two-dimensional, unswerving emblem of simple values has increasingly come to seem out of touch with reality. Bob Dole embodied just that leadership stance—the kind of leadership people in earlier times sought out.

The article by Larry Hirschhorn (1990) mentioned above identifies some of these qualities. He grounds an analysis of the leadership requirements in postindustrial settings in a similar analysis, one that focuses upon the capacity of the leader to be vulnerable and upon the leaders' ability to learn (and learn in public). To take this one step further, I would argue that leadership in New Order organizations increasingly depends upon the power of creative relationships and all that is required in establishing, sustaining, nurturing, and bearing the anxiety involved in working through the medium of creative relationships. And since the creativity in relationships is premised upon a mutual acceptance of the more subjective, irrational spheres of human functioning, these anxieties can be enormous.

## CONCLUSION

The dark side of organizational freedom and the authority to take action is insecurity and the loss of control. Without the traditional moorings of stable structures and authority relations that are embedded in structures, people must interpret, negotiate, and learn constantly in order to find their selves in their organizations, to find the meaning of their roles, and to find their competence. While this transformation of organizational life is a necessary adaptation to the emerging world, it also challenges people with the threats arising from disorientation, vulnerability, shame, exposure, and disassociation. To succeed, I believe organizations must help people avoid the regressive pulls that accompany these forces. From the perspective discussed in this paper, this means developing social defense systems that will help people achieve the kind of psychological integration required to think, to work with experience, and to link creatively with others.

## REFERENCES

Bain, A. (1994, July 2). Organizational life today: Five hypotheses [excerpts from a presentation]. Australian Institute of Social Analysis Seminar Day.

Bion, W. R. (1961). *Experiences in groups.* London: Tavistock.

Bion, W. R. (1967). *Second thoughts.* London: Heinemann.

Du Gay, P., & Salman, G. (1992, September). The cult(ure) of the customer. *Journal of Management Studies, 29*(5), 616–633.

Garvin, D. A. (1995, September-October). Leveraging processes for strategic advantage: A roundtable with Xerox's Allaire, USAA's Herres, Smithkline Beecham's Leschly, and Pepsi's Weatherup. *Harvard Business Review, 73*(5), 76–93.

Handy, C. (1995, May-June). Trust and the virtual organization. *Harvard Business Review, 73*(3), 40–55.

Hirschhorn, L. (1988). *The workplace within: Psychodynamics of organizational life.* Cambridge, MA: MIT Press.

Hirschhorn, L. (1990). Leaders and followers in a postindustrial age: A psychodynamic view. *The Journal of Applied Behavioral Science, 26*(4), 529–543.

Hirschhorn, L., & Gilmore, T. (1992, May-June). The new boundaries of the "boundaryless" company. *Harvard Business Review, 70*(3), 104–116.

Jaques, E. (1955). Social systems as a defense against persecutory and depressive anxiety. In M. Klein, P. Heimann, & R. E. Money-Kyrle (Eds.), *New directions in psychoanalysis* (pp. 478–498). London: Tavistock.

Katzenbach, J. R., & Smith, D. K. (1994). Teams at the top. *The McKinsey Quarterly, 1,* 71–80.

Khaleelee, O., & Miller, E. (1985). Beyond the small group: Society as an intelligible field of study. In M. Pines (Ed.), *Bion and group psychotherapy* (pp. 355–383). London: Routledge & Kegan Paul.

Klein, M. (1940). Mourning and its relation to manic-depressive states. In *The Writings of Melanie Klein Vol. 1: Love, guilt and reparation* (pp. 344–369). London: Hogarth Press.

Klein, M. (1946). Notes on some schizoid mechanisms. In *The Writings of Melanie Klein Vol. 3: Envy and gratitude and other works* (pp. 1–24). London: Hogarth Press.

Lapierre, L. (1989, Summer). Mourning, potency, and power in management. *Human Resource Management, 28*(2), 177–189.

McKinley, W., Sanchez, C. M., & Schick, A. G. (1995, August). Organizational downsizing: Constraining, cloning, learning. *The Academy of Management Executive, 9*(3), 32–44.

Menzies, I. E. P. (1960). A case-study in the functioning of social systems as a defense against anxiety. *Human Relations, 13,* 95–121.

Obholzer, A. (1995). *Accidents and organizations.* Unpublished paper.

Pfeffer, J. (1994). *Competitive advantage through people*. Boston, MA: Harvard Business School Press.

Pfeffer, J. (1995, February). Producing sustainable competitive advantage through the effective management of people. *The Academy of Management Executive, 9*(1), 55–72.

Porter, M. E. (1985). *Competitive advantage*. New York: Free Press.

Quinn, J. B. (1992). *Intelligent enterprise*. New York: Free Press.

Roberts, V. Z. (1994). The self-assigned impossible task. In A. Obholzer & R. V. Zagier (Eds.), *The unconscious at work* (pp. 110–120). London: Routledge.

Segal, H. (1957). Notes on symbol formation. *International Journal of Psycho-Analysis, 38*, 391–397.

Shapiro, E. R., & Carr, A. (1991). *Lost in familiar places*. New Haven and London: Yale University Press.

Trist, E. L. (1977). Collaboration in work settings: A personal perspective. *The Journal of Applied Behavioral Science, 13*(3), 268–278.

Trist, E. L., & Emery, F. E. (1965). The causal texture of organizational environments. *Human Relations, 18*, 21–32.

Turquet, P. M. (1974). Leadership: The individual and the group. In G. S. Gibbard, J. Hartmann, & R. Mann (Eds.), *Analysis of groups*. San Francisco: Jossey-Bass.

Whyte, W. H. (1956). *The organization man*. New York: Simon & Schuster.

# 5

# The Psychology of Vision

## Larry Hirschhorn, Ph.D.

Today's organizations, their leaders, and followers, face over-whelming challenges: markets are volatile; technology becomes outdated seemingly overnight; information systems link people in brand-new ways; and competition intensifies everywhere. Clients, board members, shareholders, and employees expect leaders to create and communicate a vision of the organization's relation-ship to a turbulent marketplace. The vision will presumably help people focus on the right questions, search for the right data, and take the most appropriate risks.

What are the constituents of a *good vision?* The term itself may suggest that a business vision is a dream or fantasy about the future. Indeed, vision consultants often promote such a concept. They ask executives to identify their personal hopes for the fu-ture, to imagine the ideal organization, and to do this work medi-tatively; for example, to think and feel in silence before speaking at a "vision conference."

Nothing could be further from the truth. In the world of business a "vision must be grounded in reality," otherwise it remains a dream or fantasy. What is asked by organizations of their leaders is that the "vision" be a prod to action. It must direct action and decision making. Thus, the "vision" not only provides a framework for constructing an inherently unknowable future, it is also deeply pragmatic in two ways: it helps us simplify our view of the setting we are in, and it highlights a mechanism of action, the way in which causes, effects, and actions might be linked. Its simplicity and links to action "pulls" us to see reality as presenting a potential opportunity. In turn, this potential opportunity represents the conceptual and affective bridge between the present as we have known it and the present as it might become. Leaders propose such visions—such basic ideas—and followers, "pulled" by both the leader's vision and self-confidence as well as their own desire for excitement and risk, "sign onto" the vision.

Who are the leaders generating a "basic idea" and motivating—pulling—their followers along with it? Where do their basic ideas come from, and how do people identify with them sufficiently so that they engage their passions and energies fully? What are the dangers in the complicated psychodynamics that leaders and followers enact during this process, and how can we be alert to them? These are the questions explored in this chapter.

## THE VISION AS THE BASIC IDEA

### A Leader's Basic Idea

When Bill Gates, the founder of Microsoft, first set forth in business computers, he had begun to reshape society's work and home life, but how that evolution would proceed, how "far" it would go, and what the key leverage points along the way would be, were not known. As such, his personal passion for computers was not linked to an explicit ideal image. Rather, it was nourished by three sources. First, he believed deeply that computers were universal *tools,* a belief rooted in his own experience as a high school and college student. His world became computers, and, as he lived and operated through them, he became possessed by them. In essence, computers became his psychological world, and, because of that, he could believe that the "real" world would become fully computerized.

Second, Gates' passion also was nourished by his competitiveness: this man was determined to win any game he played. While the details of his earliest family life are unknown, one can generally presume that this drive to win is rooted in early childhood experience: in his relationship to his parents and in their hope for him and their fantasies of his future.

Third, the interrelated source of Gates' passion was his basic business idea: that the company controlling computer *interfaces*—between machine languages, between machines, between machine and user—would exercise enormous market power. Gates and his Microsoft "followers" have brilliantly executed this basic idea, so that the company's stockmarket valuation is often higher than General Motors' even with revenues that are minute by comparison.

## Simplification

Visions as "basic" ideas that "pull" are *simplifying*, e.g., "control computer interfaces." These ideas are a counterpoise to the uncertainty associated with an unpredictable marketplace. While many simplifying ideas may be one-sided, overly seductive, or wrong for the marketplace, this risk is part and parcel of a simple formulation that can pull followers along with sufficient excitement so that brilliantly executed strategies ensue. In addition to Microsoft, consider the following:

> "Bring large stores to small towns"—Sam Walton's simple idea-vision led to Wal-Mart.

> "Imitate IBM (build clones), don't try to differentiate from IBM"—the simple idea-vision that built Compaq.

"Computers can be sold over the phone"—Michael Dell's simple idea of vision that triggered Dell's enormous success.

"Sell styled but low-cost knock-down furniture"—Ingvar Kamprad's key idea in founding IKEA.

In retrospect, we applaud these breakthrough visions; in fact, they seem almost self-evident. Each of them, however, challenged conventional wisdom at the time. Thus, Sam Walton took the risk that people in small southern towns would flock to big stores to find good bargains, but there were no such stores there before Wal-Mart built them, much less any guarantee that people would show up. Ingvar Kamprad could not be sure that he would be able to sell knock-down furniture that had panache and did not look cheap. Michael Dell made the unprecedented assumption that computers were commodities, and that customers would welcome speed of delivery, ease of purchase, and service warranties—and pay for it. Walton, Dell and Kamprad, like other hugely successful visionaries, articulated the simplifying idea, which pulled their organizations along with it to implement that vision.

This "pulling" occurs because the articulated simplifying idea, fashioned by the leader, creates excitement among followers and underlines the great risks the enterprise faces in executing it. *Indeed, the excitement is stimulated because people can now feel the risk of the enterprise.*

## Where Do Simplifying Ideas Come From?

Successful "visionary" leaders are deeply familiar with their technologies and resources, products or services, customers or clients, and industries or fields. They also rely on their own talent and take advantage of luck (and others' mistakes). Thus, Sam Walton could build big stores in little towns because he learned the mechanics of retailing by working for other establishments. His first store was the familiar outlet on "Main Street." Bill Gates got the right to control DOS (the disk operating system) because another small entrepreneur, whom IBM first approached, was not ready to sign a confidentiality agreement. Gates did, capitalized on the situation by securing control of DOS, and then leveraged market position to control the Windows interface.

This hard work and skillful use of circumstance, however, does not explain the origination of a basic idea or vision and its pull on those who help execute it. We need to look elsewhere to understand that phenomenon.

## Vision and the Leader's Personal History

Creators of basic ideas draw upon personal experiences that are not directly related to their business situations, but instead are aspects of their broader social identities. In developing and shaping our identities, all of us incorporate our culture's explanation of what is important, good, and valuable. The culture, in effect, helps us see the drama of life in a particular way; it helps us identify the heroes, the villains, and interlocutors.

Significantly, successful leaders, by and large, do not purposefully shape their identities; rather their "genius" is based on their ability *to be shaped* by aspects of the culture: to be in tune, remain open, draw on the ideas and passions that they stimulate, and *become the stars of their own cultural shows.* They are, in essence, not detached. Moreover, they are able to motivate others to participate in their identification with that cultural aspect and their personal dramas in it. Bill Gates identifies with an American culture of technical proficiency, of machine mastery, of getting inside the machine, and creates a vision of "interface." Sam Walton identifies with small-town America, its friendliness and frugality, and articulates a vision of big stores emphasizing friendly customer service—and bargains. Ingvar Kamprad identifies with the frugality and enterprise of the poor region in which he grew up as well as with Sweden as an international symbol of grace and lightness in design. Microsoft and Wal-Mart have legions of dedicated people who follow the particular cultural identification and attendant visions of these leaders.

Consider as well the evolution of Rupert Murdoch, who has drawn upon the widest features of his native Australian culture to build a worldwide media empire, Sydney-based News Corp. Born in a well-to-do Australian family, Murdoch took up left-wing and anti-British activities (he displayed a bust of Lenin in his Oxford room). He found Britain to be complacent and uncompetitive. The ruling class, he asserted, despised business, had damaged Britain, and obstructed change. Passionate about his native country, Murdoch brought a conception of himself as a rebel Australian and entrepreneur to the first London newspaper he acquired, *The Sun*. He saw the paper as a way of attacking the hypocrisy of the English upper class, printing a combination of sex, sensationalism, and fun. He sustained this self-conception by identifying with Margaret Thatcher's vision of an entrepreneurial Britain, where wealth would become the conduit for economic and social development, not class. This constancy of self-conception—the rebel Australian who stirs things up—has helped Murdoch build a formidable organization and sustain, by and large, the loyalty and passions of those who work for him. However we assess the quality of his efforts; we must acknowledge his willingness and ability to construct a role for himself in a wide social drama. As a visionary, he lives in a dramatic world, the content of which is shaped both by his unconscious identification with wider cultural issues as well as his conscious desires and concrete, reality-based business ideas.

## FOLLOWERS' IDENTIFICATIONS

A well-established institution has the power to motivate its members because its value is defined and sanctioned by the wider culture. People affiliated with Harvard University or the Mayo Clinic, for example, feel grateful to these institutions for augmenting their own self-esteem. People affiliated with an emerging business or organization, or an enterprise in the throes of upheaving change, by contrast, must identify with the leader and the leader's vision if it is to be successfully enacted. In effect, personal charisma replaces institutional charisma.

Leaders neither create nor own reality, but provide an interpretation of it: their vision of it. Followers identify with this interpretation in a two-step process. First, they must identify deeply enough with the leader to trust that the vision is grounded in a shared reality. That is, if a vision is grounded in general marketplace exigencies ("There's an opportunity to provide big stores for small towns"), followers must be able to access the leader's vision through their own experience of the marketplace ("That's true, there is an opportunity"). Without yet fully understanding the vision's manifestation ("How do we do it, will it work?), only its articulation, the follower transfers his or her own tie to reality onto the leader. The follower, in effect, says, "The leader is oriented toward reality in the same way that I am."

In the second step, followers internalize the vision: they make it their own so that they can begin the work of shaping, refining and applying the vision to everyday reality ("we're going to build big stores in small towns"). In other words, followers do not encounter the vision rationally by estimating its likely chance for success, but do so irrationally by believing that the leader like themselves is attached to reality.

The 1993 appointment of George Fisher, the Head of Motorola, to the CEO position at Kodak exemplifies this irrational process. In the prior decade, Kodak's earnings grew weak and net income per share was only $.11 higher at its end than it was at its beginning. The Kodak board of directors had hoped that Kay Whitmore, the CEO, would increase profits by ruthlessly cutting costs. Whitmore hired a chief financial officer, Chris Steffen, who was known for his ability to reduce costs drastically while controlling future expenditures. However, after a tenure of several months, Chris Steffen quit, suggesting that Mr. Whitmore was not truly committed to cost-cutting. The board fired Kay Whitmore shortly afterwards. Business analysts took this as a sign that the board would appoint a CEO who would now cut deeply into the company's operations. Yet to everyone's surprise, the board turned its thinking upside down and hired George Fisher. As the CEO of Motorola, George Fisher had never boosted profits by cutting costs; instead, he was known for his technical imagination, for his ability to raise revenues by creating new products.

Reflecting on the board's change of mind, one informant noted that "directors looked at his background and began to believe his dream of combining Kodak's image technology with wireless technology." To be sure, board members are not followers, but like followers they depend deeply on the skills of the CEO they appoint. Their authority is limited to hiring and firing the chief executive officer. They cannot run the company themselves. In appointing Fisher, board members could not have possibly assessed Fisher's vision in a rational manner. There were too many imponderables. Instead, they identified with his own dream, his conviction became theirs, and they became excited that Kodak, like Motorola, could create and sell new products and processes for the information age. It is less that they came to believe in his dream than that they came to believe in him.

## The Role of Fear

When a vision "takes hold" it is exciting—the vision connects passion to work. Fear, however, is an important, complex dynamic in making the vision an integral part of the relationship between leaders and followers. Successful business leaders, for example, are often willing to take great risks—not because they underestimate the odds, but because they believe they are uniquely able to recover from mistakes or discover new solutions to unanticipated problems.

   Their followers tend to possess no such absolute courage. Instead, they trade their fear of the marketplace and its unpredictability for their fear of the leader's standards. That is, they internalize the leader's strict demands for high performance to enact the vision and are made anxious if and when they expect they might fail to meet those demands. In turn, the leader maintains fearlessness because he or she is confident that subordinates will work to the highest standard. Indeed, as many leaders have an underdeveloped conscience: they are more able to make people suffer in the service of accomplishing a task. Their fearlessness is thus twofold: leaders believe deeply in the fantasy of their own success, and they are not afraid to hurt others when necessary.

In trading the fear of the marketplace for the fear of the leader, followers gain additional excitement. Followers are first stimulated because the articulation of the vision allows them to experience the risk of the enterprise. However, because the leader will manage that risk, followers are free to apply their talents to the challenges at hand. This, in turn, allows them to experience the full expression of their own powers, prodded by their anxiety about meeting demands while sharing indirectly in the leader's self-confidence.

## Jean Riboud and the Role of Fear

Until his death in 1985, Jean Riboud, president of Schlumberger, a very profitable multinational oil services company, stimulated both great anxiety and self-confidence among his subordinates. Servicing oil drilling operations around the world, the company depended on engineers and managers who could work in isolation with little supervision. In the early 1980s the company had a corporate staff of 197 people supporting a workforce of 75,000 employees. The work rewarded self-sufficient and ambitious professionals who took risks. Managers under the age of 40, for example, could direct the work of thousands of employees.

Riboud was a master of his industry. He was committed to the fundamental idea that the company was in the "information" business, supplying oil companies with a wide range of real-time information on the potential yields and actual productivity of oil wells. This single-minded focus on information enabled Riboud to steer company growth while committing most of the company's resources to work in the oil fields, research and development, and the acquisition of companies (such as Fairchild) that deepened Schlumberger's competence to secure and distribute information using automated equipment.

Riboud, however, worked to stay psychologically distant from his employees. While he loved the company and believed in the primacy of its goals, he was emotionally detached from his subordinates. This enabled him to make painful decisions on behalf of the company and its shareholders. For example, believing that he had to be consistent in his application of corporate policy, that he should not make exceptions, he asked his closest confidant, Claude Baks, whom he had known for close to 40 years, to leave the firm at the required retirement age. Baks had hoped to remain with the company and was embittered by Riboud's decision. Riboud also feared complacency and often moved successful managers, without warning, to new posts. In appointing two subordinates to the top positions in the company, one to head oilfield services and one to head measurement, control, and components, he asked each man to lead the division in which he had less experience. As one very successful company officer noted, "With him, Riboud, you never feel safe."

Riboud, however, was not a narrow person focused entirely on his company and its prospects. He was passionate about art, a close confident of François Mitterand, the head of the Socialist Party, and played a significant role in sustaining the Cinémathèque Français, the international firm library. One might say that he compensated for his neutrality and the pain he most likely felt when hurting colleagues and subordinates by focusing on art and politics. Similarly, this complicated dynamic of fear is illustrated below.

## The Case of George

When consulting to the legal department of a large consumer products company, I met "George," its senior manager, a brilliant lawyer and keen strategist. Unlike many directors of legal departments who keep their focus narrow, George determined that his staff develop a deep understanding of the company's overall business and its strategy for creating value. The department's legal strategies, he insisted, could not be created in the abstract but had to be grounded in the company's business goals and approaches. In articulating this vision of his subordinates' marrying their legal work strategy to the company's strategy—that there be no battles between "church and state"—he also implied great risks. In effect, he was challenging his subordinates to work more like line managers within the company, rather than only "legal professionals." In addition to posing this challenge to his subordinates' skills and competencies, George was frequently brutal in his criticism, dominating conversations, and even behaving ruthlessly.

I was concerned that George's followers would identify only with his narcissism and not with the challenging work he had created through his vision of the legal department's role. That is, instead of internalizing this vision through identification with George and a shared reality, they would access it only through their relationship with George, their "leader." If this were the case, the dynamic of fear would only add to the distortion. Because George could behave so brutally, rather than *trading* the fear of the "marketplace" for the fear of the leader, and thereby becoming more free to work, his subordinates would only be placating him, not meeting the new challenges his vision offered and the high standards he had set.

I discovered that there was a nuanced balance between the pleasure people felt in doing exciting, important, and highly valued work and in feeling highly valued by virtue of their relationship with George. They identified with him insofar as he represented and communicated a vision of important, high-quality work, and they internalized his standards. Additionally, they identified directly with his conviction that he was a hero in the drama of his own life, thereby partaking of his self-confidence.

In fact, George, a deeply religious man, had a complex moral stance toward his work; he perhaps compensated for his inability to acknowledge the role that intuition plays in human relationships by relying on religious precepts to regulate those relationships. In turn, his followers, in a complicated way, drew on his talents and conviction, and became psychological partners in his venture, even as they were often hurt by his brutality. Noted one lawyer in the department: "We hate the climate, but if George left, we'd all leave."

## HOW LEADERS FAIL

A vision—a basic idea—is born in the imagination of a leader, who has internalized the cross-currents of the wide culture he or she has unconsciously experienced. For that vision to be effective, however, it must be ultimately situated "between" the imagination of the leader and the reality the leader is working to interpret. It is, in psychoanalytic terms, a "transitional object": a place or space where leaders and followers, reality and fantasy, and the present "as it is" and "as it might be" meet.

Leaders fail when they do not create and sustain this transitional space. Consider, for example, the case of Joseph Fernandez, former Chancellor of the New York City Board of Education. Once a teenage heroin addict in Harlem, Fernandez eventually became superintendent of the Miami school system, and then was avidly recruited to the New York system. Despite being hailed as a hero on his arrival, and notwithstanding a string of accomplishments, Fernandez's first contract was not renewed. He was voted out by the very people who courted him. What happened?

## Joseph Fernandez

People who challenge the status quo, in the marketplace or in government, have a dramatic conception of themselves; as we have seen, they are the stars of their own shows, the heroes of their own dramas. Their stories conjure up enemies that have been vanquished. By returning to New York, the scene of his early failure and delinquency, Fernandez was, I suggest, enacting the drama of the prodigal son returning to right the wrongs. However, *he inextricably confused his own story of rising from the ashes with how New York City schools could be transformed.* Unlike Rupert Murdoch, the rebel from the outback who was able to "match" his personal story with marketplace realities, Fernandez seemed insufficiently detached from his own story to take up the appropriate work of leadership.

Significantly, in the middle of a heated controversy about such hot-button issues as condom distribution and homosexuality, Fernandez published his autobiography, which, beyond describing how he overcame adversity, disparaged the mayor of the city and labeled a school board member "a political prostitute."

This seemingly quixotic act symbolized, I believe, his overpersonalization of the situation and his distance from reality. He relied too much on his aggression and passion, as if he alone could transform the schools. Not surprisingly, he was unable to build the alliances and relationships needed to govern effectively.

## Steven Friedman

Similarly, consider the case of Steven Friedman, the director of the failed TV show *USA Today*. Under his creative direction, the show, Friedman argued, would uniquely tie information and entertainment to create "infotainment," a form of news appealing to busy Americans. The show was financed by Gannet, a communications conglomerate, produced by Grant Tinker who had retired as NBC's chairman, and was supported by an ultramodern production studio costing $40 million. The show was a flop after its first airing.

What happened? Postmortems by his staff suggested that Friedman was a charismatic but temperamental leader. Portraying himself as a rebel and outsider who would transform television news, he helped create a climate of excitement in which subordinates felt they were corporate outlaws ready to destroy the establishment. They were the modernizers, the good guys ready to attack the "bad" producers and directors who did not understand infotainment.

Friedman's arrogance undermined him. Convinced of his own superiority, he overlooked some of the most basic common practices of television production while developing a basic contempt for his audience. Because he disdained bureaucracy he appointed no coordinator to control story development, nor did he hire any professional writers. Moreover, he was convinced that the audience would be satisfied at least in the first year with simply glitz. Most importantly, in confusing his fantasies of the future of television with the reality of television production, he and his staff suppressed their common sense. As one subordinate noted, "We were like a family of alcoholics. Some of us saw what was happening but no one wanted to hear about it." Like Fernandez,

Friedman subjected reality to a private fantasy. Fernandez spun the fantasy of his own biography as an exemplar of overcoming odds, while Friedman spun the fantasy of his own visionary powers—disconnected ultimately from a vision of television news that could touch reality—that could be apprehended through common sense as well as the imagination.

## The Case of John

Consider, finally the case of John, the CEO of a large tertiary care hospital. Facing cost pressures, as all hospitals do, he wanted to create an "expense reduction target," which would guide management's efforts to reduce costs by reengineering the hospital's operations. Yet in working with him and his executive team, my consulting group discovered that few members of the team could make the case that hospital expenses absolutely had to fall. Most strikingly, the hospital was located in a high-income, high-growth suburban region, and the hospital had very few competitors. It seemed very likely that people in the region would in aggregate be spending more rather than less for health care, and that the hospital would continue to get a significant share of that increase in spending. In business terms, the hospital had significant "market power." This meant that even if some prices—reimbursement rates—fell, the hospital's total revenue would rise significantly.

There was no convincing John. For example, when we presented him with data that showed that the population in the region was not aging, or that the hospital had a significant share of all admissions in the region, he searched for counterarguments. Examples were: "Our share is high, but it is probably falling," or "People tell me that the population in the county immediately surrounding us is in fact aging." What was striking was his rigidity in the face of new data, as if his legitimacy as a leader depended on this particular version of reality.

What was going on here? I experienced John to be both a gentle but distant person. He lacked forcefulness and was certainly not an "exciting" leader. In earlier encounters with him and his team, I saw how his subordinates could "box him out" by developing their own private language for dismissing him, for rendering him unimportant. Indeed, his chief operating officer, now resigned, had been just the reverse—tough and sometimes vindictive. The COO was forceful to a fault where John was gentle to a fault. This suggests that he used rigidity as a substitute for forcefulness.

John, like George the lawyer, was also a deeply religious man. He taught Sunday school, was a leader in his church, and was an executive of high integrity. It was my sense that he could mobilize his forcefulness, his strengths, when he was God's instrument, but could not do so when he was the leader himself. We can hypothesize that instead of being narcissistic, he actually sought too little glory. This is perhaps why he also insisted that the hospital was in great danger. Just as he inhibited his aggression, he saw the hospital, powerful as it was, as a victim. John, therefore, had difficulty creating that transitional space between the present as it was and as it might be because he did not believe that reality as it unfolds is pliable, that he can could influence it through independent action. This is also why he could not and did not excite his followers.

## The Role of Followers in Failure

We argued that when followers trade their fear of the marketplace for their fear of the leader's standards they are *ceding responsibility* for assuming core risks of the enterprise. As we saw, they make this trade-off so they can more effectively take up their own work.

While doing so allows anxiety to be channeled into productive work, it also can deprive the leader of critical thinking. When carried too far, followers fear the leader rather than his standards and become either cynics or sycophants. This was what happened in the case of Steve Friedman and the *USA Today* show.

By internalizing the leader's standards, followers are not simply following the leader but are also sharing in and helping to explicate his or her vision of the present "as it might be." The vision mediates the links between the two and constantly calls on both leader and follower to do the work of acting in the world to test the vision.

When this does not happen and followers fear only the leader rather than his or her standards they may, for example, provide unreliable information to the leader. They may work only to assure that the leader's narcissism is satisfied: give the leader what he or she "wants" to hear. They may provide the leader with what makes the follower look good, or what makes another follower look bad. This is a pervasive phenomenon in business today. In the end, followers who are too anxious to please the leader may help shape what Howard Schwartz, a professor of management at Oakland University, Michigan, calls a climate of "organizational narcissism": a type of misplaced overestimation of the organization. The institution is focused only on its internal activities, not taking into account its ability to serve its customers and thereby make money. General Motors is but one example of organizational narcissism (Schwartz, 1990).

When followers are able to tolerate more risk and anxiety, they are less dependent on and less submissive to the leader's version of reality, more willing to challenge it—even sharpen it—and less likely to participate in the unhealthy inward focus that causes so many enterprises to decay. Indeed, "visionaries" like Bill Gates tolerate quite extreme amounts of aggressiveness from their followers. (The climate is set by such leaders as well, who shout at and insult their followers, giving as much as they get.) Many companies, in fact, do seem to thrive on "letting it all hang out." While there are obvious pitfalls to such an approach, the point here is that leaders secure in their vision—in no small part because it is congruent with the marketplace and the marketplace in turn has validated it—can *tolerate,* even welcome, feedback of the sharpest kind. It then becomes incumbent upon the followers to provide it.

To be sure, "challenging the boss" may appear a near-suicidal prescription in these downsizing times. However, in the psychological dance of visioning and balancing risk-taking fears, leaders and followers must become more partnerlike to enact a vision: to create and internalize new standards of excellence so that their enterprise will succeed.

## IN SUM

Business visions are neither dreams nor fantasies but, to merit the name, must be based on a deep appreciation of reality "as it is." Presenting simplified visions of the present, as we have seen, business visions must also propose how an enacted chain of causes and effects, can create a present "as it might be." Visions that "work" in a business have emerged from a view of the present, filtered through the leader, who cuts through the present's complexity. Thus, visions can be captured in a few phrases. As "reductionist statements," these business visions guide creative action, not endless analysis.

At the same time, leaders, to create effective visions, must draw upon their own drives and imagination, along with the culture in which they have matured. However, if they take only from their own drives and imagination—fantasy—they fail to perceive the business reality. They not only begin to focus solely upon the vicissitudes of their own lives but confuse these with the "life" of the organization. They become artists in the drama of their own lives, not executives in the playing out of their organization's livelihood.

For their part, followers help enact the leader's vision, even when it is stimulated by the leader's internal conflicts and hopes, if they also identify with the vision, the standards of performance it elicits, and its ongoing links to reality.

## REFERENCES

Schwartz, H. (1990). *Narcissistic process and corporate decay: The theory of the organizational ideal.* New York: New York University Press.

# 6

A Theory of Living Human
Systems as an Approach to
Leadership of the Future with
Examples of How It Works

*Yvonne M. Agazarian, Ed.D.*
*and Berj Philibossian, M.B.A.*

New paradigms of thinking are stimulating new ways of approaching leadership in organizations. A theory of living human systems is one. As a theoretical approach, a theory of living human systems has introduced some specific Systems-centered®[1] orienting principles for leadership.

The methods and orientation for Systems-centered leadership have been developed both theoretically and empirically. First came the theory, and then came the trial-and-error process of

---

[1] Systems-centered® is a registered trademark owned by Y. Agazarian.

discovering how to put the theory into practice. Today, from the original single set of concepts that defined the theory of living human systems, principles and methods have emerged which can be used to develop the work groups and the leadership necessary to address current challenges in many critical organizational areas: such as managing difference and diversity, beating the competition, and managing complex change.

One of the difficulties of presenting new ideas and new methods is that, when the words used to explain them are familiar, they do not seem so new. And when the words that are used are unfamiliar, what *is* new in their meaning can be discounted as just a new jargon. Yet, the work must be done. Translation of the theoretical concepts into words that have a special connotation must be made if they are to be defined operationally. And operational definitions are necessary if hypotheses are to be generated to test their validity and reliability in the real world of application. Thus, as new ideas develop, as new methods and techniques get generated, inevitably a new language develops to communicate them.

## A THEORY OF LIVING HUMAN SYSTEMS AND ITS OPERATIONAL DEFINITIONS

The dilemma of communicating in a new language is addressed in this chapter in a specific sequence. First a connection is made between how the ideas in the theory are defined and how these definitions in turn connect to the methods that put these ideas into practice. This sequence is first illustrated in Table 6.1, which begins with an overall statement of the theory of living human systems. The two boxes that follow the statement of theory in Table 6.1 define what is meant by the words *hierarchy* and *isomorphy*. Hierarchy is then further defined in terms of "context," and isomorphy in terms of "structure" and "function." The methods of "contextualizing," "subgrouping," and "boundarying" follow as the bridge between the theory of living human systems and its systems centered practice. The table ends with references to

## TABLE 6.1
### A Theory of Living Human Systems and Methods for Systems-centered Change (adapted from Agazarian, 1997)

A theory of living human systems defines a hierarchy of isomorphic systems that are energy organizing, self-correcting, and goal directed

| | | |
|---|---|---|
| **Definition of Hierarchy:** Every system exists in the context of the environment of the system above it and is the environment for the system below it. | **Definition of Isomorphy:** Systems within a hierarchy are similar in structure and function and different in different contexts. There is an interdependent relationship between the function and structure within, between and among the systems of a hierarchy. | |
| **Definition of a Systems Centered Hierarchy** defines the contexts of (1) "member systems" that exist as organizational roles; (2) subgroup systems that contain both sides of conflict in the group as a whole; and (3) the system as a whole which is the interface between its internal systems and its environment. These systems are isomorphic at every level of the hierarchy. | **Definition of Structure:** Systems centered structure defines boundaries in the context of space, time, reality and role. <br><br> **Method: Boundarying** is the systems centered method used to reduce the restraining forces to communication; influencing what to communicate and how to communicate towards system goals. | **Definition of Function:** Systems centered systems survive, develop, and transform through the process of discriminating and integrating differences. <br><br> **Method: Subgrouping** is the systems centered method for conflict resolution that enables differences to be contained and explored as a resource for problem solving rather than used as political ammunition. |
| **Method-Contextualizing:** Predicting the impact of change from different perspectives of different levels in the organizational hierarchy. | | |
| Contextualizing interventions are discussed in example 3. | Boundarying interventions are discussed in examples 2, 4, & 5. | Subgrouping interventions are discussed in example 1. |

examples, given later in the chapter, of what it looks like to put these methods into practice.

Table 6.1 illustrates the direct link between the ideas framed in a theory of living human systems; the methods that have been developed from these ideas; and the effect in the real world of putting them into practice. The methods of contextualizing, subgrouping, and boundarying interventions are expected to induce observable changes in the predicted direction. Outcome, therefore, serves as feedback to the leader on the one hand, and as a test of the validity of the theory and the reliability of its practice on the other.

Thus systems-centered interventions are like hypotheses that test whether or not there is an identifiable change in the predicted direction. Examples of some of the hypotheses currently being tested follow. (1) Given that the system of the subgroup exists in the environment of the system as a whole and is the environment for its members, it is more efficient to direct change interventions to the subgroup rather than to an individual. (2) Given that through the method of subgrouping, conflicts over differences are contained in the system as a whole rather than within or between the member systems, subgrouping will increase the ability to identify and address work related conflicts within a meeting and will reduce the scapegoating response to conflict outside the meeting. (3) Given that there is an inverse relationship between noise in communications and the probability that the information in the communication will be transferred,[2] reducing noise in communication through boundarying techniques will increase the level of work-related communication (Agazarian & Janoff, 1993).

Table 6.1 is followed by a discussion of how definitions of the theory are useful to systems-centered leaders as they orient themselves to their work. We then turn to illustrations of how systems centered ideas are applied. Five examples are given, each one of which describes the context of a change intervention, and what happened when one or another of the techniques that define these methods were used by an internal consultant to an existing organization. After the examples, the chapter introduces the force field as a tool that may help some leaders lead, and ends with a reprise of the theory.

## More about Hierarchy

*Hierarchy* is a common word that has a particular meaning for systems-centered leadership. Thinking in the context of hierarchy

---

[2]The hypothesis that there is an inverse relationship between the transfer of information and the amount of ambiguity, redundancy, and contradiction

is important for systems-centered leadership because "every system exists in the environment of the system above it, and is the environment of the system below it." Systems are ideas that exist only in the mind, they do not exist in the real world like people do. Looking at an organization through systems eyes means that what you see at any one time depends upon how you look at it. In other words, what you see depends upon the context that frames what you see. Shifting contexts means shifting levels in a hierarchy of abstraction as well as levels of an organizational chart. There is, for example, a hierarchical relationship between a team or a department or an organization and also for the different member roles within a team or a department or an organization.[3] Thus thinking about any one living human system means thinking about the whole hierarchy of systems as well as each system that makes it up.

For example, thinking about systems is useful when it helps one to plan in ways that one might not be able to plan so easily if one's thinking was confined to the people in an organization. Let's take the "member" system, for example (remembering that the word *system*, like the word *member*, stands for an idea and not a person). Context defines what is relevant to think about when one thinks about "member" as a living human system rather than the living person that is occupying the role. A team "member" is a different "system" from the "member" of a department or the "member" of the organization. At each level of the hierarchy, the "member" has a different role, different goals and different relationships to the other systems of the hierarchy. Indeed, it is the same person who occupies all three roles (team member, department member, member of the organization) but how you think about the impact of the person will change as his role

---

(entropic noise) in a message is derived from Shannon and Weaver's information theory (1964).

[3]When managers think hierarchically, their understanding shifts according to the level of hierarchy they are thinking about. In other words, as the context changes, so do the requirements and implications for change. It is, of course, extremely important to keep in mind the impact of change at any one level of an organization on other levels of the organization. A useful change at one level is not always useful to the organization if it interferes with the efficiency at another level.

changes, because how you think about a person depends less on him or her personally and more on the context that you are working with. Every manager knows this intuitively. Every systems-centered manager always keeps it in mind.

What is important about thinking hierarchically in systems-centered leadership is that it keeps in mind that every communication from any system will influence every other system. How this applies to influencing change within an organization is that any specific intervention is best considered not only in terms of the specific system that you are influencing but also in terms of its impact on other systems in the hierarchy. Examples of this are discussed later in this chapter.

## More about Isomorphy

Isomorphy means that every system in a defined hierarchy is similar in structure and function (von Bertalanffy, 1969; Durkin, 1981). Isomorphy is the word that is used when the structure and function of all systems in the hierarchy have been defined using the same principles and are therefore equivalent. In other words, the way that boundaries give structure to any one system will be common to all living human systems; and the principles by which any one system functions will be common to all living human systems. Thus the practice of systems-centered leadership provides a consistent framework for all leadership influences, whether the influence is toward change or toward stability, in that systems-centered leaders think isomorphically about all systems at whatever level or complexity they exist.

Isomorphy is an important and powerful idea for systems-centered leaders to keep in mind. Understanding the principle of isomorphy enables leaders to pay attention to how their change strategies influence both the structure and function of the system in the context of the hierarchy. Thinking "hierarchy" and "isomorphy" leads to the understanding that however different a team may look from a department, or how different a department may look from the organization of departments as a whole, each in fact has certain common factors which can be recognized in their structure and in their function. The importance of this lies in the fact that a systems-centered orientation applies to any level system intervention, whether it be a team member, a team, a work unit, a department, or the organization as a whole. (For example, the bearer of bad tidings in example III will be shot, no matter which level of the hierarchy he bears his tiding to!)

## Making Isomorphy Operational

In the process of discovering how to make the definitions of isomorphy operational, specific methods were developed—"boundarying" and "subgrouping." These define specific approaches to the management of the structure and function of an organizational system. A series of specific techniques are suggested in order to implement these methods. Most of the techniques are simple to understand and to use, and their effect is often complex and far-reaching. Both subgrouping and boundarying have to do with managing communication within and between groups that make up the hierarchy of systems that form the organization as a whole. They will be discussed at greater length under the sections on structure and function below.

## More about Structure

Systems-centered leaders define system structure in terms of boundaries.[4] Boundaries in space and time make the difference

---

[4]**Structure:** The structure of a system is formed by its boundaries: boundaries between, among, and within all the systems in the hierarchy of like living systems. Work organizations are living human systems: individuals, operating and staff groups, and the departments that contain them. Boundaries occur at the interface of these different system levels. The structural boundaries of the system contain the energy of the system. Systems-centered managers monitor boundary permeability by helping to speed up or slow down the process of communication. Too much information floods a system with ambiguity. Too little information stalls the system in redundancy. Contradictory information challenges the system's ability to recognize similarities and differences and to integrate the information usefully. There is an inverse relationship between the transfer of

between whether a team or a department or an organization actually exists in the real world or whether it exists only in the mind; whether the work energy is contained and directed toward the goal or whether it is dissipated. For example, a team meeting that keeps a time boundary and starts and stops on time is a very different system from one that does not. A team meeting that contains all its work energy within its boundaries for the duration of its working time, without distractions and irrelevancies drawing the energy away into nostalgia for the past or negative predictions about the future, will have a different quality of work life and potential for reaching its goals than one that does not. It will also have a different climate and a morale.

Boundaries that are "impermeable" to irrelevant interruptions during work time make a great difference to how the energy of the system remains connected to the work. Boundaries that are so permeable that the internal working organization of the system can be disrupted unpredictably and frequently, by phone calls or "crises" from the outside, "leak" out the energy that is required for the work.

There is another kind of permeability that results in the loss of work energy that is more easily recognized if one thinks about boundaries from a systems perspective. Systems boundaries exist in space and time—they mark the thresholds between the outside and the inside; the past and the future and the present; between fantasy and reality. Inappropriate diversions into anecdotes or gossip about the world outside; diversions into how much better it was in the past, or how things won't work so well in the future; or constructing a view of the boss based on negative predictions and fears; not only leak energy across the boundaries away from the here-and-now task, but also leave less and less room in the present for testing out the realities of work.

Once again, the way the people on the team work will have more to do with the context of their work—more to do with the morale and the climate and the way the boundaries are managed, than it will with the people themselves. Who anyone is at any one

---

information and the ambiguities, redundancies, and contradictions in the communication (Shannon & Weaver, 1964).

time has more to do with the way the working system "is" than who they "are."

## Boundarying: Making Structure Operational

Systems-centered boundarying is the activity of deliberately influencing the structure of the system by influencing the way boundaries are managed in space and time. Boundarying also applies to the management of boundary permeability between the system and its environment, as well as within the system. A systems-centered orientation to managing boundaries often makes the difference between a working system that relates to its goals, and one that is related to other goals, like safety or survival or status or inertia or sabotage.

Boundarying methods systematically organize the way that information is communicated within and between systems so that the restraining forces of ambiguity, contradiction, and redundancy in the communication pattern are systematically reduced. As ambiguities, redundancies, and contradictions in a message create "noise" in the communication (Shannon & Weaver, 1964), reducing them reduces "noise" and makes it more likely that the work related information in the communications can get across (examples 2, 4, and 5).

## More about Function

Systems-centered leaders define a well-functioning system in terms of its ability to discriminate and integrate differences. Actualizing the system potential for discrimination and integrating governs how well the system survives, how well it develops, and determines the quality and quantity of work energy that is available to direct is energy toward its goals. All living human systems require both stability and change if they are to survive, develop, and organize. Functional stability comes from the system's ability to maintain its existing organization. Functional change comes from the system's ability to change its existing organization so that it can take in and integrate new information. All living human systems have a greater tolerance for differences within what is already acceptably similar than they do for similarities in what is already unacceptably different. Differences that are not too different can be absorbed into the status quo because they do not introduce information that is "different enough" to require the system to change the way communication is organized. Unless the system has good methods for managing differences that are too different, however, the information that they contain will either be ignored or "stored." When systems "ignore or store" information (and the "deviant" people who own the information!) it is as if they have closed their boundaries to communication. These systems then tend to stereotype or ghettoize not only the communications, but also the communicators. Learning how to recognize and integrate differences leads to organizational change.

## Functional vs. Stereotypic Communication

Functional communication is directly related to the purpose of work and is therefore a driving force in relationship to the system goals. Stereotypic communication is indirectly related to "not rocking the boat" or other kinds of "political" communications which serve as restraining forces in relationship to the goals of work.

Communicating across every boundary requires sending a message from one place to another. Every communication contains an aspect of the message that is familiar and can be easily integrated. Every communication also contains information that is less familiar or even unfamiliar. Integrating unfamiliar information is not so simple.

All human organizations tend to maintain an existing integration or organization that works, to accept similarities and to reject differences. Every difference threatens the status quo. At the same time, organizations survive, develop, and transform from simple to complex through their ability to accept and integrate the differences that reflect the needs of changing times and to reject the differences that don't.

Systems-centered leaders therefore pay fundamental attention to the response to differences in the workplace. The problem to be solved is how to interfere with the natural tendency to fight off differences. For example the typical response to anything new is an immediate, "Yes—but...." Technically this requires a method that stops the natural tendency to close out differences in order to maintain the status quo, and at the same time to increase the tolerance for differences so that they become a resource in problem solving instead of a threat. Functional subgrouping is the method that systems centered managers use to address this.

## Functional Subgrouping: Making Function Operational

"All living human systems tend to come together and join around similarities and to split and separate around differences." Once this process is completed, differences are typically kept in their place by stereotyping—and stereotype subgroups are formed. As systems function best when they can recognize differences and integrate them, rather than stereotype or scapegoat them, the management of differences by functional subgrouping is fundamental to systems-centered leadership.

The method of functional subgrouping was developed from operationalizing the definition of systems-centered function: "Survival, development, and transformation depends upon the single process of recognizing and integrating differences over time." Functional subgrouping is a conflict resolution method that deliberately interferes with the tendency to form stereotype subgroups around similarities and to split off differences.

Functional subgrouping flies in the face of the typical tendency to split around differences and come together around the splits thus creating stereotype "in-group" subgroups and scapegoated "out-groups."

Functional subgrouping manages conflict in the process of managing change by splitting and containing differences in separate subgroups on the one hand, which then function to develop an increasing ability to integrate differences on the other. By requiring subgroups to build around similarities, when differences emerge they are more likely to be tolerated than attacked. In this way, a lot of differentiation can be explored without making too many waves. Then as the differences become recognized in what was apparently similar within each subgroup, the similarities become apparent between each subgroup. In this way, the two subgroups work down to what is common in the conflict that can serve as a platform for resolution rather directing most of the energy toward the differences.

Functional subgrouping capitalizes on these two predispositions. Before the system can split around differences, the systems-centered leader deliberately interferes with the process: deliberately splits the conflicts between two functional subgroups. The functional subgroups come together on their agreements and "contain" the two different halves of the disagreement separately between them while the work group as a whole contains the split.

## APPLYING SYSTEMS-CENTERED METHODS

In the section that follows, the techniques that have been developed to operationalize the ideas above will be discussed in terms of what happened when they were applied to the business of organizational change. Simple as the illustrations appear, their power is in the deliberateness in which the change strategies were thought through before they were initiated, the conscious management of boundaries and the communication process, and how specifically the probability of outcome could be assessed in terms of the success or failure of the intervention.

Systems-centered leaders deliberately influence the way the organization functions by influencing the way the energy is organized and directed—in other words, by influencing the way the people behave. The major focus of influence is on the communication behavior that crosses the boundaries. At every boundary, the issue is what and how to communicate in order to get the message across. Systems-centered managers increase the probability that information will be directed toward solving problems and organizational goals, not only by monitoring what people say but by establishing communication patterns that are lower on ambiguities, redundancies, and contradictions. In other words, for systems-centered managers, how something is communicated is at least as important as what is communicated.

Any "yes–but" conflict, however small, is a signal to systems-centered managers to subgroup. The information that is contained in the "yes" is just as important as the information contained in the "but"—and much of the information is likely to be lost if it remains contained in a concealed yes–but conflict: hence functional subgrouping. In functional subgrouping, one subgroup is encouraged to explore the various meanings of "yes" and the other to explore the many meanings of "but." As both subgroups come together around similarities, each provides a supportive climate. As similarities are explored, so differences in the apparently similar are recognized, a process which develops both differentiation and increased integration of the system. As each subgroup becomes increasingly differentiated, so similarities in what was so apparently different between subgroups are recognized. In other words, the "yes–but" is taken out of the individual and "contained" in the work group. The end of the process of functional subgrouping is an integration of the "yes" and the "but"; and the conflict that it represented; which in turn leads to an understanding of the function of the conflict for the group as a whole.

The "yes–but" conflict makes an excellent first illustration of the application of systems-centered thinking in that it is both simple and obvious. The purpose of systems-centered thinking is to vector change through the most obvious and direct route, wasting as little time as possible and eliminating the side roads which, though interesting and frequently relevant, are unnecessary if there is a more direct route to change. The consultant below, as he tells his story, is putting into practice a great deal of understanding about isomorphy and hierarchy—hence his direct intervention which meets the systems-centered criteria of both simple and direct common sense. How this works in practice will be discussed next in the example of the "can do it/can't do it" subgroups, where the conflict is taken out of the individual and contained in "can do," "can't do" subgroups in the work group as a whole where it becomes an important step in doing preliminary work in orienting the department to its goals.

## Example 1: The "Can Do It/Can't Do It!" Subgroups

**Subgrouping: containing conflict in the work group rather than in the individual member by splitting the yes and the but into separate subgroups for exploration. Establishing functional subgroups and testing the reality of negative predictions with clarifying questions.**

The context is a planning meeting of the executives and managers of a major line operating department. A week prior to the meeting, each manager had received a notebook full of information relative to goals and tasks that were to be completed before the end of the year, which was about 8 months away. In preparation, the managers were asked to review the goals and tasks and be prepared to state what information and resources they would need to ensure that the goals were met before the year end. The meeting was chaired by the senior executive of the department and one author (B. P.) was there as a facilitator. The senior executive opened the meeting by asking the managers if they had all had a chance to review the goals and come to a conclusion about what was needed to achieve them by year end. One manager responded by saying: "Yes—but there's just too much to do, we can't do it all."

To contain an initially negative input without losing the information it contained, and to keep the communication boundaries open to both the yes and the but, I started the work of establishing functional subgroups. The first step in subgrouping is to contain the yes–but impasse before it stalemates the process and to encourage instead the splitting of the conflict into two working subgroups that come together around similarities first and explore them before any differences are processed.

So I started the process by finding out first how big the pessimistic subgroup was. I asked: "Who else is in that boat and feels that it can't be done?" About half the group raised its hands.[5] I

---

[5]This incidentally was a relief. Had the whole group raised its hands I would have had to split the conflict and develop functional subgrouping along

then addressed the other half of the group. "So who is in the boat that feels that there is a chance of getting it done?"

Most of the rest of the group raised its hands. That left me with the "I don't know" or the uncommitted subgroup. As it is important not to lose any potential work information, I reminded them that their work was to find a way to enter the work.

"That leaves us with the I don't know yet group! Don't forget, that what you don't know yet is the information that is going to be most important next. So as we do our work, stay alert for when you have something to say on one side or the other. We don't want to miss out on any resource when the decision is as important as this one."

I now had two subgroups formed, those who felt the goals were achievable, and those who felt they were not, and a third subgroup at the ready, waiting until they felt they had something to contribute to either side. Typically, at the beginning of any work, it is the "but" that contains most of the work energy—and only later when the work vectors in relationship to the goal does the energy shift to the yes. So I asked the "buts" to lead off first. I said: "Let's explore first with those who feel there's too much to accomplish, what the issues are, and then we can work on the next steps for the group as whole. Art, you say that there is just too much to do. Can you expand on that and then let's see who else can join you or build on the points you make."

This is the second step in forming subgroups. Encouraging people not only to build upon similarities but also to join in with contributions of at least comparable weight. He responded: "I would need some systems support and some extra people to get my processing rate up to meet these goals and we know that that's not in the cards." To test the negative prediction and bring the

---

different lines. For example, as problems must be solved in reality terms, rather than addressed from a framework of either negative or positive predictions about what will happen in the future, an exploration into prioritizing along the lines of feasibility would be a reality orienting first step. This work done, it would then be relatively easy to subgroup around the costs and benefits of meeting some but not all of the tasks. With a cost subgroup and a benefit subgroup exploring the issues, the potential for meeting as many of the goals as possible would be increased. Had some goals in fact been dropped, the decision would have been based on reality rather than on negative predictions.

discussion into the here-and-now I asked a reality testing and clarifying question: "You're saying you will need support and help and will not receive it. Can you, or anyone else expand on that. He said: "We have had constant pressure over the last year to watch costs and in terms of systems support they are backed-up as it is."

This started a vigorous and active exploration among the "can't do" subgroup about limits in people and equipment processing capacity. By the time they had finished they had made many points, that included the following:

Not enough computer system support

Limits in processing capability tied to limits in equipment capacity

Not enough staff to keep the work moving

But that was not all that was made. Some members of the group were not as concerned about some of the points as they were about others, and others of the "can't do" members brought in some "can do" ideas. As soon as I judged that the "can't do" subgroup had supported enough differentiation among themselves to be able to pay attention to the "can do" subgroup, I pointed out a potential similarity between the two subgroups.

I said: "It seems that although all of you have some doubts about what can and can't be done, I notice that what most of you agree on is that there are resources for some of the issues even if we don't all agree as to which! Let's ask the "can do" subgroup if they have any ideas about that. "Is this the way it is, or can additional resources and help be made available?" The "can do" subgroup spoke up and the first member said: "What's been identified as difficulties are all true enough. But mostly that's how it's been in the past." The senior executive joined in: "I'm ready to push as hard as I need to get the resources or help we need. I'm confident that if we have a solid plan to achieve our goals and make a good case for the help we need that we will get it.

Things have changed. Good planning and initiative on our part will be responded to."

By the end of the "can do" work, the managers in the "can't do" subgroup felt that their concerns and perceptions around resource availability were addressed.

The group as a whole was then in a position to work constructively and efficiently on the next steps.

## Example 2: "Negative Predictions"

**In Table 6.1 boundarying is defined as the method which operationalizes system structure: identifying and working with boundaries that are acting as barriers to communication; keeping the group work energy focused on the realities of the here-and-the-now and redirecting it when it takes flight into the past or the future or the irrealities and negative predictions around the present.**

The context of this example was a 2-day meeting of all of the executives and managers of a major line department. The department had just completed a major restructuring and was meeting to clarify its direction and goals for the coming year. The group was meeting in a climate of hope and concern. The department was making measurable progress after some setbacks, but the road ahead was sure to be challenging and stressful. The purpose of this opening segment of the 2-day meeting was to give the attendees an opportunity to clarify any questions or concerns that they had relative to the restructuring and its implications, personal and organizational.

At this point, the meeting has been in progress for about an hour. I (B. P.) am acting as the facilitator of the meeting. The executives and managers are sharing their concerns for the future. In the following narrative, what I will be focusing on is an example of identifying and working with a boundary that is acting as a barrier to communication (in this case the reality/irreality boundary). A manager voiced a concern by saying "Things never change, new executives come and go, do their thing, but things don't get any better." This kind of global and negative statement often acts to divert a group's communication and energy into complaining and blaming and then into hopelessness and passivity. It is what, in systems centered language, is called a negative prediction. The emotional work climate that negative predictions generate is often mistaken for reality rather than for what it is, the negative feelings that are generated by negative thoughts. If left unaddressed, the emotional climate then acts as barrier or restraining force to the group channeling its energy into constructive communication and effective problem solving. I responded with a reality focusing question:

"Is that accurate? I just heard the managers here today report that there have been several gains in the past year: higher output, lower error rates, and better training!" He responded, "Well, yes, some things have improved." I then asked a clarifying question, "Could you be saying that in your area there has been less improvement?" He said, "Hmm, yes, that's what I'm saying."

I responded with a statement designed to maintain the reality focus and to differentiate the subgroups in the group. I said, "I think it's important to keep communicating, differentiating, and clarifying both sides, what's okay in addition to what's not okay."

To further clarify the boundary between past and present, reality and irreality, and to clarify and differentiate what is okay from what is not okay or needs improvement, I polled the whole group. I asked the participants to identify which subgroup they were in, the "things are better" subgroup or the "things haven't changed" subgroup.

This allowed the group to identify, contain, and constructively share its differences. It also focused the group on a here-and-now reality based assessment of what has improved or not improved and what the next best steps are.

In summary, this is an example of identifying and working with boundaries that are acting as barriers to communication and hence problem solving. In this case we worked with the past/present, reality/irreality boundaries. The point that is being emphasized here is that to assure that valid communication and effective problem solving takes place in the here-and-now the leader must help the group stay focused on the present, and on objective reality vis-à-vis subjective and often distorted reality which we call irreality.

## Example 3: "The messenger is shot"

**In Table 6.1, the method for operationalizing the concept of hierarchy was defined as bringing the context into focus and the methods for operationalizing the concept of isomorphy were defined in terms of boundarying and subgrouping which have already been discussed above. This example illustrates the focus on context rather than content: seeing the problems from different perspectives in the organizational hierarchy. The concepts and methods of hierarchy and isomorphy are used to clarify the goals of work within the context of reality; identifying the restraining forces to communication.**

The context of the example given here is a meeting between the executives and managers of a major line department who had already been introduced to the idea of isomorphy in the communications up and down the hierarchy. The goal of the meeting was to address the tendency for some key problems to remain unacknowledged until they had grown to almost unmanageable proportions. My systems-centered management agenda was to identify ways to make the boundary between levels more appropriately permeable to the communication of potential problems and of performance related information by employees to their supervisors.

As a first step toward identifying ways of improving upward communication, we decided to identify what the group currently saw as the restraining forces to upward communication by supervisors.

In order to identify the restraining forces to communication, I asked the manager subgroup: "What do you know about what keeps the supervisors that report to you from giving more advanced notice or more early warning of problems they are having? Why do they keep trying to fix the problem themselves and end up waiting too long before they involve you in trying to do something about it?"

A manager responded: "You could ask us the same question. You could ask us why we as managers wait so long before we involve the executives in a problem, rather than involve them before it gets too big?"

This statement demonstrated that the manager was aware that the problem was isomorphic: that it existed on at least two levels of the hierarchy (managers and supervisors). It was with a feeling of great satisfaction that I responded: "Well you make an important point. You as managers do create the context and rules that govern the response of the supervisors so let's go up a level in the hierarchy and ask the same question. Why don't you as managers provide more advance warning of the problem, or in other words speak up sooner?

Another manager responded: "Because more often than not the messenger gets shot! Instead of being received neutrally the bearer of negative news or information frequently experiences a critical response from the next level and hence gets reluctant to provide information upward unless its positive or unless you have some strategy all ready for definitely fixing the problem."

Since "the next level" the manager was talking about was the executive group in the meeting I asked a reality testing question, but first, in line with the normalization that is built in to all systems-centered thinking, I first framed it in terms of the familiar. "Well, maybe we are continuing a long-standing tradition. I believe that the bearers of bad tidings actually were killed among the ancient Greeks! Is that still true here? Do the executives here tend to not be open to, or even be critical of, negative information unless it is accompanied by a definite way of fixing the problem." An executive responded. "That has been the case until recently and we are working to change that kind of response. We do want managers to feel free to give earlier warnings of negative information to us (and the supervisors to them!). We don't want people waiting until they are near the point of no return before extra resources are pulled in."

To make sure that both subgroups were located in terms of the communication goal I underlined the importance of upward and downward communication in the hierarchy with a goal clarifying statement: "Is it accurate to say then, that our goal is to improve the upward communication of supervisors by improving the downward communication within the system as a whole? That we will seek ways for executives as a group to encourage upward communication from managers and that will provide a model for the managers' communication with supervisors?''

As will be seen from the example above, there were no particularly dramatic happenings in the meeting. However, this simplicity, speed, and directness of the work (the interchange above, though edited, took no more than a few minutes) rested on some significant systems-centered practices.

First there was the introduction of the idea of isomorphy. The managers looked up and down the organizational hierarchy and discovered that many of the difficulties that they were experiencing in their own communication upwards to the executives as well as downwards to their line staff was mirrored at the executive levels as well as at the supervisor/line staff level.

Second, there was the communication training seminar with the executives and managers in which they had been introduced to the idea of the communication force field. The communication force field is a simple model that has some profound implications both theoretical and practically. In a force field training seminar, members are asked to place their fists against each other and to push as hard as they can. What is immediately apparent is there is a deadlock—however much they increase the force, neither fist moves. It is then suggested that, while maintaining the pressure, they suddenly weaken the wrist of one hand. Predictably, the fist that maintains the force shoots forward in the direction of the force.

This simple illustration demonstrates the major principle of the force field. It is more effective to weaken the restraining forces than to increase the driving forces when one wants to vector change toward a goal.

When this is applied to communication across the boundaries of systems in the hierarchy, another simple principle is applied. There is an ever-increasing probability that the information in the communications will get across if the ambiguities, contradictions, and redundancies are reduced. Again, although the theoretical principles behind both these approaches were many years in the making, their application is simple.

## Example 4: "The Fork in the Road"

**In this example, methods are discussed for directing energy across two levels of the organizational hierarchy through (1) monitoring and managing boundary permeability, and (2) maintaining open communication by managing boundary permeability. Managing the scope, complexity, and rate of processing information addresses the first point. Opening and closing communication boundaries appropriately to manage the rate of information flow and avoid overload addresses the second point.**

The context of this example was a management meeting of the top two levels (executives and managers) of a line department. The purpose of this segment of the meeting was to (1) identify the major goals for the coming year, and (2) plan and schedule a meeting to communicate and further formulate the department's goals with the next management level (line supervisors).

In a systems-centered context we are dealing with three levels of human organizational systems—executive, manager, and supervisor. Each level is the environment of the system below it and exports and (one hopes) imports information with it. For example, the "manager system" operates within the environment of the "executive system," and is the environment for the "supervisor human system."

My role in this meeting was to facilitate the work of the total group (executives and managers). The group had come to the point where it was ready to clarify its major goals for the coming year. The head of the department and I were working with the group to begin to identify the major goals and sets of goals.

As I listed the major goals on a chart, the list became longer and longer. It included organization-wide goals, department, quality improvement, productivity, and cost improvement goals, goals driven by the next generation of processing equipment, and internal and external auditor recommendations. When the list was finished, I put down my pen, faced the group and said, "Well, what do you think? How's it look?" There was a deep silence as the group looked at the length of the list of things that they had to work on in the coming year. A participant responded, "This gives me a much different understanding of what the department is facing, I have never seen the total picture like this. It's interesting and it feels awesome."

There were nods of agreement. This was the first time that the leadership group as a whole had seen everything in one place at one time. Many of the management team had seen most of the pieces over time, either in major chunks or small fragments, but almost no one had seen the whole thing at one time in one place. The management group now had a new perspective on what the department was facing and how different things related.[6]

At the same time, the group was taken aback by the scope, complexity, and overlap of what they had to do. In this sense, the information was still disorganized and therefore appeared contradictory and overwhelming.

The group's first reaction was that there was no way that they could schedule and plan for the next step with the supervisors. They had to get clear for themselves first, what were the goals, what where the priorities, and where overlap existed.

## The Fork in the Road

From the systems-centered perspective, the department head and I were clearly at a "fork in the road."[7] On the one hand, we could rally the management team, push ahead with the original plan, and schedule and plan the meeting with the supervisors. After all, the executives and managers as a group were now more informed and more interested than before. On the other hand, we could respond to the group, and defer the supervisory meeting until the group got itself better oriented.

---

[6]The group had moved to a new level of understanding and interest (increased boundary permeability).

[7]The "fork in the road" is a specific SCT technique which requires containing the frustration of not knowing which way to go to manage a conflict, while both roads are explored. This simple technique interrupts the typical response of prematurely making a choice in order to get rid of the conflict. Once a work group is halfway down the road, it is often very difficult to remember that there was an alternative choice. Halfway down a road, it is much harder to turn back. The fork in the road technique, therefore, delays action until the action is well considered.

In systems-centered terms, the group was in both ambiguity and contradiction, which characterizes information overload. Its capacity to sort, order, organize, integrate, and absorb the information was at its limit. Pushing ahead at this time ran the serious risk of generating resistance and reducing receptivity to new information or direction (or in other words reducing boundary permeability). It was time to slow down the process of communication. It was better to err on the side of taking a couple more weeks on the front end of the plan rather than potentially undermining the execution or implementation of the total plan.

In summary a major task of the group leader is to maintain open communication by managing boundary permeability. In this case, appropriate boundary permeability was a two-step process. The first step was to open the boundaries to all the information that was relevant to the task at hand. This was done by identifying the total field of goals by listing all of the major goals in one place at the same time for everyone to see. However, in this case the boundaries were too permeable and the information entered the system too fast. The result was an information overload that was experienced as both ambiguous and contradictory, and the reaction was, "Can I possibly cope with this, understand it all, do it all, and do it well?" Thus a prior step was required before the information could be used—the information had to be organized and integrated. The rate of information flow was slowed down by delaying the scheduled meeting and making space for additional meetings to give the executive and manager team a chance to absorb, process, and integrate the new information. The number of meetings were not prespecified, rather a clear goal was set of organizing the information so that it could be clearly communicated. The executives and managers, both separately and together, reviewed all of the goals as a totality; clarified the goals and standards; reviewed resource requirements in terms of dollars, people, and time; identified the resources needed; and set appropriate priorities. It took three additional meetings to reach the interim goal. The group as a whole was then ready to take the next step with the supervisors.

What is illustrated is the importance of keeping the boundaries closed between the levels of the hierarchy until the system that is responsible for communicating the information has a clear integration of the information. In this way, upward and downward communication is as congruent as possible with the goals of the communication. This avoids the problem of ambiguous and contradictory communications of information that then introduces stress at other levels of the system.

## Example 5: "Staying in the Here-and-Now"

**This example illustrates a different aspect of boundarying: reducing the restraining forces at the boundary to influence and maintain the positive communication energy that drives the forward movement of the group. As does crossing the boundary from the future to the here-and-now, staying at the appropriate hierarchical work level and context, undoing negative predictions, and a concealed "yes-but" fight climate.**

The context is a problem-solving and planning meeting of managers of a major production operation. The purpose of the meeting was to identify ways to deal with the costly aspects of turnover in terms of work disruption, reduced capacity, and maintaining quality and output. My role in the meeting was to facilitate the discussion; to arrive at possible alternatives to explore in the future with the next senior level of management.

At this point of the meeting the group was identifying some possible alternatives for dealing with the turnover issue such as cross-training employees so that they could be called on to take up the slack when someone left, or generating more career advancement paths to provide employees with greater motivation to stay. One of the managers offered up another alternative. "Instead of replacing one person at a time when someone leaves, why don't we hire groups of three or four, train them as a group, and then we will have an immediate pool to draw from when people leave? Our turnover is predictable and the extra employees would be absorbed fairly quickly, and the added salary costs would be more than offset by avoiding the cost of poor quality and disruption of production."

A second manager immediately replied with a yes-but: "That sounds like a good idea, but senior management would see this as overstaffing and they would not even consider the idea."

This looks like a relatively simple response and one that is quite typical in a management meeting. However, within our framework, there is a great deal going on in this statement in terms of restraining forces that must be addressed to maintain positive communication energy and forward movement of the group and the problem-solving process. The statement contains the following restraining forces: First in terms of the major purpose of this example it crosses the boundary from the manager level of the working hierarchy to the senior manager level. It takes it out of the context of the here-and-now manager group working with the task-goal of generating alternatives to the future context of a senior management group with the goal of making judgments about alternatives and choosing. Second, it crosses the time boundary from the present into the future (for example "Senior management would see this as overstaffing"). Third, it makes a negative prediction (for example, "They would not consider it a good idea").

Finally, the statement contains the possibility of shifting the group climate from problem solving to fight by introducing a "but" or difference rather than an agreement.

To neutralize the four restraining forces above, and to keep the problem solving and communication in the context of the here-and-now of the manager level, I made the following intervention:

1. First I neutralized the possibility of a fight developing by rein-forcing the goal of the group which was to generate alternatives and not evaluate them. I addressed the "but" by saying, "Our goal for today is to generate alternatives before we evaluate them. Your but is an evaluation, John. Could you not forget it, and hold it for later?" (He answered affirmatively.)
2. Next, I made an awareness-generating and norm-setting inter-vention to neutralize the negative prediction and move from the future to the present by saying to the group: "Do we see that we've made a negative prediction that moves us from the

present to the future and into a possible problem with senior management (as well as a shift both in the hierarchical level and the context) and that this would divert us from our goal here today?" The group nodded affirmatively. "It's very important for the success of this meeting to stay in the here-and-now versus going into the future and to avoid making negative predictions that make us feel negative."

3. Finally, I focused the discussion in the group on its goal and working level of the hierarchy by making a goal clarifying statement and by bringing some new information into the group. "I think its important to reinforce that today, our goal is to generate alternatives from our perspective as managers, which is our level of the hierarchy. We must be careful not to move the discussion to a different level of the hierarchy that would change the context. Senior management has different goals and perspectives from us in this meeting. This is especially important because the senior management of this department has just changed and we really don't know if their point of view will be similar or different from the past and where it will be similar or different."

In summary we looked at how to help a work group system to stay focused on the here-and-now task by differentiating information that is relevant to the other levels of the working hierarchy from information that is specifically relevant to their level. We also saw how many of the systems-centered issues are interwoven (avoiding negative predictions, staying in the present versus the future, avoiding "concealed fight" statements).

When systems-centered change is managed within the parameters defined in theory and operationalized within the strategies that make the methods operational, it can be predicted that change will largely take place in a way that the system as a whole changes in the direction of its goals.

The task of systems-centered practice is to bring the work energy into the group as a whole and direct it toward the system goals, thus enabling the system hierarchy to transform from simple to complex.

To bring the work energy into the group-as-a-whole system by:

- Bringing into existence systems-centered member systems, who function to import the work energy across the boundaries of space and time, reality and role;
- Weakening the forces that restrain the work energy from crossing the space boundary from the outside to the inside of the system;
- Weakening the forces that restrain the work energy from crossing the time boundary from the past and future into the present;
- Weakening the forces that restrain the work energy from crossing the role boundary from outside social roles into a systems-centered role of functional subgrouping;
- Weakening the forces that restrain the work energy from crossing the boundary from irreality into the context of the here-and-now as it relates to goals of survival, development, and environmental mastery and the transformation from simple to complex.

## Tools That Help Systems Centered Leaders Lead

Systems-centered leaders rely on some form of communication training to manage this, one of which is the Sequential Analysis of Verbal Interaction (SAVI) observation system developed from information theory which serves as a map for determining the patterns of communication and their different potential for making problems or solving them (Simon & Agazarian, 1967). Another tool that is available to systems centered leaders is the force field (K. Lewin, 1951). The force field is a simple way of organizing complex phenomena so that the restraining forces that are easiest to reduce can be identified and weakened, with the understanding that it is more efficient to solve the problems that lie in the way of the goal than it is to increase the pressure toward the goal (Howard & Scott, 1965).

The force field presented in Table 6.2 is a simple representation that serves as a blueprint in practice for operationalizing all three of the theories above.

**TABLE 6.2**
**Adaptation of Lewin's Force Field Model (Agazarian, 1992)**

Force Field of Driving and Restraining Forces
in Influencing Boundary Permeability to Communication

| *Driving Forces* → | ← *Restraining Forces* |
|---|---|
| | ← *Indirect Questions* |
| *Asking Direct Questions* → | ← *Leading Questions* |
| | ← *Sarcastic Questions* |
| | ← *Avoiding Answering* |
| *Answering Questions* → | ← *Changing the Subject* |
| | ← *Answering a Question with a Question* |
| | ← *Preempting Ideas* |
| *Building On Ideas* → | ← *Yes-Butting* |
| | ← *Interrupting* |
| *Proposing* → | ← *Blaming & Complaining* |
| *Owning Own Feelings* → | ← *Putting Self Down* |
| *Supporting Self and Others* → | ← *"Oughtituding"* |

These are the tools that influence the "function" of the communication as it crosses the boundaries between, within, and among systems in the hierarchy. As all systems exist in the environment of the system above them and are the environment of the systems below them, every communication that is sent out will affect the environment of the organization which in turn will affect the systems that take it in. For example, when a corporation downsizes, if middle management assumes the victim position and communicates that is has been "done in" the organization as a whole will take on the same tone. Conversely, if middle management takes an assertive stand, that downsizing will make the company "leaner and meaner," a more constructive organizational image of "survivor" rather than "victim" will orient the change.

Techniques for reducing the restraining forces to goal-oriented communications at the boundaries of the system include:

- Identifying and working with boundaries.
- Keeping the group work energy focused in the realities of the here-and-the-now and redirecting it when it takes flight into the past or the future or the irrealities and negative predictions around the present.
- Subgrouping: splitting and containing conflict in the work group rather than in the individual member by splitting the "yes" and the "but" into separate subgroups for exploration.
- Focus on context rather than content: seeing the problems from different perspectives in the organizational hierarchy; and understanding the impact of decisions from the perspective of upper management, middle management, and workers on the line.
- Differentiating between the exploration and explanation phases of problem solving and learning to identify and produce the language of exploration and explanation as resources that reach the goal.

## A THEORY OF LIVING HUMAN SYSTEMS: REPRISE

Living human systems are related hierarchically and isomorphically. Every living human system is isomorphic in that it can be recognized and defined in terms of its similarities in structure and function. Living human systems are related hierarchically in that each living human system exists in the environment of the system above it and is the environment of the system below it.

Like subsystems come together around similarities and come to recognize differences in the apparently similar. As differences in the apparently similar are recognized within the subsystems, so similarities in the apparently different are recognized across the subsystems.

The process of transformation depends upon system recognition and integration of both similarities and differences: both differences in the apparently similar and similarities in the apparently different.

Because systems are isomorphic in structure and function, the process of discrimination and integration is the underlying principle by which the hierarchy of living systems transforms from simple to complex. Systems centered members contain the conflicts encountered along the path to the goal by functional subgrouping, thereby managing conflict by splitting and processing differences into like subsystems.

The goal of each and every living human system is to survive, to develop, and to influence its environment so that the potential for survival and development is increased. System goals are hierarchical: survival is a necessary (though not sufficient) condition for development which is a necessary (though not sufficient) condition for influencing the environment.

Each and every living human system survives, develops, and influences its environment through the process of discrimination and integration. Through discriminating differences and integrating them, living human systems transform from simple to complex.

Every system contains its own potential for transformation. How it actualizes its potential determines how it influences the nature of its environment (the living human system above it) and also determines the nature of the environment of the system below it. How each and every system actualizes its potential influences the transformation potential of the hierarchy of living human systems.

Just as any one system as a whole contains the potential to transform from simple to complex through discrimination and integration, so does the system hierarchy-as-a-whole, and each and every system relationship in it. The goal of systems-centered change strategy is to make boundaries appropriately permeable to communications between one system and another in the hierarchy of living human systems. This is achieved by reducing the restraining forces to communication at the boundaries. Systems-centered managers enable systems to locate themselves in this process by clarifying the goals of work within the context of reality.

Systems-centered leaders deliberately influence the way the organization functions by influencing the way the energy is organized and directed[8]—in other words, by influencing the way the people behave. In systems-centered thinking, directing communication energy requires keeping the goal in focus so that all communications are related to the goal. The major focus of influence is on the communication behavior that crosses the boundaries. At every boundary, the issue is what and how to communicate in order to get the message across. It is no small thing to keep reminding a group what the goal of the work is and how much time there is left to reach it, and it makes a big difference (Raven & Rietsema, 1960). Directing communication energy also requires reducing the communications that are not relevant to the goals (Agazarian, 1992). Speed of communication is managed by reducing the kinds of communications that are likely to reduce the probability that the information within the communication will be received. This is done by deliberately reducing the ambiguities, redundancies, and contradictions in the communication (Shannon & Weaver, 1964). In practice, as we have demonstrated, this can be as simple as deciphering "yes-but," shifting from vague to specific, or requiring a direct rather than an oblique answer to a question.

## Systems-Centered Leadership in the Twenty-First Century

Systems-centered leadership requires paying as much attention to developing the environment as a potentiating force as it does to creating an internal environment that supports a problem-solving and goal-oriented culture. Systems-centered practice is predicated on consistently reducing entropy[9] throughout the system hierarchy by reducing the ambiguities, redundancies and

---

[8]Communication as energy: reducing the loss of energy in communication due to ambiguities, contradictions, and redundancies in the message.

[9]Shannon and Weaver (1964) determined that the probability that information contained in a message will be transferred is in inverse proportion to the ambiguity, contradiction, and redundancy in the communication environment. They also determined that their formula was the reciprocal of the formula for

contradictions in the communications within, between, and among the systems in the hierarchy.

The major challenge for systems-centered leadership in the 21st century will be the requirement that leaders not only view all levels of organization from the perspective of hierarchial[10] iso-morphy,[11] but also enable the various levels of leadership to take responsibility for the effect of their communications both within their own working systems as well as in the environment of their systems.

The principle is not new. It is the same principle that arouses concern for the environment today: the recognition that every system that pollutes its environment decreases the probability that it will thrive in its environment.

The advantage of the theory of living human systems is that it formulates few principles, and the methods for putting these principles into practice are relatively simple. The methods them-selves are quite simple to learn. They are often also quite simple

---

entropy, which made it possible to define the communication process itself as relatively entropic or neg-entropic, independent of the information that was being conveyed in the messages communicated. Simon & Agazarian (1967) developed the SAVI system (Sequential Analysis of Verbal Interaction) to diag-nose the problem solving potential in communication patterns. The SAVI sys-tem is also used to build neg-entropic communication skills as part of systems-centered leadership training.

[10]*Hierarchy:* The hierarchical nature of the organization of living human systems means that every system in the hierarchy exists in the environment of the system above it and is the environment for the system below it. Thus all communications from a system influence its environment, and all communica-tions from the environment influence the system. Any change, therefore, at any level in the hierarchy will have an impact both upon the systems above and below, and most strongly upon those immediately above and below. The impor-tance of organizing information and relating it to the goals *before* communicat-ing it across the boundaries, even at the cost of delaying the next steps in the service of this preliminary task is well illustrated in Example 4: "The fork in the road."

[11]*Isomorphy* is the most important of systems concepts in that it states that every system mirrors every other system in its structure and its function. Think-ing isomorphically has several important implications. It implies that the more one learns about any one system in the hierarchy, the more one has learnt about the structure and function of the system-as-a-whole. It implies that under-standing any single system at any level of an organization will provide important information about all systems in the organization and the organization-as-a-whole as a system in its environment.

to do. For example, a small change, like a "yes-and" instead of a "yes-but" can make a big difference. What remains to be seen is whether or not the satisfaction that comes from implementing a systems-centered in lieu of an individual-centered orientation will carry sufficient weight with 21st century human beings.

## REFERENCES

Agazarian, Y. M. (1992). A systems approach to the group-as-a-whole. *International Journal of Group Psychotherapy, 42,*3, 177–205.

Agazarian, Y. M. (1997). *Systems-centered therapy for groups.* New York: Guilford Press.

Agazarian, Y. M., & Janoff, S. (1993). Systems theory and small groups. In I. Kapplan & B. Sadock (Eds.), *Comprehensive textbook of group psychotherapy.* Waverly, MD: Williams & Wilkins.

Bertalanffy, L. von. (1969). *General systems theory* (Rev. ed.). New York: George Braziller.

Durkin, James E. (Ed.). (1981). *Living groups: Group psychotherapy and general system theory.* New York: Brunner/Mazel.

Howard, A., & Scott, R. A. (1965). A proposed framework for the analysis of stress in the human organism. *Journal of Applied Behavioral Science 10,* 141–160.

Lewin, K. (1951). *Field theory in social science.* New York: Harper & Row.

Raven, B., & Rietsema, J. (1960). The effects of varied clarity of group goal and group path upon the individual and his relation to his group. In D. Cartwright & A. Zander (Eds.), *Group dynamics research and theory* (2nd. ed.). New York: Elmsford, Row, Peterson.

Shannon, C. E., & Weaver, W. (1964). *The mathematical theory of communication.* Urbana, IL: University of Illinois Press.

Simon, A., & Agazarian, Y. (1967). *S.A.V.I., Sequential analysis of verbal interaction.* Philadelphia: Research for Better Schools.

# 7

# Mental Health and Leadership in the Twenty-First Century

## Marvin R. Skolnick, M.D.

> The whole world is our hospital
> Endowed by the ruined millionaire,
> Wherein, if we do well, we shall
> Die of the absolute paternal care
> That will not leave us, but prevents us
>     everywhere.
> —T. S. Eliot, *Four Quartets*, 1943

H, a 26-year-old single computer operator, an employee of the Universal Personnel Information Data Systems (UPIDS) was transported from work by an employee assistance vehicle to the Mental Health Central Receiving Center with a provisional DSM-XXX diagnosis of 20,009.765. He was described by employee's assistance report as troublesomely introspective but otherwise a team player. He was the son of the former president of the company, now deceased. His uncle, who had married H's mother after his father's death, was now president of the company. In the past month it had been noted by several observers that H frequently sat in front of his computer screen transfixed, mumbling to himself, "To be or not to be—that is the question," also muttering that there was "something rotten" in UPIDS. He had complained vigorously to his supervisor that the information that he was being fed through the computer were lies designed to conceal a nefarious conspiracy. He was also seen talking to thin air, explaining when questioned that he was conversing with his father's ghost. He also broke off relations with his girl friend who also was reported to be very unstable.

An employee assistance early warning system had been triggered a few weeks earlier by a significant slip in H's work–productivity profile. A system check of the citizen personality databank revealed nothing unusual about TV or VCR usage, spending to earning ratio, credit irregularities, politically correct index, driving record, or irregular utilization of medical or personality rectification services over the past 5 years. Neighbors and friends had nothing alarming to report.

Past history was unremarkable except for an eruption of deviancy in the 10th grade, when H was frequently seen smirking when reciting civic lessons and on several occasions challenged the credibility of American history textbooks. During one incident, after shouting that history was being destroyed, H smashed a clock on the teacher's desk. A thorough mental health assessment performed at that time revealed an imbalance between acetylcholine and serotonin neurotransmitter systems, history of unprovoked attacks on H's mother, and antisocial behavioral tendencies. H's assertions that his mother was having an affair with his uncle and that there had been abusive treatment by coaches were unsubstantiated and discounted as antisocial diversionary tactics to undermine legitimate authority. H requested to meet with a psychotherapist but this also seemed to be a defensive maneuver and was not implemented, particularly since psychotherapists were in short supply. A behavioral retraining program was instituted along with dietary alterations to reset the neurotransmitter balance. Within 2 months deviant behavior and other symptoms disappeared. H on subsequent retesting revealed no chemical imbalance and on psychosocial testing conformed with the National Institutes of Mental Health (NIMH) parameters for normal childhood development. Until the present episode H's record had been unblemished, attesting to the success of the early childhood intervention. However, it was the general consensus that H had not lives up to his promising early potential.

Mental Health authorities at the retraining center utilized the most modern techniques available in their neuropsychiatric assessment and treatment of H (considerable advances had been made since the first Mental Health intervention with him 15 years ago). In addition to the total body scan, PET scan, MRI, and chemical analysis, a computerized EEG dream analysis revealed bizarre patterns with psychopathic tendencies and potential for kindling and excessive blood flow to the limbic system. A report from the genome project revealed a translocated gene on chromosome 13 strongly correlated with dereistic thinking and low violence threshold. This data, plus his total life personal data, was fed to the Master Frame Super Biopsychosocial computer which delivered in 10 seconds a complete DSM-XXX diagnosis on all 25 axes, treatment goals, and a treatment plan. The treatment plan included dietary alterations to help reset the neurotransmitter imbalance and five 10-minute sessions with the biopsychosocial supersimulated counseling computer (the efficiency of which being remarkably enhanced, completed in 5 sessions what formerly required 10). A further recommendation was for three hours of enculturating TV programming per day. The plan was automatically faxed to the managed care outlet at the computer corporation where H worked and implemented by a Harvard MBA case manager. Zacpro, the newest neurotransmitter equilibrator and antisocial abater was added to the regimen since analysis revealed a clear Zacpro deficiency disorder in H's chemical constitution. Sadly, the treatment plan failed to effect a retraining. H continued to hurl epithets at whomever came near and continued to perseverate on "to be or not to be." A quality assurance computer check revealing that there were no problems in treatment delivery, concluded that H was idiosyncratically resistant and noncompliant to this latest and best form of rectification. Fortunately, an even more powerful neurotransmitter equilibrator and antisocial abater drug Lofzo was currently undergoing an expedited approval protocol at the FDA. In the interim, after consultation and authorization from his uncle, H was sent to the cryogenic holding tank for freezing until the Lofzo could be added to the retraining regimen.

The preceding narrative case history of H could be read as a futuristic nightmare of mental health in the 21st century or a wish-fulfilling dream of a scientific, rational culture on the path toward cost effective solutions to the problems of being human. Whether dream or nightmare, the story of H is not as removed as one might think from contemporary reality.

I began my psychiatric career at Yale in the 1960s. Now as I approach my sixtieth year I am still sorting through the results of the ongoing encounter between myself, psychiatric training, and life. So far, I believe that like H, I have been relatively untrainable. This belief is based on my own assessment and on unsolicited feedback from authoritative sources within the psychiatric profession. I feel that there is a skepticism that seems wired into my soul. I have been influenced by others who also seemed to me to be untrainable—Dr. Wilfred Bion, two analysts, numerous patients, members and staff of A. K. Rice Group Relations Conference members and staff, and Daniel Levinson, a professor in the Department of Psychiatry at Yale University. Although I never knew him personally, Dr. Levinson has a special place in my pantheon of skeptics. As a psychiatrist in training, I was encouraged to keep my eyes trained on the patient, but Dr. Levinson continually decentered this view by his provocative comments in Grand Rounds and his writing, drawing attention to the power of the social process to shape the individual and also shape the way we perceive others. He helped open a space in my mind to grapple with the interplay between the inner and outer world that subverts any fixed explanation of disease as just an individual matter.

Perhaps drawn by my kindredness with the untrainable, I have devoted much of my psychiatric energies over the past 25 years to the development of a therapeutic community, the P St. Day Treatment Therapeutic Program, for people like H, considered schizophrenic or chronically mentally ill. In this work I have not only encountered sickness but also powerful social, political, and economic forces that have much to say about who becomes sick and who stays sick. In this 25-year period beliefs about the nature of mental illness and the sociocultural context in which treatment is embedded have changed dramatically. As we approach the 21st century, change is accelerating and threatens to make the P St. program, with its emphasis on the psychosocial dynamics of human development, obsolete.

Not all change is progress, of course. It can be driven by unexamined assumptions masquerading as science. Just as the appreciation of personal history is essential in helping a patient gain perspective on his present reality and future possibilities, an appreciation of historical process is essential for society and work leaders. What is driving the changes in mental health institutions and practice today? Is it scientific progress? Expediency or retreat from disturbing insights? In my role as founder and clinical leader of the P St. program, I have had considerable encouragement from many to agonize over whether my struggles to sustain the therapeutic community in the face of rising tides of opposition from institutional and biological psychiatry have been in the service of human development or in the service of my countertransference or of the basic assumption group that resists new ideas and progress in order to preserve the group regardless of the cost.

Bion has suggested there is nothing like an answer to ruin a good question. In sorting through 25 years of clinical experiences, I don't feel I have an answer, but I do have strong opinions. I will attempt to make the case that while the P St. program may seem to be inefficient and outmoded in the eyes of critics who like managed care, in fact it offers a model for a more humane antidote to the collapsing space for Being for the serious psychiatric causalities of this postmodern age than the most modern technological solutions.

Nancy Adreasen (1984), a leading neuropsychiatrist, claimed in the *Broken Brain* that if Hamlet could have had access to lithium salts he well might have been spared his dark agonies. Mental illness as we approach the 21st century is being increasingly placed in the biological domain and away from the domain of the mind. Recent NIMH initiatives to address the increasing level of violence in our society, particularly in poor urban areas, has focused on the biological causes of violence (Breggin, 1991). While there is a rich developing psychoanalytic and sociological body of knowledge about man as subject with a mind who relates to other subjects in a nonmaterial universe of meaning, this perspective is largely relegated to a corner. Man as object takes center stage. Dysfunctions of the brain, genetic aberrations, behavioral disorders, chemical imbalances, and corrective drug treatments are the dominant fields of study by powerful institutions such as NIMH, the pharmaceutical industry, and most university departments of psychiatry. *The Diagnostic and Statistical Manual,* the sanctioned classifier of mental illness in our society, reflects this bias.

This perspective is embraced by the media with frequent references to chemical imbalance as the cause of mental illness as though it were established fact. New miracle drugs have appeared on the covers of newsmagazines, news stories report studies that claim genetic breakthroughs, or the superiority of computerized counseling over live psychotherapists, but studies that shed serious doubts on these claims are seldom mentioned. The embracing of managed care schemes for the treatment of mental illness that disregard confidentiality between psychotherapist and patients also underscores the dominance of the model of the patient as a disordered, disconnected object rather than a troubled subject embedded in a field of conflicting interests with other subjects.

This effort to conquer mental illness through a positivistic science approach can be seen as a derivative of the Western Enlightenment that began in the 17th century. *Positivism,* a term coined by the 19th century philosopher Auguste Comte, posits that truth is attained through objective observation and reason. In this paradigm the "objective" observer or experimenter utilizing data from the senses subjected to analysis by reason (split off from the irrational, the mystical, and subjective) arrives at truth while essentially standing outside of the process that he is researching. Giants like Bacon, Newton, Descartes, Kepler, and Copernicus casting off the chains of dogma passed down through the dark ages resting on the inaccessible authority of God, the church, and dead icons, installed the authority of their own reason and scientific empiricism as the new standard for truth.

The transformative process set in motion by this new science collided with the established belief systems and the hierarchially arranged social order, but stirred hope that reason and science promised an earthly utopia that could not only solve old problems but also the new problems created by "progress." Positivistic science burst on the scene like a Promethean gift to man that could harness the unlimited forces of nature. The optimism about the conquest of darkness is captured by Alexander Pope's eulogy of Newton: "God made Newton and then there was light." Positivistic science and its technological offspring have transformed the planet and almost every facet of life. The reliance on machines to heat, cool, light, drive, communicate, calculate, mass produce has become comparable to our reliance on the beating of the heart.

The Enlightenment also generated hope that the power of reason could liberate man from the tyrannical social controls of the middle ages and allow for the emergence of the free, rational individual—a new construct in human history. Why couldn't the disordered human being with a dysfunctional brain, as in the case of H, be amenable to the science of modernity? Why should it not be the last and perhaps the most important frontier to conquer in the 21st century? Cost effective, efficient, computerized systems, based on reason, brain chemistry, physiology, and behavioral principles uncontaminated by psychological speculation seem like a logical extension of the Enlightenment and a positivistic rational science dream come true.

To Nietzsche, Heidegger, Buber, and Foucault, psychoanalysts, psychotherapists, and others concerned about the realm of meaning in human relations, the story of H might seem a nightmare come true. From the postmodern perspective, the effort to frame mental illness or emotional disturbance and suffering as a disease spilt off from the historical, anthropological, social, philosophical, spiritual, economic, and political realms of being is a Cartesian sleight of hand in the service of power and denial. Dr. Thomas Moore, a struggling psychiatrist in Walker Percy's (1987) novel *The Thanatos Syndrome* spends a year in prison. After his release he returns to his community and finds his old patients, friends, and enemies transformed. Gone are the neurotic or psychotic problems, the tensions, but also missing are irony, humor, and emotion. The townspeople now have a robotlike genius for calculating, contract bridge, and an uncanny ability to know precise longitude and latitude. Eventually, Dr. Moore uncovers a secret NIMH experiment with a lithiumlike substance that has been added to the town reservoir. This is a pilot project for a grander design.

The more light shed by science and reason, the greater the length and breadth of the shadow cast. The Romantic movement of the early 19th century in art, music, and literature constituted a revolt against the encroachment of the industrial revolution and rationalism on the human subject. However, it was Nietzsche who systematically probed the paradox of the enlightenment (Breisach, 1962; Levin, 1987; Magill, 1990). Accompanying his pronouncement that God is dead, Nietzsche warned that there was little to replace God and religion's enchanted mythology that had served as the center and source of meaning for Western man. In its place were the shallow mythologies of the state or the marketplace, a bleak nihilism looming on the horizon. Freud reputedly said of Nietzsche that he knew more about himself than any human being who had ever lived or was ever likely to live. While Nietzsche might have been skewed more toward the paranoid than Freud realized, Nietzsche as the "master of suspicion" knew more about the deceptions and labyrinths of covert power packed into what passes for objective knowledge, morality, and truth than anyone before him. In his genealogical detection he found irrationality embedded in reason, immorality lurking behind morality, and covert, power-shaping, socially sanctioned knowledge. While the Enlightenment promised to many the triumph of reason over the irrationality of the Middle Ages with its subjugation of the individual to the will of tyrants and superstition, Nietzsche detected the emergence of an insidious new tyrannical power wielded by the modern establishment. This new, more covert tyranny threatened to render the individual a nonsubject without willpower to compete with the pervasive power of the marketplace and the state. The centrality of power from the beginning of the Enlightenment is captured in Bacon's definition of knowledge that emphasized mastery. Machiavelli's *The Prince* (1952), a handbook for leadership, seems to be the primary handbook in our age—not just for tyrants but for important political and business leaders as well. It stresses the imperatives of power with little or no concern for the means necessary for its acquisition.

The covert influence of power dynamics in the natural and social sciences, philosophy, art, literature, education, economics, politics, psychology, and psychiatry is a prominent theme of postmodernist thought, echoing Nietzsche's concerns about nihilism and the plight of the individual (Levin, 1987). Kafka and Orwell provide chilling fictional portrayals of the demise of the individual in the modern world that resonated with Nietzsche's (1956) and Hiedegger's (1962) warning of the imminent destruction of the human in man through the insidious effects of technology and the fury of nihilism. Kuhn (1962), a contemporary philosopher of science, has also noted that paradigm shifts in science occur not so much from the persuasiveness of reasoned or empirical evidence but from shifts of power within the leadership of a discipline. Why the dramatic shift in psychiatry to a biological perspective? In a book entitled *Voltaire's Bastards: The Dictatorship of Reason in the West,* John Saul (1992) asserts that the hope that reason would bring justice and freedom to human affairs has been derailed. Rather than becoming an instrument of truth, reason has evolved into structures that organize and disguise the exercise of power. Saul cites "number crunchers" and prophets of the reasonable like Robert McNamara and Henry Kissinger as modern counterparts of the courtiers of kings. Edward Said (1993), in his book *Culture and Imperialism,* argues that the West's efforts to subjugate and exploit the non-Western world has infected every culture that it has touched, installing the struggle for power as the dominant force eroding cultural legacies built up over the preceding centuries. Feminists have argued that the masculine ego, in its appropriation of reason and denigration of feeling and the subjective as feminine, has utilized this split to subjugate women and maintain patriarchal systems formed around phallic power.

Foucault (1965) defines madness as "that constantly changing region of human experience which defies any regulating intentionality; which speaks in the language of the fantastic and the passionate; which dwells not merely in historical time but also in a violent timeless stream of subversion, flooding the secure banks of all that is positively known about the order of the self and the world" (cited in Bernauer, 1987, p. 349). In *Madness and Civilization* he asserts that individuals defined as mentally ill, the scientists who classify them, and the doctors who treat them may be used by the establishment to instill values and ways of being that suit the prevailing power structures and silence an unsettling but creative dialogue with the repressed, split-off, or suppressed.

Foucault has challenged the conventional wisdom that modern psychiatry has rescued the "mad" from the cruel and inhuman treatment of the dark ages. He argues that the "mad," despite the presence of cruelty and superstition in the Middle Ages often had more of a place and voice in community affairs—as prophet, mystic, wise fool—than they do today as moral degenerates or biological defectives. The mentally ill who aren't able to function as participants in the production–consumption process of modern life often become commodities themselves in a mental health industry that loses sight of their human worth and the meanings of their narratives (Barham, 1984).

For Nietzsche the remedy for nihilism and the demise of the individual was to fight fire with fire—to become an "over-man"—a superman who doesn't succumb but creates himself through his own will to power. Heidegger, grappling with a similar grim prognosis, points in a somewhat different direction (Magill, 1990). He recommends confrontation with the anxieties, guilt, and uncertainties inherent in personal choice and responsible involvement with one's community. "Authentic becoming" also means shedding the denial of time, history, and the inevitability of death. Unfortunately, Heidegger himself apparently succumbed to the seductiveness of raw power in his alliance with fascism, which has undermined his reputation and the credibility of his thought.

Freud's (1921/1955) discovery that an unconscious mind driven by irrational instincts and transference distortions profoundly influences thinking and perceptions of external reality, added a psychological depth to Nietzsche's suspicion of appearances. Freud hoped to develop psychoanalysis into an enlightened science that would fit respectfully under the tent of the prevailing positivistic science of his day. However, Freud's discovery itself rendered this hope obsolete. How could the scientist or the psychoanalyst ever objectively stand outside of the field of observation, when he too had an unconscious? Freud used mechanistic metaphors about physical energy at the core of his metapsychology and envisioned a day when the mind could be objectified in terms of the physical sciences, while at the same time he was the intrepid intuitive explorer of the ineffable mysteries of the unknowable psyche.

What is external? What is internal? Fact? Fantasy? What is objective? What is subjective? What is subject to the will and what is determined? These are questions that have defied answers, frustrating the positivistic ambitions of Freud's psychoanalysis. However, the unanswerable questions have also catalyzed the pursuit of understanding in human relations through the nonpositivist lens of intersubjective exploration to view the elusive human condition in terms of the complex interplay between the individual, the group, the intergroup, and the society. The trajectory of the positivism of the Enlightenment discounts the value of this lens. As Einstein warned, the technical achievement of smashing the atom hasn't touched the destructive ways we think and relate as human beings.

## MENTAL HEALTH IN THE DECADES OF THE 1960s AND 1970s

In the 1960s and 1970s it seemed as though a window had begun to open to explore the interdependent systemic nature of human relations. The social order was challenged on many fronts. A new generation of provocative thinkers and activists in a variety of fields moved to transform race, gender, class and generational relations, politics, economics, medicine, and education. What had been a relatively fixed social order threatened to unravel under the pressure of provocative new ideas or old ideas in new energized forms. In Bion's terminology the contained (ferment caused by new ideas) was stretching and challenging the social containers. Paradoxically, out of the social churning new linkages and relationships between what had previously been partitioned into separate domains in the social consciousness began to emerge. In contrast to the prevailing Cartesian tendency toward splitting, complex and often subterranean, recursive interdependent relationships between reason and irrationality, between the mad and the sane, between the individual and the group, between history, culture, politics, economics, and the individual, between cultures, and between the mind and the body, entered the public mind.

The mental health field began to develop a comprehensive biopsychosocial developmental model (Strauss & Carpenter, 1981) that provided a framework with which to integrate the explosion of knowledge about the brain, psychopharmacology, child and adult developmental research, and cultural and social factors in mental illness and health. Winnicott (1969) focused on the mother's "holding" function of empathically making environmental provisions, transitional objects, and space for play to enable her infant to have a sense of "going on being." He demonstrated parallels with the environmental provisions and transitional space necessary for therapeutic developmental work with children and adults. Researchers demonstrated links between mental illness, economics, and class (Hollingshead & Redlich, 1958). Family system therapists showed how disturbed families unconsciously select a specific member to embody family sickness and become the designated patient (Bowen, 1978). Anthropologists and sociologists studying mental hospitals elucidated connections between unprocessed staff conflict and patient agitation (Stanton, Stanton, & Schwartz, 1954), and links between authoritarian, hierarchically structured institutions and the fostering of chronicity (Goffman, 1961). Organizational structure thought to be rationally determined was discovered also to be shaped by unconscious attempts to defend against the anxieties generated by work, even if by such defensive maneuvers real work is destroyed (Menzies, 1975). Epidemiology researchers demonstrated links between mental illness and sociocultural conditions (Leighton, Harding, Machlin, Macmillan, & Leighton, 1963). The quality of the social milieu in mental hospitals was shown to impact on the success or failure of treatment. This led to the development of communities structured on therapeutic principles (Jones, 1953; Main, 1975). A surge of interest in mental health spurred by the Kennedy family spawned the community mental health movement that provided government funds and incentives to build community mental health centers across the nation. These not only provided direct care in the community as an alterative to institutionalization, but attempted to address and treat interrelationships between pathological economic, political, and social conditions and mental illness.

## THE P ST. DAY TREATMENT THERAPEUTIC COMMUNITY

The P St. Day Treatment Therapeutic Community, started in 1971, grew out of this ferment, therapeutic optimism, and idealism. Influenced by these developments, I approached the P St. project armed with a faith close to zeal that even the most severely ill psychiatric patients could be restored to a quality life in the larger community if provided with support, time, understanding, dignity, and opportunities to grow with a community of others free from the iatrogenic toxicity of impersonal institutions. We began by transporting chronically psychotic patients and staff from a locked psychiatric ward in a large city hospital to an unused elementary school building located in the hub of the larger community. Spending their days in the school building and returning by bus to the psychiatric ward in the evenings, the patients found this shuttling from one location to another disorienting in a concrete sense. However, for patients and staff it was the distance between social belief systems symbolized by the hospital versus the school that had the most profound and unsettling impact. This back and forth trip resonated with conflicts within each patient and staff member about their roles, authority, and place in the social order. Eventually the busing was discontinued as patients returned to their families or found living arrangements in halfway houses or on their own, and we admitted new patients directly from the community, but the tension between two different social constructions of mental illness remained.

My idealistic determination not to replicate the estranging dichotomy of ill patients and healthy staff, and therapeutic optimism about the healing potential of a cohesive community, provided a jump start for the program. However, will and good intentions proved insufficient to contend with the challenges of sustaining a therapeutic community in the face of the gravitational pulls of our collective psychopathology, the madness generated by group life, and the subversive negligence or attacks of the larger institution.

## THEORETICAL FRAMEWORK

In the midst of catastrophic change, a good theory can be an essential ingredient that enables a group to reestablish boundaries and reorganize at developmentally higher levels rather than sink into chaos. We applied the work of Melanie Klein (1959), Bion (1961), Winnicott (1965), and Tavistock group relations and social systems theory (Miller & Rice, 1967) that stresses the relational, developmental, and hermeneutic dimensions of psychoanalysis as road maps to emerge from bogs of emotion toward a more coherent appreciation of the dynamic links between the inner worlds of individuals, the group, the institution, and society.

By extrapolating from her psychoanalytic play therapy with young children, Melanie Klein delineated an inner world in which experience of self and others is organized through unconscious phantasies that rely on splitting and projection. These defensive operations protect the child from the threat that hate, envy and greed generated by the inevitable frustrations of the mother–child relationship will spoil the self or the nurturing other on whom the child must depend. The child attributes all that is unacceptable to a persecuting bad breast, preserving the mother's "goodness." She called this defensive operation projective identification and its mode of experience, the paranoid–schizoid position. At first this was thought to be a primitive developmental phase through which children pass on their way to the more mature depressive mode, in which one owns impulses and ambivalent feelings toward others seen as both good and bad. However, later work by Klein and her followers proposed that the paranoid–schizoid mode exists in modified form throughout life in dialectic interaction with the depressive mode and that failures to contain projections and achieve balance between the two are implicated in serious social dysfunction and psychosis. Bion believed that adult anxieties generated by group membership are comparable in their centrality and intensity to the anxieties of the infant–mother relationship. His Kleinian perspective on group dynamics emphasizes the blurring of boundaries and the role of projective and introjective identification in the formation of unconscious collaborative defenses against anxieties evoked in group—the Basic Assumptions. This perspective has proved extremely useful in the therapeutic community in elucidating the social factors that foster psychotic phenomena. In his later work, Bion (1970) recognized that insight into group dynamics, while essential as a step toward rectifying the collusive and pathological effect of boundary distortion involved in massive malignant projective and introjective processes, was not sufficient in itself. The therapeutic other, like the good-enough mother (in this case the community), must have the capacity to allow projections to unfold in a shared transitional space, and to process them so that individuals can reintroject what has been projected in nontoxic form. It then can stimulate emotional growth and movement from the paranoid–schizoid position toward the depressive.

Tavistock social systems theory (Miller & Rice, 1967), a synthesis of Bion's psychoanalytic insights into group and general system theory (von Bertalanffy, 1968) has enriched our thinking about how to construct and maintain a social system which has the requisite holding and containing characteristics necessary for therapeutic and developmental work with psychotic patients. The delineation of the primary task, roles, and boundaries, and an appreciation of their interrelatedness, provides the structural frame that makes experience available for sorting and processing. Social systems analysis has revealed how institutions and societies use social structure to defend against the anxieties and pain inherent in the task through maladaptive boundary management, distribution of authority, and pathological projective identification in ways that seriously undermine the task (Jaques, 1974). This lens has been particularly useful in determining whether resistance to work is emanating from within the therapeutic community or from the environment (i.e., institutional context in which the program is embedded).

One can conceive of the project of a community of patients and staff struggling to move through madness toward human development in an uncertain surrounding environment as analogous to the task of a lifeboat full of surviving passengers and crew struggling to reach land on an unpredictable sea. There are three main dimensions which must be dealt with on the journey. The structural (containing) aspects of the lifeboat must be maintained. The individuals' morale and relationships, particularly involving authority issues, require attention. And there are the environmental factors–the weather, currents, and essential resources necessary for survival at sea. Leadership must struggle with all these dimensions and their impact on the primary task—moving the lifeboat toward land.

## STRUCTURE, CONTAINING, AND HOLDING

The conventional contemporary means to "contain and hold" severely disturbed psychiatric patients has been to literally detain them in closed hospital structures that control potentially destructive behaviors with mechanical or chemical restraint, and deliver treatment through a somewhat impersonal parentified medical model. The social context created by these means exerts a calming order, but throws up barriers to communication. By contrast at P St. we attempt to contain and hold through use of psychosocial principles which stress the importance of respect for individual autonomy, open-mindedness to experience, faith that the expression of destructive, envious, jealous, loving and sexual feelings can be survived, processed, and empathically understood. A matrix of authentic nonhierarchical personal relationships provides a platform on which the community stands. The clear delineation of time, task, role, and group boundaries adds to the holding capacity of the group. The use of boundaries as a frame of reference should be distinguished from imposition of rules to enforce behavioral conformity. From an open systems perspective, boundaries are not stone barriers, but permeable membranes that can be blurred, crossed, and reformed that delineates a creative space between rigidity and chaos. However, the prohibition of physical violence and a commitment to confidentiality (so often disregarded with psychotic patients) are boundaries that must approach barriers. Without them the community cannot be safe enough for spontaneous expression and regression necessary for deep therapeutic work. A 5-day-a-week program rather than 24 hours, 7 days per week, reduces the risk of enmeshing the patients in an institutionalized way of life that engenders pathological dependency. Leaks in the boat or in the containing holding structure invariably occur and must be continually spotted and repaired to keep the therapeutic project afloat.

## THE INTERNAL PROCESS—INTERACTION BETWEEN THE INDIVIDUAL, SUBGROUPS, AND THE THERAPEUTIC COMMUNITY AS A WHOLE

Many of the patients who enter the P St. community have suffered catastrophic collapses of their inner worlds and capacity to function. Their idiosyncratic attempts to reconstitute an inner world that restores a sense of meaning and bearable feeling states often are met in the treatment setting with a nonempathic medical diagnosis, medication, and control measures. This response to the patient as a disordered object rather than a suffering subject reinforces the patient's defensive tendencies to retreat inward. The resulting relationship between the treater and the treated too often becomes a construction of estranged paranoid–schizoid worlds of mutual nonrecognition. The patients and nonpatients create a wall from behind which they suspiciously view each other.

At P St. we have tried to create a safe enough environment that the latticework of unconscious projections and introjections that form walls can be brought into awareness as a crucial step in reopening communication. Group and community dramas allow the emergence of repressed or suppressed affect (Hinshelwood, 1987). Community meetings, small-group psychothcrapy, psychodrama, movement therapy, art therapy, task groups, recreational outings, and patient government become the stages on which the dramas are performed, often stirring intense anxieties and complex intergroup processes. Transforming deadening defenses into live experiential theater provides an opportunity to reclaim what has been projected, and free what has been encapsulated, creating new plays with better endings. This is the daily challenge.

As with the occupants of the lifeboat, the abilities and vulnerabilities of all members must be recognized, whether patients or staff, and integrated into the work. Particularly challenging are the processing of staff pathology and the use of patient strengths. Roles for patients that carry authority, such as determination of treatment goals and meaningful responsibilities in community government, as well as roles for staff that include self-scrutiny and following as well as leading, help to counteract the pull of a treatment community toward dichotomies of health and illness.

Psychotropic medications can play a vital role in treatment by making the unbearable bearable, but they are not curative and can have serious debilitating side effects like tardive dyskinesia and reduction in capacity for experiential learning. There are also less obvious pitfalls. Too much emphasis on the psychopharmacological dimension of treatment reinforces the definition of patients as disordered machines waiting passively to be fixed. Many patients are enticed by the potential magic of medication and the relief from the pain and responsibility inherent in development. The doctor and staff are often tempted to relieve themselves by sedating the disturbing patient. Exploitation of the illness model and transference to the doctor can increase compliance to medication regimens, but it can also sentence patients to a hypothetical chronic disease that ignores their autonomy and the wisdom of their bodies. At P St. weekly medication groups provide patients with the opportunity to explore their experience with medication, give the doctor feedback, and learn about what is known about psychopharmacology. It is a more complicated but more collaborative prescription process.

## THE ENVIRONMENT—THE INTERACTION BETWEEN THE THERAPEUTIC COMMUNITY AND SOCIETY

Often the efficacy of psychiatric treatments are assessed without regard to the environment in which they are embedded (Klein &

Gould, 1973; Singer, Astrachan, Gould, & Klein, 1979). This is like evaluating surgical procedures without considering cleanliness or sterility of the operating room.

Like every other program, the P St. Therapeutic Community exists in a context of interdependent relationships across an open boundary with a nexus of other groups and institutions. In the case of the P St. community these relationships include the city mental health department, families of patients, and agencies involved with housing, welfare, social security, and employment. Both patients and staff are also simultaneously members of other groups and organizations which may pose conflicts of interests with their roles as therapeutic community members. Social systems theory has been invaluable in raising to consciousness the pervasiveness of intergroup phenomena inside the boundaries of the program. Maintaining permeability in the external boundary to allow collaborative work across it, while resisting pressures to blur the boundary through homogenization with antitherapeutic values and norms of outside groups often feels like a delicate dance through a gauntlet.

Examples of such pressures are:

The tendency of families to locate all family disturbance in their designated patient;

The tendency of mental health departments to acquire funds from federal and city sources by establishing patient disability status as a priority, rather than supporting the patients' striving for autonomy;

The tendency to adopt inadequate time frames for treatment not determined by realistic therapeutic principles but by pressures from third-party payers;

Society's investment in establishing a chemical imbalance theory of mental disorder, thus avoiding shared responsibility and complex links between child rearing practices, economics, political, and social values.

Surviving the struggles on the boundary is one of the greatest tests of leadership. Like the lifeboat that can be carried off course by invisible currents, the therapeutic community without vigilant leadership can easily drift toward an antitherapeutic culture. As with one of the first therapeutic communities started by Bion in 1945 (Bridger, 1985), many creative and effective programs have gone by the wayside because of inadequate attention to the inter-action with the external environment. The therapeutic commu-nity is also at risk of projecting unaddressed internal conflicts into an "enemy" outside. Twenty-five years after its beginning, the P St. therapeutic community struggles to maintain its commit-ment to its values. I have grown to more fully appreciate the painful distance that must be continually traveled between the assertion of ideals and their realization. The recovery from falls into paranoid–schizoid and autistic processes, as a seductive way to circumvent the pain and complexity of the work of develop-ment, is a daily challenge.

## SKETCHES OF THE WORK WITH PATIENTS

When B joined the community he formed a deep attachment which enabled him to regress to an almost inert embryonic pos-ture, then slowly came back to life through the experience and expression of rage that he previously could only tolerate in disso-ciated psychotic states. P gradually reconstructed his character by using different parts of the program over 17 years, culminating in graduation from college and marriage. M, a devoutly religious middle-aged woman, joined the program after a psychotic epi-sode precipitated by stress at work. She used the community for support, while discovering that her terror of roasting in hell was linked to her assumption that anger at her boss was fused with anger at her mother and God that warranted the most drastic eternal punishment. With the community's help, M saw that her boss was in fact sadistic, and distinguishable from mother and God. Her sadistic superego and psychotic core could be kept in check by a job change, taking low doses of a neuroleptic, and continued support of the therapeutic community. She broke a revolving door pattern of hospitalizations even though the core of her psychotic process was only partially reached. T joined the community in an acute paranoid state which had grown out of an abused childhood. Though T was initially very responsive to the interest and concern of other patients and staff, he soon became suspicious and hostile. In an intense community drama he came to embody for others what was menacing in the community, while he perceived other patients and staff as persecuting bad objects. When these processes congeal into a dramatized community pattern, it can be the beginning of a long but fruitful discovery leading to greater integration of split-off parts of the selves of all participants, and an opening to a healing dialogue. However, for T and the community the drama became a fixed pathological organization that resisted interpretation or other efforts. T became utterly convinced that there was something irredeemably rotten in the community and many in the community became hardened and despairing about reaching him. T refused help, including neuroleptics, and fled to another city, convinced he was leaving his persecutors behind. The community breathed a sigh of relief that it had gotten rid of what was menacing. The community's relief was short lived, however, as new menacing figures emerged.

Many of the patients who have participated in the program over its 25 years seem to have derived significant benefits in the form of reduced hospitalizations and medication and better quality of life and increased connectedness with others. Some of the schizophrenics who seemed most hopeless have made profound development progress. While many have not undergone dramatic changes, they have held their own and avoided the downward pull of chronicity.

## THE INTERACTION OF THE P ST. PROGRAM AND THE CHANGING SOCIAL CONTEXT

If H were to be admitted to a P St. therapeutic community in the year 2000 after suffering a psychotic episode, I hope that he would be given an opportunity to tell his story to others who are "inefficiently" listening rather than simply diagnosing; that he would not only be assessed for signs and symptoms of pathology, but also for his gifts and strengths; that family, workplace, and society factors would be explored; that he would meet with patients and staff to do his own interviewing before joining; and that he would have the support, time, and space to *be*.

The window of support in our society that opened in the 1960s for programs like the P St. therapeutic community seemed to gradually close in the seventies as federal support for community mental health centers began to narrow, and then slam shut in the eighties as politics turned to the right. Fish are the last to discover water, and scant attention is paid to the context in which we make "scientific" judgments about who is mentally ill, why, and what should be done about it. As the centers of political power shifted from liberal to conservative, research funding, diagnostic manuals, education, and treatment priorities skewed sharply toward the "bio" and away from the "psychosocial" in the biopsychosocial model. The shifts in mental health practices in the last two decades are related more to political cultural shifts than they are to the persuasiveness of scientific evidence.

During the eighties, the P St. therapeutic community began to lose support. Federal grants were not renewed. Staff positions were lost. The Citizen Advisory Board which had energetically supported a day treatment facility in its community lost its enthusiasm as deinstitutionalized patients without adequate treatment began to wander aimlessly in larger numbers down its streets. The city Mental Health Department, caught between court mandates to provide least restrictive care to increasing numbers of patients with diminishing financial resources, tried to increase efficiency with bureaucratic procedures and central control of programs. The result was increased layers of bureaucracy preoccupied with litigation, public relations, and reducing costs. Decisions passed down to clinical programs became more removed from the necessities of clinical care, curtailing the authority of clinicians and program directors to maintain meaningful treatment. The effort used to build trusting therapeutic relationships was considered wasteful by the bureaucracy. The delivery of time-limited prepackaged programs that relied primarily on drug treatment compliance, computerized paperwork, and management of patients rather than treatment proliferated. Patients were relegated to the bottom of a hierarchy driven by bureaucratic imperatives, reducing clinicians to middle managers. Underscoring this schizoid impersonality, a bureaucratic directive ordered clinicians to refer to patients as "consumers" and themselves as "providers" in all future memoranda.

The P St. Therapeutic Community began to feel more and more like an enclave of counterculture rebels under siege. When staff left there were no funds to hire replacements. As the therapeutic community model was less in vogue with training departments, students and volunteers diminished to a trickle. Leaking ceilings, broken air conditioners, dilapidated furniture, and general maintenance neglect undermined the sense of a reliable holding environment.

The therapeutic community values such as personal and social responsibility, respect for the autonomy of the patient, and the value of relationships, collided with the larger institution's values stressing authoritarian exercise of power. Dissent was labeled pathology. Patient efforts to exercise their authority through the publication of a newsletter and activism on mental health policies affecting them evoked responses from high-level bureaucrats in the Department of Mental Health that addressed the patients as if they were insubordinate employees on the bottom rung of the hierarchy. Autonomy was further eroded by strong pressure for patients to apply for maximum disability benefits and Medicaid. The impact on their treatment of autonomous strivings was treated as irrelevant.

Commitment to the philosophy of treatment deteriorated within the staff as clinicians were caught between loyalty to the principles of the therapeutic community and implicit and explicit threats from the larger institution to promotions and careers. Conflict within the staff became so compelling that it often preempted work with the patient. Patients and their families seemed increasingly beguiled by the promise of a fix for a chemical imbalance that would free them from guilt, responsibility, and the need to actively struggle with the pains of development.

## An Episode

In 1992 P St. and the Mental Health Department had a dramatic collision. The administrator of adult services for the entire system issued a directive to discharge all patients who had been in the program longer than 18 months. This was to be accomplished within 2 months in order to make room for a stream of new patients being forced by court order out of the state hospital. Since plans to develop several other needed day treatment programs had not been implemented, P St. was left as the only day program to accommodate a large number of patients being discharged from the hospital. This last minute plan also involved converting the P St. Therapeutic Community into a short-term behavior modification program. It seemed reasonable to expect that many of the patients to be summarily discharged from P St. would probably regress and return to the hospital. A short-term program design for many of the seriously disturbed chronic patients leaving the hospital could offer no more than a token treatment. However, the administration, under pressure from a court order to provide community placements for institutionalized patients, devised their plan without consultation with the clinicians who would staff the radically transformed new program.

The Therapeutic Community Patient Government responded to the notice of discharges and conversion of the program with letters of protest to the administrator's office emphasizing how much they valued and depended on the program. A patient–staff committee also formulated a plan that would allow increased admissions to the program while preserving its philosophy and circumventing the need for forced discharges. The administrator's office replied by a memorandum that the patients were not following proper channels. The patients persisted. The administrator's office accused the patients of excessive dependency in not submitting to the inevitability of appropriate discharge. My efforts to work within the system as an advocate for what I felt was the soundness of the patients' position was seen as disruptive and uncooperative by the administrators of the larger institution. I was systematically being stripped of formal programmatic authority in favor of a program manager with no clinical training or inclination to question orders from above. However, as the psychiatrist, I still retained the authority to prescribe and write admission and discharge orders and remained the de facto clinical leader within the program. Like the character in Melville's prophetic story *Bartlebly,* I became an obstacle to the bureaucracy's need for compliant paper pushers. When I refused to write discharge orders on patients whom I felt would be harmed by precipitous discharge this exacerbated tension within the staff, afraid that resistance to the changes would invite retaliation.

Rumors circulated that I was to be replaced. However, news of the impasse reached the court monitors of the mental health system who sent a clinical representative to audit the program. The auditor concluded after meeting with patients that unlike most programs within the system the Therapeutic Community patients were deeply invested and believed they were being helped. This led to changes within the administration, cancellation of discharges of patients, and rescue of the Therapeutic Community. Modifications proposed by the patient-staff were adopted.

## Concluding Reflections

Despite the lack of financial resources and political clout, and the generally inhospitable larger institution in which it is embedded, the program has continued to survive precariously for at least 10 of its 25 years. Its survival seems particularly remarkable since on any given day the community may be struggling with sagging or precarious morale, frustrated expectations, painful experiences that rival Dante and Virgil's journey through the inferno, and serious reservations about whether the Community is at all therapeutic. Despite their fragility and deep suspicion of relationships, the patients' emotional investment in the Therapeutic Community has often been the crucial factor in keeping the Community going. The staff perhaps make their most important contributions by joining the patients rather than taking refuge in "clinical" detachment in the often painful ongoing community drama of being and becoming.

It is difficult to define what is therapeutic. The treatment that H received at UPIDS can be understood as a negative resolution of the question, "to be or not to be." The Therapeutic Community's capacity to endure love, hate, destructiveness, and creativity while continually reflecting on itself helps avoid stagnation in a fixed idea of "normality." Bion's (1977) "F" factor (faith) may point most eloquently to the therapeutic. "F" is the conviction that if one remains in relationship and emotional contact with self and fellow humans in the pursuit of truth, developmental transformations will occur.

Habermas and the Frankfurt School of Philosophy have argued that normative standards of society, like the psychiatric DSM, are most likely to be based on coercion that benefits the powerful and punishes the less powerful, unless the normative standards are constructed out of an ongoing discourse of unencumbered free speech by all affected parties (Levin, 1987). The positivistic approach to psychiatric patients clearly tends to close off dialogue, particularly with the most vulnerable or disturbed individuals, by assuming that their disturbing or dissenting narrative is based primarily on the aberrations of their brains. The attempt of the P St. Therapeutic Community is to reopen dialogue that does not confine its focus to the "healthy" converting the "sick," but includes the uncovering of coercion and exploitation by the "healthy." Social spaces like P St. which attempt to recover the lost speech of the disenfranchised mentally ill, may provide opportunities for corrective experiences that are pertinent to society as a whole.

In the mental health field there has been an explosion of information that one might safely anticipate will continue into the 21st century. From what underlying assumptions and values will this information be evaluated as it is transformed into sanctioned "knowledge?" It is striking that while leading thinkers in the philosophy of science and in the physical sciences are moving away from the confines of logical positivism (Prigogine & Stengers, 1984), psychiatry seems at this moment to be in a headlong trajectory toward it. In order to address the most important questions in mental health in the next century, leadership should not be oblivious to the often subtle currents of politics, economics, and sociocultural forces that skew our judgments about health and disease in ourselves and our patients. However, since no leader is immune from self-serving distortions and the pull of the basic assumptions, I struggle to stay open to painful questions often posed to me in my role at P St. Is my struggle with institutional authority pursuit of the treatment task, countertransference, my problem with authority, or arrogance?

If our whole world can be viewed as a hospital, as T. S. Eliot suggests, how are we using those individuals we call patients? What is hiding in the "scientific" evidence and treatment practices that may obscure our collective illness? In the 19th century, canaries reactive to changes in air quality were used by coal miners to offer an early warning sign of a toxic atmosphere. When vulnerable individuals become "mentally ill," to merely "treat" their disorder without regard to what it may signify, puts us all at risk of suppressing symptoms and missing the deeper shared disorder.

## REFERENCES

Andreasen, N. (1984). *The broken brain*. New York: Harper & Row.

Barham, P. (1984). *Schizophrenia and human value*. New York: Basil Blackwell.

Bernauer, J. (1987). Oedipus, Freud, Foucault: Fragments of an archaeology of psychoanalysis. In D. M. Levin (Ed.), *Pathologies of the modern self* (pp. 350–384). New York: New York University Press.

Bertalanffy, I. von (1968). *General systems theory*. New York: George Braziller.

Bion, W. R. (1961). *Experiences in groups*. New York: Basic.

Bion, W. R. (1970). *Attention and interpretation*. London: Tavistock.

Bion, W. R. (1977). *Seven servants*. Northvale, NJ: Jason Aronson.

Bowen, M. (1978). *Family therapy in clinical practice*. Northvale, NJ: Jason Aronson.

Breggin, P. (1991). *Toxic psychiatry*. New York: St. Martin's.

Breisach, E. (1962). *Introduction to modern existentialism*. New York: Grove.

Bridger, H. (1985). Northfield revisited. In M. Pines (Ed.), *Bion and group psychotherapy* (pp. 87–107). Boston: Routledge & Kegan Paul.

Eliot, T. S. (1943). *Four quartets.* New York: Harcourt, Brace, Jovanovich.

Freud, S. (1955). Group psychology and the analysis of the ego. In J. Strachey (Ed. and Trans.), *The standard edition of the complete psychological works of Sigmund Freud* (Vol. 18, pp. 65–143). London: Hogarth Press. (Original work published 1921).

Foucault, M. (1965). *Madness and civilization.* New York: Pantheon.

Goffman, E. (1961). *Asylums.* Garden City, NY: Anchor.

Heidegger, M. (1962). *Being and time.* New York: Harper & Row.

Hinshelwood, R. (1987). *What happens in groups.* London: Free Association.

Hollingshead, A., & Redlich, F. (1958). *Social class and mental illness.* New York: Wiley.

Jaques, E. (1955). Social systems as a defense against persecutory and depressive anxiety. In M. Klein, P. Heimann, & R. E. Money-Kyrle (Eds.), *New directions in psychoanalysis* (pp. 478–498). London: Tavistock.

Jones, M. (1953). *The therapeutic community.* New York: Basic.

Klein, E., & Gould, L. (1973). Boundary issues and organizational dynamics: A case study. *Social Psychiatry, 8,* 204–211.

Klein, M. (1959). Our adult world and its roots in infancy. *Human Relations, 12,* 29–303.

Kuhn, T. (1962). *The structure of scientific revolutions.* Chicago: University of Chicago Press.

Leighton, D. C., Harding, J. S., Machlin, D. B., Macmillan, A. M., & Leighton, A. H. (1963). *The character of danger—Psychiatric symptoms in selected communities.* New York: Basic.

Levin, D. M. (1987). Clinical stories: A modern self in the fury of being. In D. M. Levin (Ed.), *Pathologies of the modern self* (pp. 479–537). New York: New York University Press.

Machiavelli, N. (1952). *The prince.* London: William Benton.

Magill, F. (1990). *Masterpieces of world philosophy.* New York: HarperCollins.

Main, T. F. (1975). Some psychodynamics of large groups. In L. Kreeger (Ed.), *The large group: Dynamics and therapy* (pp. 57–86). London: Constable.

Melville, H. (1952). *Selected writings of Herman Melville: Complete short stories, Typee, and Billy Budd.* New York: Modern Library.

Menzies, I. E. P. (1960). A case-study in the functioning of social systems as a defense against anxiety. *Human Relations 13,* 95–121.

Miller, E. J., & Rice, A. K. (1967). *Systems of organization: Task and sentient systems and their boundary control.* London: Tavistock.

Nietzsche, F. (1956). *The will to power.* New York: Doubleday.

Percy, W. (1987). *The thanatos syndrome.* New York: Ballantine.

Prigogine, I., & Stengers, I. (1984). *Order out of chaos.* New York: Bantam.

Said, E. (1993). *Culture and imperialism.* New York: A. Knopf.

Saul, J. (1992). *Voltaire's bastards: The dictatorship of reason in the West.* New York: Free Press.

Singer, D. L., Astrachan, B. M., Gould, L. J., & Klein, E. B. (1979). Boundary management in psychological work with groups. In W. G. Lawrence (Ed.), *Exploring individual and organizational boundaries.* New York: Wiley.

Stanton, A., Stanton, M., & Schwartz, M. (1954). *The mental hospital.* New York: Basic.

Strauss, J. S., & Carpenter, W. T. (1981). *Schizophrenia.* New York: Plenum.

Winnicott, D. W. (1965). *The maturational processes and the facilitating environment.* New York: International Universities Press.

Winnicott, D. W. (1969). The use of an object and relating through identifications. *International Journal of Psycho-Analysis, 50,* 711–716.

# Part II

**Transformational Leaders:
Vulnerability, Diversity,
and Connection**

# 8

# When Women Lead

## The Visibility–Vulnerability Spiral

*Kathy E. Kram, Ph.D.*
*and Marion McCollom Hampton, Ph.D.*

"New Kinds of Leadership Required" say the headlines in management journals and the business press. Practitioners and scholars alike are recognizing that organizations struggling to survive in an increasingly complex and changing environment need leadership that is transformational, collaborative, and relationship-oriented (Bennis & Nanus, 1986; Hammer & Champy, 1993; Handy, 1990). Writers agree that if organizations are to become more adaptive and responsive to tumultuous and competitive environments, they will have to become flatter and more flexible

*Acknowledgments.* We would like to thank the following individuals for their very helpful comments on earlier drafts of this paper: Clay Alderfer, Jean Bartunek, Marcy Crary, Joyce Fletcher, Tim Hall, James Hunt, Mark Leach, Gerry Leader, David McClelland, Vicky Parker, Peter Yeager, and Mary Young.

193

and to rely more on teams as critical integrating structures. The consensus is, organizations need leaders who offer a new vision of the effective organization and who can model the skills and attitudes necessary to enact that vision.

It is easy to notice that the leadership traits that are extolled in this contemporary discourse generally match those that have been described as the characteristically "female" approach to management, an approach that is theorized to spring from sex-role socialization and contemporary sex-role expectations (Baker Miller, 1991; Gilligan, 1982; Hegelson, 1990; Huff, 1990). The capacity to care for others, listen, empathize, and search for collaborative solutions regularly surface in studies of women managers as the qualities that enable women to be effective in organizational roles (Belenky, Clincy, Goldberger, & Tarule, 1986; Marshall, 1984; Rosener, 1990). Indeed, it has been noted frequently that the operative approach women typically adopt in relation to their work is distinct from the agency approach typically found among traditional male leaders—and this is now considered good news for organizations and for women (Bakan, 1966; Marshall, 1984; Urch Druskat, 1993). The time appears right for women to succeed as leaders in formal organizational roles.

Why, then, is it still so difficult for women to move into and succeed in leadership roles in organizations? The need for new forms of leadership has been consistently espoused, yet women continue to encounter obstacles as they ascend organizations. The purpose of this chapter is to lift up for examination the unique challenges posed to women leaders by the combined and interacting effect of (1) the heightened visibility women experience in leadership roles, and (2) a perceived and actual vulnerability they accept when they occupy these roles. While it is true that the differentiation, and resulting visibility, that attaches to all leaders makes them vulnerable to criticism and attack (Slater, 1966), we offer here a theoretically based argument for how these conditions may be exacerbated for women.

We begin by drawing on theory to propose an explanation for the mostly invisible processes that pose a critical challenge to women in leadership roles. Using object relations theories from the psychodynamic literature (Wells, 1995), we explore the kinds of projective processes that are stirred when women are placed in formal organizational leadership roles. These dynamics almost guarantee (and research has shown) that women leaders will be experienced as violating traditional role expectations, either of leaders or of women or both. These dynamics result in role overload, role confusion, threats to the leader's self-esteem, and strained relationships, all of which can undermine effectiveness in a leadership role.

To illustrate these dynamics, we have drawn on our own experiences in assuming leadership roles in an academic setting. Not only have we personally experienced the substantial challenges that come with heightened visibility in this setting, but it is also true that in academia—as in many contemporary organizations—women have difficulty surviving the climb from junior to senior levels. Women are underrepresented among tenured faculty, and the culture is dominated by traditionally male values. Not surprisingly, many of the personal accounts that we hear from female clients in the corporate world closely parallel our own experience and that of our female graduate students and faculty colleagues.

The opportunity to reflect on our own experiences in leadership roles is particularly timely for both of us. As women who have reached midlife, we find ourselves moved to reexamine our major life choices and to assess their consequences. And, unlike earlier periods of adulthood, this stage allows the emotional dimension of our experiences at work—including anxiety, vulnerability, ambivalence, and anger—to be accessible for exploration. Rather than only denying and splitting off unpleasant feelings, we are more able to study and gain insight into their origin and impact. Indeed, the work of this chapter facilitates a critical developmental task of midlife—that of reassessment—that could not have been done earlier (Levinson, Darrow, Klein, Levinson, & McKee 1978).

Our analysis suggests that women must find ways to leverage the experience of vulnerability that comes with our heightened visibility, by seizing the opportunity to learn about self and to diagnose organizational dynamics while keeping our integrity and self-esteem intact. We will illustrate how women (and men as well) may treat the experience of vulnerability, and how some responses to vulnerability can undermine effectiveness. Finally, we pose a scenario in which vulnerability can actually enhance leadership capacity and turn threats to leadership into growth, learning, and greater efficacy in the role.

## THE DYNAMICS OF VISIBILITY AND VULNERABILITY: A THEORETICAL MODEL

While both men and women assume risk when they take on leadership roles in organizations, a wide range of organizational forces—including minority–majority group dynamics, sex-role stereotypes, ethnocentric intergroup relations, and unconscious fantasies about organizational leaders—combine to heighten the risk for women leaders by compounding the inevitable threats to their effectiveness as leaders (Cox, 1993; Kanter, 1977; Morrison, White, & Van Velsor, 1987). Here we propose an explanation for these complex processes; the argument is based on Kleinian object relations theory, which we summarize below.

### The Theory Base: Object Relations

Object relations theory is a psychodynamic theory of early childhood emotional development expounded most prominently by Melanie Klein (Segal, 1992; Wells, 1995). Essentially, Klein proposed that humans at a very early age utilize two psychological mechanisms to cope with unpleasant emotions: splitting and projection. In order to "preserve" the experience of a caring, attentive mother in the (inevitable) situations in which the mother is not fulfilling all the infant's needs (to eat or to feel dry, for example), the infant mentally creates two mothers: a bad one, at who to be rageful, and a good mother, to be the all-caring protector and comfortor that the infant needs. This psychological mechanism is called splitting, "an action undertaken in fantasy that can be used to separate things that belong together" (Segal, 1992,

p. 36). This mechanism allows the infant and, later, the adult in stressful situations, to cope with anxiety by separating the "self" from painful feelings.

Projection, or projective identification, the second mechanism, is closely related. Klein proposed that infants learn to distance themselves from destructive feelings by disowning them and actively "placing" those feelings in someone else.

> Projection can be thought of as *perceiving* someone else as having one's own characteristics: projective identification involves a more active *getting rid of* something belonging to the self into someone else. . . . Projective identification involves a very deep split, where the aspects of the self projected into others are very deeply denied in the self. (Segal, 1992, p. 36)

There is extensive precedent in the organizations literature for application of Kleinian theory to groups and organizations. At the group level, researchers have used splitting and projection frameworks to explain group dynamics in which group members collectively deny difficult emotions and project them onto one vulnerable group member ("scapegoating"—Wells, 1995) or onto a "rival" group (ethnocentrism—Alderfer, 1986). In addition, a school of organizational analysts relies on these theories to analyze irrationalities in systemwide organizational processes (Hirschhorn & Young, 1991; Kets de Vries, 1991; Krantz, 1995).

In this paper, we propose that fantasies (unconscious wishes and fears) and projections about leadership combine with fantasies and projections about women to produce a spiraling effect in the anxiety-laden organizational environment. The spiral, which we will describe in more detail, is roughly as follows: the more visible a woman becomes as a leader, the more she is subject to scrutiny and criticism. This enhances her vulnerability to the collective dynamics of splitting and projective identification. Once these dynamics have been set in motion, her behavior and person become even more visible as people, with a variety of motives, find it necessary to keep close tabs on her. The challenges that come with this scrutiny can either undermine her success or, if overcome, allow her to climb higher in the organization, where she is even more in the minority and, therefore, more visible and vulnerable to the next round of the spiral.

## Visibility

The minority status of women in organizations, and particularly in leadership positions, creates the first step in what we have called the visibility–vulnerability spiral. In many areas of management, women are still a novelty, particularly at senior levels in organizations. We know primarily from Kanter's (1977) work, that skewed numbers among organizational groups of any type produce subtle yet potent dynamics that undermine the group that is represented at the "token" or "minority" level. With minority status comes a documented set of experiences, including heightened visibility, intense scrutiny of performance, and pressure to assimilate into the majority culture (Kanter, 1977).

Kanter developed a simple but eloquent "case" using X's and O's to illustrate her point about minority–majority dynamics. Looking at an O in a group of X's tells the story: the O becomes the object of attention because it is different; the O's performance is closely scrutinized because the X's have never worked with an O before; the O feels isolated but finds it futile to try to fit in with the X's; the O feels its performance reflects on the capabilities of other O's and theirs on it. Research supports this story; the simple fact of being demographically "different" from the majority of others is correlated with a variety of negative outcomes, including low social integration in the work unit and greater turnover (Tsui, Egan, & O'Reilly, 1992).

In this chapter, we focus our analysis in particular on the dynamic impact of one of these experiences—visibility—as it seems to drive many of the other processes Kanter identifies. And organizational literature confirms that women leaders regularly experience heightened visibility, especially at senior positions, where their numbers are fewer (Morrison et al., 1987; Owen & Todor, 1993).

The experience of visibility by itself is not necessarily negative. All leaders depend on it for recognition and influence. Visibility ensures that a leader's performance gets noticed; if the role
is performed well, this recognition can propel an individual into
positions of greater status and authority. We argue, however, that
women leaders are likely to experience visibility more negatively
than their male counterparts, in part because they face a far more
complex array of conscious and unconscious expectations for
their behavior.

For example, while male leaders are expected to be strong,
aggressive, and competitive, women who display similar characteristics are criticized for being "too aggressive" and "too masculine" (Morrison et al., 1987; O'Leary & Ickovics, 1992; Powell,
1993). At the same time, women in masculine environments who
bring more "feminine" qualities to their leadership roles—a caring, nurturing, collaborative style—may be labeled as "wishy-
washy" and not fit for the leadership task (Harragan, 1977; Lindsay & Pasquali, 1993).

To understand these competing role expectations, we need
to look more carefully at the projections carried, first by women,
and then by organizational leaders. This helps us understand the
confusion when women take organizational leadership roles.

## Vulnerability

It is necessary to restate an obvious but unpalatable fact of contemporary society in order to make this argument: women are
still perceived to be the weaker sex. While this "fact" is true
along some dimensions (women are physically weaker and more
frequently victims of violence), it has recently been understood as
a stereotype, a cultural perception reinforced by, and reinforcing,
historical social structures and norms (for example, about appropriate sex role behavior) (Bayes & Newton, 1985). Much of the
change in thinking about gender roles since the 1970s has been
a broader recognition that women are not as weak as the culture
has painted them: women are now seen as capable of taking care
of themselves financially, for example, and able to represent

others' interests in professional roles. However, despite these changes, women are still likely to be perceived as vulnerable, perhaps easily victimized and therefore in need of protection.

As vulnerability is an unpleasant emotion, under stressful conditions, individuals will tend to split their own feelings of vulnerability off and project them onto others; this allows us to feel that others, rather than ourselves, are vulnerable. Sex-role socialization prepares women to experience and handle this difficult emotion (Jordan, Kaplan, Baker Miller, Stiver, & Surrey, 1991). Indeed, women are generally quite familiar with the experience of vulnerability; typically, they can describe the discomfort and have learned how to manage it (usually via relationships with others).

In contrast, men are far more likely to disown a sense of vulnerability. Object relations theory suggests that these gender-distinctive orientations toward vulnerability will produce a collusive dynamic in intergroup settings, in which men project their vulnerability and women all too easily absorb it. Smith and his colleagues have described this dynamic in detail (Smith, Simmons, & Thames, 1989).

Work organizations provide exactly the kind of setting in which feelings of vulnerability are likely to provoke a splitting and projective process. Contemporary work organizations derive historically from military organizations and retain aspects of the military culture (for example, in the ideas of hierarchy, chain of command, and discipline in carrying out orders). Vestiges of this history are evident in metaphors and imagery in use by managers when organizations face major changes (Hirsch & Andrews, 1983). This suggests that organizational conflict, whether it is among groups inside the organization or across the organizational boundary, is experienced as competition ranging in intensity from sports competition to warfare. From this perspective, the prospect of defeat is the equivalent of humiliation (at best) or extermination (at worst).

Research confirms that organization members hold powerful unconscious expectations of the leaders to defend their groups, to carry the flag for their group, and to win on these conscious and unconscious battlefields (Smith & Berg, 1987). To the extent that leaders lose the various struggles they undertake (for re-sources, market share, reputation) they are likely to be criticized, scapegoated, and/or unseated. When organizational or group survival is at stake, the intensity of the attack rises with the level of anxiety experienced by group members (Hirschhorn & Young, 1991).

What happens then when women take on leadership roles in organizational settings? In overly simplified terms, unconscious stereotypes about women collide with unconscious expectations of the leader role (Bayes & Newton, 1985; Eagly, Karan, & Makhi-jani, 1995). The appointment of a female leader, by this logic, must inevitably raise the anxiety of group members: if she is a woman, she is vulnerable; if she is vulnerable, then the survival of our group is in jeopardy.

What is particularly complex about the dynamics of vulnera-bility for women leaders is that it is both real and projected. On the one hand, all leaders take a real risk (to career, to reputation) by virtue of the role they occupy. On the other hand, women leaders are far more likely than their male peers to be the target of projected vulnerability, given the social roles they carry and the splitting and projection process, which requires that the object of the projections is to be seen as either all powerful or completely vulnerable. This means, we argue, that the real vulnerability of women leaders in role is greater than the vulnerability experi-enced by most men in those same roles, due to what we call the visibility–vulnerability spiral.

## The Spiral: Real Vulnerability

The spiral starts, as we have said, because women are in the minor-ity, and therefore visible. Assuming unconsciously that she is vul-nerable, and perhaps projecting their own vulnerability onto her, followers will watch their female leader closely to make sure she can withstand attack from other groups (which probably have male leaders). Peers will scrutinize her to see how strong an oppo-nent she will be, if things heat up. Even well-meaning superiors will watch her closely if they feel guilty about putting her in jeopardy by giving her a leadership role.

This intense scrutiny—some of it well-intentioned—creates what we are calling real vulnerability, or risk of failure in role, for the female leader for several reasons. Under such intense scrutiny, small errors—that male leaders might be able to cover or repair—will be noticed sooner, examined more closely, and criticized more often (Aker, 1983). In addition, Kleinian theory would predict that men are more likely to notice errors or question the judgment of women than of other men, because splitting dynamics tend to lead people to locate fault in the "other" group rather than in their own. Finally, and paradoxically, behaviors that are not sex-role appropriate (i.e., too aggressive or competitive) will be noticed immediately and criticized. Such gender-specific expectations are likely to result in negative attributions of women leaders, particularly in highly prescriptive organizational cultures in which appropriate sex-role behavior is clearly—and narrowly—delineated (Cox, 1993). This combination of dynamics means that, in general, a woman's performance in a role is more likely to be negatively evaluated than a man's, especially in male-dominated organizations where the evaluators are likely to be male (Eagly, Makhijani, & Klonsky, 1992).

Under these circumstances, women leaders may experience substantial risk in acting on personal authority in their role, narrowing their repertoire of leadership styles, and thus limiting their effectiveness. Ultimately, such close scrutiny is likely to undermine self-confidence, a critical psychological state for any leader undertaking a new challenge. And, because women characteristically derive their sense of identity and self-esteem from relationships with others (Baker Miller, 1976; Jordan et al., 1991), criticism increases their internal experience of real vulnerability as well (Eagly et al., 1995).

These real sources of vulnerability combine with projected vulnerability—particularly from those who are anxious about their female leader—to produce a spiraling dynamic. As a leader's vulnerability (real and projected) increases, people watch them even more carefully.

## The Visibility–Vulnerability Spiral in Action

As we have said, the dynamics of visibility and vulnerability are pervasive in settings where women are underrepresented in leadership roles and there is a need felt to tap female talent. Whether the motivation is to put a good face on a gender imbalance in managerial ranks or to provide genuine opportunities for women professionals to demonstrate their competence, the spiral is set into motion as women are disproportionately asked to "represent" their gender by taking on a variety of visible, formal roles as well as relatively invisible, informal roles (Baker Miller, 1976; Fletcher, 1996).

Ironically, these opportunities to take on new roles are just what women and people of color have been seeking. Yet unless the visibility–vulnerability spiral is understood and effectively managed, individual self-esteem, well-being, and performance will suffer. In particular, the opportunity for women to flourish in a leadership capacity is often undermined by substantial role overload, close scrutiny of leadership style, and increasingly strained relationships, all the products of the visibility–vulnerability spiral. We draw on our own experiences as women in academic settings to illustrate each of these typical dilemmas.

## Role Overload

The range of roles that we have been invited, selected, and/or subtly pressured to assume have created opportunities for leadership *and* made us highly visible. In reflecting on our personal experiences we discovered that both of us are "on display" regularly—in program catalogs, in orientation sessions for new students and alumni, in facilitating and presenting at critical events such as faculty retreats. While some of these require little effort, others require considerable involvement. All of them combined make us highly visible.

Additionally, in a setting such as ours, where women are underrepresented in senior ranks, we are regularly asked to take on a variety of formal roles: to chair particular committees, to join a committee in order to create more diversity in membership, and/or to take on substantial administrative roles (e.g., Marion to be MBA faculty director and Kathy to be department chair). These leadership opportunities have allowed us to create vision, to mobilize resources, and to have an impact within the school. What we also notice is that we seem to have been chosen for these roles at a relatively junior stage, before our informal status in the system allowed us the leverage required to feel fully authorized in the roles. While such appointments are offered to junior men as well, these opportunities increase our vulnerability more substantially, since individuals in the system can attribute the appointments to diversity pressures rather than to our competence.

Less obvious, but equally potent in their effects, are the informal roles we are tacitly expected to fulfill. We find ourselves, like other "scarce" professional women, fully immersed in mentoring, counseling, and nurturing faculty colleagues and students (Sekaran & Kassner, 1992). Examples of such relational practice (Fletcher, 1996) abound: an undergraduate student invites us to coffee to talk about his relationship with his father; a faculty member calls us to talk at length about his personal development plan; or, individual faculty members stop by to process difficult meetings with us, seeking advice and comfort.

While we view this work as important, it drains us of personal and professional time and energy. And, as Ann Huff (1990) describes, we are all too willing to collude with others who expect us to always be available to fulfill these critical emotional needs. Indeed, we tend to want to meet others' needs, and we have the relationship skills to do so (Fletcher, 1996).

The visibility–vulnerability spiral is set into motion when we assert our boundaries and become temporarily unavailable for counsel (i.e., close the office door, screen telephone calls, or say no to a lunch invitation). While necessary for professional survival, these actions paradoxically invoke disappointment, criticism, and/or anger as we violate unconscious, ingrained gender expectations (Gutek & Cohen, 1987). Department colleagues, for example, at first could not understand Kathy's decision not to attend a department retreat during her sabbatical year.

Similarly, we find ourselves taking up other psychodynamic roles in groups, roles that give voice to otherwise highly sensitive matters. Marion, for example, the only junior faculty member in an otherwise male group of faculty meeting with the dean, assumes the role of explaining to the dean why the group has acted contrary to his wishes; senior, tenured men are silent. A group-level analysis helps to understand this process: women are unknowingly selected to surface conflict because we are the low-power players in the group, and also because we are comfortable with difficult emotions so it feels "safer" for us to express them (Baker Miller, 1976; Smith et al., 1989). Too often, rather than resist the unspoken expectation, we readily collude with it. This dynamic—men splitting off difficult emotions and women absorbing and expressing them—sets the visibility–vulnerability spiral in motion. Ironically, while women serve a critical function for the group, we may also be criticized for being too emotional, too sensitive, or not team players. We should also note that women are full participants in the process that gives them these roles.

## Close Scrutiny of Leadership Style

In listening to other women reflect on their experiences, we have noted that many of us feel closely scrutinized during most of our efforts to lead. The visibility–vulnerability spiral starts working when we sense the scrutiny and internalize the discomfort and criticism as a reflection on our competence. The opportunities for this dynamic abound in the department chair role, where there is little formal authority but wide-ranging expectations about what is to be accomplished, particularly during periods of organizational transition. What is noteworthy about Kathy's experience in this role is that considerable discomfort seemed to surface regardless of the style she chose. An entry from her personal journal illustrates this clearly: "When I chose a participative style to complete the business plan for the department, some thought I should take charge more. When I acted more decisively regarding several resource allocation issues I was viewed as too autocratic."

When one is new to a role, it is all too easy to internalize criticism as data that one is not competent. Yet discussions with male department chairs at other universities, combined with written accounts of other women's experiences in university administration (Sekaran & Kassner, 1992), suggest that male department chairs receive less criticism of lesser intensity in response to the same styles of influence and decision making. While all leaders are likely to be criticized as they attempt to influence others (regardless of their styles), the nature of these reactions are shaped and fueled by unconsciously held gender expectations (Morrison et al., 1987; Owen & Todor, 1993). That is, the same behavior (e.g., an autocratic style) coming from a female leader will be more highly criticized. This, combined with women's tendency to "take in" the criticism, heighten our experience of vulnerability.

In preparing to write this chapter, we recalled a significant dialogue in a meeting with doctoral students several years ago. A high level of trust and openness in our community at the time allowed expression of the shared view that Kathy was "the more nurturing one" and Marion was "tougher and more distant." We were the only two women faculty in the department at the time, portrayed as two extremes. In reality, Kathy had tough standards, and Marion had a caring and supportive side, but students could not comfortably hold more complex and rounded views of each of us. Interestingly, the male faculty's styles did not draw comment.

It appears that whatever style is enacted, we are either not feminine enough (not sufficiently nurturant when wielding authority) or not masculine enough ("wishy-washy" or "touchy-feely" when using a participative style). It is possible that our own tendency to be open, to sense others' reactions, and to encourage others to talk about their experience make discomfort with our styles discussible, while discomfort with our male colleagues remains unspoken. However, the actual discomfort with women's leadership styles, combined with a greater willingness to make them public, ultimately heighten our visibility and vulnerability.

## Strained Relationships

It appears to us that as we have assumed leadership roles, historically supportive relationships have become strained. Mentors, peers, and junior colleagues have had a variety of reactions to our attempts to lead, many of which are discomforting. These strains seem to affect not only us and those that we deal with regularly, but also relationships between men and women in the larger system.

For example, as we have moved into leadership positions, we have begun to outgrow the need for the kind of coaching and protection that our mentors provided earlier. Not only is change experienced as a loss (for both parties), but there is increasing discomfort as we necessarily enact styles and strategies that are different from those used by our male mentors. While all protégés experience this (Kram, 1988), our hunch is that women in minority leadership roles—and our male mentors—experience this separation more intensely.

There are several forces that may combine to make this a more intense and difficult transition than in male–male mentorships. Most importantly, it seems to us, is the extent to which the father–daughter alliance is familiar and satisfying to both parties. And, since women protégées are, in fact, increasingly vulnerable as they advance in their organizations, continued paternal concern about our welfare is not unwarranted. Second, while male protégés can find success in emulating their mentors' styles, this strategy doesn't work for us because of the sex-role expectations previously outlined. We have repeatedly discovered that if we try to use our position and authority as our male mentors do—for example, by declining a request to take on another committee assignment—we are viewed as harsh, arrogant, or aggressive.

From our perspective, we are profoundly disappointed at the realization that the alliance with senior males does not make our leadership style acceptable (we are still not X's). In the end, the transition to a more peerlike relationship is difficult, in part, because the visibility–vulnerability spiral undermines both parties' sense that the relationship has successfully prepared us for leadership. While all mentor relationships experience difficulty as they transition to more peerlike alliances, the texture of the transition is likely to be of a different quality when the mentor is male and protégée is female. Indeed, sons are expected to act increasingly independently and to succeed at doing so, while daughters are expected to need protection—and actually do—even as they become more independent, since the organizational world is less hospitable to them.

Other senior colleagues also seemed more comfortable with us when we were in the apprentice stage; we have both experienced strain in relationships with senior colleagues as we became more independent and outspoken. As long as we are asking questions and seeking advice and support, these relationships flourish. When we begin to offer differing views or to turn down offers of "help" (Marion turned down a junior role on a research team in order to focus on her own research), we sense discomfort. All junior faculty sense such discomfort as they embrace their own authority, but the increased autonomy and assertiveness of junior men may be greeted with less ambivalence than ours.

Similarly, our junior faculty colleagues and students seem to react with ambivalence to our increasing status and authority. While they may be pleased that competent women are ascending in the organization, they notice that, as we advance, our perspective changes to reflect our more senior status. We necessarily become less accessible as our responsibilities increase and the challenges mount. Junior women, in particular, seem to feel particularly disappointed and angry when we appear less nurturing and less available to them (Parker & Kram, 1993; Urch Druskat, 1993). They blame senior women rather than the system for violating their expectations and having such a difficult time staying on top of their responsibilities. This projection of inadequacy onto women leaders may allow junior women to believe that their own fate in the system will be different.

The more established and confident women become in leadership roles, the more our male peers seem to perceive us as a threat. For, as we feel more assured of our competence and begin to assert our vision and style, it is more difficult for them to project their vulnerability onto us and to assume a protector role much like our male mentors have done. For example, in a meeting of a faculty group designing an executive program curriculum, Marion, a newcomer to the group, expressed displeasure at the jargon the group was using. A senior male in the group, assuming that she was doubting her competence to deal with the material, "reassured" her that she would do very well in this program. Marion reacted angrily, clarifying that she was not asking for reassurance but rather expressing annoyance with the group and the leader for not managing the design process well. Dealing with women as equals requires men to own their vulnerability rather than project it, and to confront the possibility that we may have strengths that they envy.

These relationship strains enhance the vulnerability women feel, particularly since our development and self-concept is nurtured primarily through connection with others (Baker Miller, 1991; Gilligan, 1982). Paradoxically, the challenges posed by increasing visibility and vulnerability so consume our energy that we can lose touch with our female and male peers who might empathize and act as a sounding board.

Somehow we—and other women—have managed to transcend these relationship strains and experience at least some success in leadership roles. When women fail in leadership roles, however, the relationship strains are of a different sort. Our male colleagues may experience guilt for having "killed off" a vulnerable person, a guilt that can quickly become rationalized in the confirmation (for some) that women really cannot stand up to the demands of leadership. This rapidly affects the visibility, and vulnerability, of other women in the system, who may blame the men for failing to protect their female colleague but also feel angry at her because her failure makes our own lives more difficult. In either scenario, there is projection of blame—by the individual onto the system, or by the system onto the individual. Both real and projected vulnerability increase as well.

The discomforts described here absorb lots of energy, and generally go undiscussed. Perhaps we would feel less vulnerable if somehow these relationship strains were made discussible and all of us could learn through joint inquiry about the complexities

posed in heretofore satisfying relationships when we ascend organizations and begin to lead.

## RESPONSES THAT STRENGTHEN
## AND RESPONSES THAT DERAIL

The dynamics we have described here require women in leadership roles to attend to a number of challenges—including role
overload, close scrutiny, and strained relationships—that
threaten to undermine our self-esteem and personal effectiveness. Whether the subtle yet potent visibility–vulnerability spiral
actually derails our leadership potential is a function of how we
choose to respond. Our analysis suggests that there are three
basic responses to heightened visibility and vulnerability, each
with its own consequences (see Table 8.1).

### The Internalizing Response

Research suggests that women are socialized to respond to excessive scrutiny and criticism by devaluing, or splitting and denying,
the parts of themselves that produce discomfort for others (Baker
Miller, 1976, 1991; Jordan et al., 1991; Lindsay & Pasquali, 1993).
We intuitively respond by looking inward at what we may have
done to evoke such negative responses to our actions. This reflex-
ive response—based on a desire to meet others' needs and expectations—results in attempts to accommodate by altering our
fundamental style, by devaluing important aspects of our self-
identity, and ultimately by leaving the organization. This response, as we have experienced it, represents a substantial threat
to our self-esteem.

For example, when peers and junior colleagues have reacted
negatively to our assertion of boundaries (in order to prevent
burnout from role overload), both of us have questioned our
actions and wondered if we were too self-oriented. Or, when we

**TABLE 8.1**
**Responses to Heightened Visibility and Vulnerability**

|  | Internalizing | Externalizing | Integrating |
|---|---|---|---|
|  | Looking inward | Looking outward | Looking inward and outward |
| Basic Stance | Blaming the self | Blaming the system | Using interpretive skills for complex understanding |
|  | Accommodating | Confronting | Listening, empathizing, empowering self & others |
|  | Suppression of valued parts of self | Limited personal learning | Enhanced personal learning |
| Consequences for the Individual | Loss of self-esteem | Self-esteem maintained | Self-esteem enhanced |
|  | Pressure to conform | Personal beliefs and style are maintained | Adaptability |
|  | Risk of derailment | Risk of derailment | Better assessment of organizational dynamics |
|  | Loss of a valuable resource | Loss of a valuable resource | Better leadership |
| Consequences for the Organization | Diversity in leadership is discouraged | Adaptability in leadership is minimal | Organizational learning from a variety of leadership styles |

have raised sensitive and heretofore undiscussible issues and others have suggested we are overreacting, we question whether this may be true. And, when relationships become strained as we become leaders, we wonder if the costs of continuing to fill these roles are worth it.

This pattern of response is costly for both the individual and the organization. Internalizing criticism not only enhances vulnerability, but also discourages women from enacting their own individual styles. Self-doubt leads us to accommodate more, to follow a "safe" path, rather than asserting a different perspective. The organization thus loses a valuable leadership resource.

## The Externalizing Response

An alternative response to heightened visibility and criticism involves shifting blame outside the self to explain why one's actions seem unacceptable to others. This appears to be a more common response among men who, as a result of their socialization, have been taught to respond with a "thick skin" (Kimmel, 1987; Pleck, 1981). Frequently, this response is angry and narcissistic, motivated more by a fundamental desire to win or be right than by connection and collaboration (Baker Miller, 1991; Gilligan, 1982). The externalizing response is protective of self-esteem but also can enable leaders to stay with unpopular (and often correct) decisions.

Rather than look inward for explanations or blame, those with this response look for forces in the system that are responsible for criticism or attack. Thus, for example, resistance to one's ideas or style, criticism of one's lack of accessibility, or discomfort with one's bold actions will be interpreted as others' limitations rather than as a reflection on one's personal effectiveness (Sheppard, 1992).

This pattern of response—typified by externalizing blame and criticism—minimizes vulnerability, both real and projected. However, this response also limits the opportunity to learn about self, about one's impact on others, or about the system one is attempting to influence. Those who use the externalizing response generally do not invite more data from others through active listening, empathy, and sensitivity to others' affect. They are unlikely to better understand the assumptions, values, and/ or needs underlying negative responses to their actions.

While self-esteem is more likely to remain intact, this response does not enable one to expand one's own repertoire of influence on behaviors, or to learn how to address systemic resistance to acts of leadership. Ultimately, individuals who are unable to learn about self and about the organization too often fail to effectively adapt to challenging circumstances, and are then derailed (McCall, Lombardo, and Morrison, 1988). Not only do individuals fail to achieve personal goals, but the organization loses much needed leadership potential.

## The Integrating Response

Questioning one's actions, as in the internalizing response, is not necessarily self-undermining. Indeed, it is through such self-reflection and sensitivity to the impact of one's behavior that personal learning and growth can occur. In order to understand how women have been successful as leaders—despite the dilemmas outlined here—we have tried to describe a response, which we have observed occasionally in ourselves and in others, in which vulnerability actually becomes a source of strength. In this response, the experience of heightened visibility and vulnerability is leveraged for learning: about self, about others, and about the system one is attempting to lead. Those who enact this response have the capacity to sense and empathize with others' reactions, to empower others to voice their concerns, and to develop personal and organizational insight from others' criticism and attack. Rather than allowing vulnerability to derail self-esteem and competence, those who take an integrating approach turn this capacity to absorb others' reactions into a strength.

In practice, the integrating response assumes there is a third kind of vulnerability (we have discussed real and projected): proactive vulnerability, or openness, to others' reactions. Individuals examine reactions to leadership attempts for what might be learned about the impact of one's actions, others' needs and values, and systemic forces such as cultural imperatives and other sources of resistance that might be shaping them. Relationship strains and close scrutiny by others are viewed as opportunities to learn rather than (or, more realistically, in addition to) threats to self-esteem and effectiveness.

This response is similar to the internalizing response in that it heavily relies on the capacities to listen, empathize, and empower others to voice their concerns. Given gender socialization, women may be particularly well suited to incorporate this response. Indeed, research suggests that women tend to experience relationships as a source of learning more frequently than do their male counterparts (Van Velsor & Hughes, 1990).

However, the integrating response also requires the ability to stand back and utilize intuitive, diagnostic, and interpretive skills to develop multiple perspectives on the challenges posed by the visibility–vulnerability spiral. It is a more considered response in which, for example, internalized reactions to vulnerability, although present, do not interfere with developing complex understandings of how sex-role stereotypes—and our collusion in them—are serving to reinforce resistance to new forms of leadership. This measured response helps to label and make discussible the complex array of subtle dynamics that undermine women's efforts to lead.

This response has much in common with what others have described as essential to effective leadership in contemporary organizations. The ability to seize opportunities to learn about self—one's strengths and weaknesses—and then to effectively alter one's strategy is a competence that is shared by successful leaders (Bennis & Nanus, 1986). And, as Argyris (1982, 1985) clearly articulates, double loop learning—the capacity to modify basic assumptions and frameworks in response to feedback—is what enables individuals to effectively adapt to complex organizational environments.

The integrating response is characterized by greater complexity than both the internalizing and externalizing responses (Lindsay & Pasquali, 1993). Individuals who take this approach will not be satisfied with interpretations of events that take only internal or external forces into account. They will examine personal, group, and organizational forces that are shaping responses to their leadership actions. This balanced approach minimizes threats to self-esteem, preserves what is unique and potentially valuable about one's style, and enhances understanding of complex organizational dynamics that can only result in more effective action.

## CONCLUSIONS

The integrating response is essential if women (and men) are to understand and effectively manage the visibility–vulnerability spiral. Yet, it is not easily enacted. Far too often, we react to the anxiety and difficulty of our situation by internalizing or externalizing. Neither of these promotes much learning, and the internalizing response—most often observed in women—is likely to undermine self-esteem and, ultimately, derail us from leadership tracks.

Our analysis leads to the conviction that the capacity to be vulnerable in a proactive sense—that is, open to others' responses—is actually a critical leadership competence. Vulnerability is a strength when it enables personal and organizational learning. Only when men and women develop and effectively utilize this competence will a broader range of much needed leadership styles emerge in organizations.

The path to building this competence is likely to be different for men and women, given our distinctive socialization experiences, sex-role expectations in the workplace, minority-majority demographics, and intergroup dynamics of splitting and projection. For example, women who regularly experience vulnerability need to learn how to develop a more measured response in which alternative explanations for criticism of our actions are thoroughly considered. Similarly, men who are good at externalizing criticism and attack may need to learn how to experience vulnerability rather than projecting it and to be more inquiring about others' reactions.

Our view is that self-inquiry and joint inquiry with same- and opposite-gender colleagues are good starting points for this difficult and important work. For example, women in dialogue with each other about common experiences can challenge one another to consider alternative explanations that take external, systemic forces into account. And, in conversation with each other, men and women can expand their repertoires of responses by witnessing how others—who, because of their gender, encounter different expectations and experiences at work—handle the challenges posed by vulnerability and visibility.

Both men and women leaders will become more effective as they begin to view their vulnerability as a potential strength rather than only as a liability. By doing so, they will be more able to learn and develop new strategies in challenging situations. As more leaders engage in this personal work, the visibility–vulnerability spiral can be transformed, women leaders will be less often derailed, and organizations will finally benefit from (much needed) new styles of leadership.

# REFERENCES

Aker, S. (1983). Women, the other academics. *Women's Studies International Forum, 6*(2), 191–202.

Alderfer, C. (1986). An intergroup perspective on group dynamics. In J. Lorsch (Ed.), *Handbook of organizational behavior* (pp. 190–222). Englewood Cliffs, NJ: Prentice-Hall.

Argyris, C. (1982). *Reasoning, learning, and action: Individual and organizational.* San Francisco: Jossey-Bass.

Argyris, C. (1985). *Strategy, change, and defensive routines.* Boston: Pitman.

Bakan, D. (1966). *The duality of human experience.* Boston: Beacon.

Baker Miller, J. (1976). *Towards a new psychology of women.* Boston: Beacon.

Baker Miller, J. (1991). The development of women's sense of self. In J. V. Jordan, A. G. Kaplan, J. Baker Miller, I. P. Stiver, & J. L. Surray (Eds.), *Women's growth in connection* (pp. 11–26). New York: Guilford.

Bayes, M., & Newton, P. (1985). Women in authority: A sociopsychological analysis. In A. Colman & M. Geller (Eds.), *Group relations reader* (Vol. 2, pp. 309–322). Jupiter, FL: A. K. Rice Institute.

Belenky, M., Clinchy, B., Goldberger, N., & Tarule, J. (1986). *Women's Ways of Knowing.* New York: Basic.

Bennis, W., & Nanus, B. (1986). *Leaders.* New York: Harper & Row.

Cox, T., Jr. (1993). *Cultural diversity in organizations.* San Francisco: Berrett-Koehler.

Eagly, A., Karan, S., & Makhijani, M. (1995). Gender and the effectiveness of leaders: A meta-analysis. *Psychological Bulletin, 117*(1), 125–145.

Eagly, A., Makhijani, M., & Klonsky, B. (1992). Gender and the evaluation of leaders: A meta-analysis. *Psychological Bulletin, 111*(1), 3–22.

Fletcher, J. (1996). Relational theory in the workplace. Work in Progress Series #77, Wellesley College Centers for Research on Women, Wellesley, MA.

Gilligan, C. (1982). *In a different voice: Psychological, theory and women's development.* Cambridge, MA: Harvard University Press.

Gutek, B., & Cohen, A. (1987). Sex roles, sex role spillover, and sex at work: A comparison of men's and women's experiences. *Human Relations, 40*(2), 97–115.

Hammer, M., & Champy, J. (1993). *Reengineering the corporation.* New York: HarperCollins.

Handy, C. (1990). *The age of unreason.* Boston: Harvard Business School Press.

Harragan, B. (1977). *Games mother never taught you.* New York: Warner.

Helgesen, S. (1990). *The female advantage: Women's ways of leadership.* New York: Doubleday Currency.

Hirsch, P., & Andrews, J. (1983). Ambushes, shootouts, and knights of the roundtable: The language of corporate takeovers. In L. Pondy (Ed.), *Organizational symbolism* (pp. 145–156). Greenwich, CT: JAI Press.

Hirschhorn, L., & Young, D. (1991). Dealing with the anxiety of working: Social defenses as coping strategy. In M. F. R. Kets de Vries, et al. (Eds.), *Organizations on the Couch* (pp. 215–240). San Francisco: Jossey-Bass.

Huff, A. (1990). *Wives of the organization.* Working paper presented at the Women and Work Conference, Arlington, TX.

Jordan, J., Kaplan, A., Baker Miller, J., Stiver, I., & Surrey, J. (1991). *Women's growth in connection.* New York: Guilford.

Kanter, R. (1977). *Men and women of the corporation.* New York: Basic.

Kets de Vries, M. (1991). *Organizations on the couch.* San Francisco: Jossey-Bass.

Kimmel, M. (Ed.). (1987). *Changing men: New directions in research on men and masculinity.* Newbury Park, CA: Sage.

Kram, K. (1988). *Mentoring at work: Developmental relationships in organizational life.* Lanham, MD: University Press of America.

Krantz, J. (1995). Group relations training in context. In J. Gillette & M. McCollom (Eds.), *Groups in context: A new tradition of group dynamics* (pp. 215–234). Lanham, MD: University Press of America.

Levinson, D., Darrow, C., Klein, E., Levinson, M. & Mckee, B. (1978). *Seasons of a man's life.* New York: Knopf.

Lindsay, C., & Pasquali, J. (1993). The wounded feminine: From organizational abuse to personal healing. *Business Horizons, 36*(2), 35–41.

Marshall, J. (1984). *Women managers: Travelers in a male world.* New York: Wiley.

McCall, M., Lombardo, M., & Morrison, A. (1988). *The lessons of experience.* Lexington, MA: Lexington Books.

Morrison, A., White, R., & Van Velsor, E. (1987). *Breaking the glass ceiling: Can women reach the top of America's largest corporations?* Reading, MA: Addison-Wesley.

Owen, C., & Todor, W. (1993). Attitudes toward women as managers: Still the same. *Business Horizons 36*(2), 12–26.

O'Leary, V., & Ickovics, J. (1992). Cracking the glass ceiling: Overcoming isolation and alienation. In U. Sekaran & F. Leong (Eds.), *Womenpower: Managing in times of demographic turbulence* (pp. 7–31). Newbury Park, CA: Sage.

Parker, V., & Kram, K. (1993). Women mentoring women: Creating conditions for connection. *Business Horizons, 36*(2), 42–51.

Pleck, J. (1981). *The myth of masculinity.* Cambridge, MA: MIT Press.

Powell, G. (1993). *Women and men in management* (2nd ed.). Newbury Park, CA: Sage.

Rosener, J. (1990, November-December). Ways women lead. *Harvard Business Review, 68*(6), 119–125.

Segal, J. (1992). *Melanie Klein.* Newbury Park, CA: Sage.

Sekaran, U., & Kassner, M. (1992). University systems for the 21st century: Proactive adaptation. In U. Sekaran & F. Leong (Eds.), *Womenpower: Managing in times of demographic turbulence* (pp. 163–191). Newbury Park, CA: Sage.

Sheppard, D. (1992). Women managers' perceptions of gender and organizational life. In A. Mills & P. Tancred (Eds.), *Gendering organizational analysis* (pp. 151–166). Newbury Park, CA: Sage.

Slater, P. (1966). *Microcosm: Structural, psychological and religious evolution in groups.* New York: Wiley.

Smith, K., & Berg, D. (1987). Intergroup influences: The paradoxes of scarcity, perception, and power. In D. Berg & K. Smith (Eds.), *The paradoxes of group life* (pp. 182–204). San Francisco: Jossey-Bass.

Smith, K., Simmons, V., & Thames, T. (1989). Fix the women: An intervention into an organizational conflict based on parallel process thinking. *Journal of Applied Behavioral Science, 25*(1), 11–29.

Tsui, A., Egan, T., & O'Reilly, C. (1992). Being different: Relational demography and organizational attachment. *Administrative Sciences Quarterly 37,* 549–579.

Urch Druskat, V. (1993). Gender and leadership style: Transformational and transactional leadership in the Roman Catholic church. *Leadership Quarterly, 5*(2), 99–119.

Van Velsor, E., & Hughes, M. (1990). *Gender differences in the development of managers: How women managers learn from experience.* Greensboro, NC: Center for Creative Leadership.

Wells, L. (1995). The Group-as-a-whole. In J. Gillette and M. McCollom (Eds.), *Groups in Context* (pp. 49–85). Lanham, MD: University Press of America.

# 9

---

# Discourse and
# Corporate Leadership

## Transformation by or of the Feminine?

*Susan Long, Ph.D.*

Women are increasingly moving into leadership roles in corporate life, perhaps bringing with them new ways of viewing and acting in those organizations. This chapter addresses whether and how these organizations will be transformed by this, or whether the predominant discourse and culture in the organization transforms the women.

It is difficult to enter the debate about gender in organizational life. A lot has been researched and written. Many may believe that it has been done to death, and it has now needed a point where gender has become one issue amongst others under the general rubric of "diversity." Indeed one writer recently called her paper "Sex and the MBA" rather than gender and the

MBA, admitting that she used the word *sex* primarily to get away from the perjorative and uninteresting term *gender,* even though it was on gender issues that she mainly focused; that is, the masculine stance of most MBA programs and female students' experiences of this (Sinclair, 1995). Notwithstanding the separate but linked and mostly unexplored issue of sexuality in organizational life, there is still much to be explored around gender. However much we have had our consciousness raised, there are still questions to which we have little answers. In terms of leadership, a central question is whether or not it is primarily the entrenched system of roles typical in our organizations, that is, the more or less hierarchical systematization of management (Chattopadhyay, 1995), the organization of power, status, and authority, and the symbolic management of meaning emergent from organization dynamics per se, that creates our organizational men and women (Kanter, 1977a). Or, might these themselves be just another symptom of a more generalized difference between the genders and their relatedness, played out in organizational life. In other words, is the culture emergent from a basis of patriarchy that could be changed? If the latter proves to be the case, then there may be reason to watch with interest the emergence of a critical mass of women in corporate leadership, because this will allow for the emergence of a more feminine discourse in a place where masculine discourse has predominated.

In order to discuss this issue, I will first present an outline of what is meant by discourse. This will be developed within a context of the psychoanalytic theory of Jaques Lacan (1977) and will follow Foucault's (1972) ideas of discourse and discursive practices. The discourses of gender will then be examined and related to the prominent discourse of modern organizations. A major argument to be presented is that men and women enter the social arena as subjects and agents of different gender discourses and cultures which has effects at individual and group levels. It has effects in the ways that men and women relate to one another, and how each works with different institutions-in-the-mind (Armstrong, 1995), and hence takes up and experiences different emotional positions within the organization. It also has political effects in terms of cultural dominance.

It will be suggested here that feminine discourse, historically submerged in corporate life, may increasingly become important as organizations require that leaders able to acknowledge their vulnerabilities as well as their strengths, to develop management upwards and sideways as well as downwards in hierarchies, to work more fully with consensual methods, and hence to more readily position themselves in alternative positions in the "corporate management discourse."

The arguments developed here, although guided and supported by theory, derive predominantly from my own experience in working with organizations as a consultant, in working in management education with managers from a diverse set of industries, and in working as a psychotherapist with people struggling with the problems of bringing together their complex family and work lives. They also derive from my experience as a woman having myself to bring together issues of sexual and gender identity as they influence and join with my work roles. For sure, the questions I pose and attempt to illuminate here have personal relevance to my own career progress through the organizations in which I work. The theoretical perspectives that I use have impressed themselves upon me (with a clarifying force that seems almost their own) as enabling the right questions to be asked. As well as being cognitively helpful by drawing pertinent conceptual distinctions, they aid my intuitive grasp of many of the experiences that I have had, and that others have described to me.

## THE IDEA OF DISCOURSE

A discourse is a set of symbolic relations. It is the ground from which new ideas, new perceptions, and hence new objects emerge. All speech and speaking together takes place within and between particular discourses. For example, over the past century the discourse of psychology has created objects such as "the mind" or "motives" and concepts such as "reinforcement of behavior." The discourse legitimates people who can speak it with some authority, such as psychologists and psychology professors, and it has its own rules for choosing how theories and methods of exploration should develop. Moreover, there opens up, through history, the possibility for individuals and groups to be "positioned" or to take up positions within discourse so that they might be subject or object for specific discourses and hence be in relation to one another (Henriques, Holloway, Urwin, Venn, & Walkerdine, 1990). Positioning may be multiple, changing, and contradictory, so that individuals, through personal histories, come to contain, as well as be contained by, multiple discourses.

According to Foucault (1972), discourse is broader than Kuhn's idea of paradigm (1962). A discourse has power to set the conditions of human relations because it implicitly and unconsciously sets down rules for defining terms in language, and behaviors in social contexts. It is not simply a natural language or a science or philosophical position, but a whole process of social legitimation for how a language is used, who uses it, where and when. It implements an interface between language and behavior. It becomes reproduced (Henriques et al., 1990) through those discursive practices that are, in a circular fashion, produced by the discourse. For example, the modern discourse of femininity produces the glossy pictures of slim models which reproduce the desire of women in relation to their bodies, even to the extent of starving themselves. This occurs not withstanding the additional explanations produced through medical or psychoanalytic discourses of anorexia.

Following Lacan (1977) human experience may be understood as being simultaneously registered in three different ways. First there is the field of the Symbolic, whereby experience is registered through those systems of signifiers founded in cultural law. Language is the quintessential symbolic system (hence Lacan's idea of the unconscious being structured like a language through processes similar to those of metaphor and metonomy). Language is not created by any one individual but is the result of cultural history interpenetrated with the capacity to symbolize. It is a system of signifiers, each defined and valued in terms of other signifiers and the system as a whole (note that a dictionary defines words and phrases in terms of other words and phrases; also the symbolic systems of mathematics and money have this closed self-referring quality). From such a finite system infinitely new numbers of signifying chains can emerge (cf. Chomsky's 1965 idea of how transformational grammar is able to create an infinite number of sentences and meanings from a finite lexicon). In this way meaning and human subjectivity arise. Both are constrained by significant cultural law (such as the incest taboo and Freud's discovery of the Oedipus complex) yet are modified by experience within those constraints. An individual's personal history, or that of a group (Long, 1991, 1992a) can be regarded as a signifying chain at the level of the Symbolic. Meaning is developed as each important event, thought, or feeling is linked (often unconsciously) to others.

The second register of experience is that of the Imaginary. In Lacan's scheme, the field of the Imaginary covers most of what is consciously apprehended (and hence most of what modern psychology deals with), as well as unconscious aspects of the ego, which include unconscious identifications, defense mechanisms, and so on. It is the field of the "effects" of the Symbolic organization of the psyche. This register includes most of what we normally understand by psychological experience: memory, perception, imagery, thoughts, phantasy. An example of the difference between the Symbolic and Imaginary registers is evoked by understanding the difference between the symbolic father and the imaginary father. Symbolic fathers are equivalent in any one culture because the relation between "father" and "son" or "daughter" is the same between different families. Each of these signifiers stands in relation to the other in a closed way, and it is the relation that counts. The imaginary "fathers," "sons," and "daughters" may, however, be widely disparate. Each may be experienced as good or bad, as proud or humble, and so on depending upon specific personalities and specific relationships. In the Imaginary, it is the personal history of the individual or group that counts. The Imaginary is seen as an effect of the personal signifying chain established from within the constraints of the symbolic, cultural system.

The third register of experience is the Real, which, although variously theorized by Lacan at different stages, contains that field where unsymbolized experience is registered. Like Bion's (1962) "beta elements" the experience registered is unsymbolized, and hence unable to be thought about within the normal constraints of a culture. Experience registered in the Real has a hallucinatory quality—raw, ineffable, and direct.

Although a theory and method of psychoanalysis in itself, the Lacanian scheme might also be regarded as a metatheory or philosophy. The three registers of experience formally identify Freud's work as being beyond psychology, and provide a framework for understanding the practice of psychoanalysis and the idea of discourse at personal, group, and cultural levels. Given this perspective, it could be said that a discourse is a *practice* that forms:

1. Its own objects at a symbolic level (rather than employing pre-existing objects), e.g., in the discourse of modern corporations "a manager" is created—although it is by no means certain that this discursive object is experienced or constructed in the same way by men and women or for people from different classes or ethnic backgrounds. That is, the object at the imaginary level of the experienced effects of underlying symbolic organization, may be diverse. (This is so even though the symbolic level remains fixed; for example, as indicated above, whether he is experienced as good, bad, or indifferent, a father is a father is a father);
2. Those positions from which its statements may be enunciated with authority, e.g., corporate leaders, management academics, and consultants;
3. Its own conceptual field of regularities and constraints; its own signifying chains, e.g., in Western corporate discourse, managers have authority over subordinates who are accountable to those managers, whereas in other cultures accountability might be to those holding political power (Long, 1995);
4. Its own theoretical domain and strategies for choice of theory and method, e.g., methods of management consultancy, organizational change or fiscal policy.

The discourse of modern corporations has worked to form new objects. These are the objects of, e.g., "managerial hierarchies" and of "shareholders." The discourse talks of "motivation," "remuneration," and "superannuation," "profits" and "losses;"

and legitimates management training, the authority of the C.E.O. and the rules of corporate takeovers. It may be enlightening to think of your manager as a product of corporate discourse, especially when he/she has just delegated (a discursive strategy) a mammoth task (a discursive objective) to you (a modern victim of corporate discourse!)

## GENDER DISCOURSE AND ITS RELATION TO CORPORATE DISCOURSE

At the level of the Imaginary, gender discourse differences have been widely explored (Gilligan, 1988; Maltz & Borker, 1982; Rosenthal & Jacobsen, 1968; Spender, 1992; Tannen, 1991). The overall consensus of opinion from such studies points toward the ways in which men and women communicate differently and are regarded as coming from different subcultures. For example, men are generally regarded as content focused, whilst women are more interested in process and relationships; women tend to use questions whilst men tend to make statements (Maltz & Borker, 1982; Tannen, 1991); male self-image is formed primarily through a growing capacity to develop autonomy, detachment, and objectivity, whilst female self-image is formed through a growing capacity to develop empathy, attachments, compromises, and self-transformation (Chodorow, 1978; Gilligan, 1988). Both genders tend to address boys and girls differently, focusing more on the boys who make their presence more noticeable (Rosenthal & Jacobsen, 1968; Spender, 1992). Many explanations of these results are framed in terms of social learning. But is this satisfactory?

Sayers (1986) questions the explanatory power of socialization theories alone, arguing that they do not account for the continued presence in women of both their subjugation and their resistance (and perhaps their ambivalence toward power). Following Freud (1961a) and Lacan (1977) the imaginary dynamics documented through gender research may be said to emerge from the differentiation of the sexes within the symbolic field where the feminine is unconsciously structured as castrated masculine and the sexual drive is considered as one drive with two forms—the active and the passive (Freud, 1961a; 1961b). Such symbolization renders the feminine as both *lacking* the symbol of sexual differentiation and power, the phallus, and hence having a more diffuse identity; and, *having* a subjective position where a portion of feminine desire is outside the social law, being not subject to the threat of castration (Mitchell & Rose, 1982; Sayers, 1986). This leaves the feminine swathed in mystery. Such symbolic structuration of the genders positions males and females differentially in sexual discourse and in its Imaginary effects. At least this is the case in patriarchy where social law is derived from the father and the "feminine" has only the choice of taking up a passive position in relation to male libido or to becoming masculinized through father identification (see, however, Irigaray [1974] for a critique of the Freudian position on femininity; and Sayers [1986] for her view that psychoanalysis can only go as far as reconciling the patient to reality, whilst social change is a step beyond to one of changing reality).

What then is the structure of corporate and management discourse, and how gender-tied is it? This question has driven research that results in conclusions such as the following from Bayes and Newton (1978). "We suggest that, because of the fantasy and fear of women's power, both men and women are socialized to accept a strongly held stereotype of women as possessing legitimate authority only to nurture" (p. 321). The power they refer to is derived from the mother of early infancy. Theoretical positions such as those put forward by Dinnerstein (1976) and Chodorow (1978) consider the question of socialization more deeply and link gender differences to the early object relations between infants and parents in ways that seem to support these conclusions. Although both sexes begin life in a close identification with their mother, the male gains his sexual and gender identity through differentiating from his mother, whilst the girl must continue her identification with mother, finding it difficult to individuate because of this. Bayes and Newton extrapolate this dynamic into corporate life, posing it as an explanation for the type of authority generally given to women.

An associated question to the above is, does Western corporate discourse create gendered managers? Or put differently, does such a discourse create only one gender for managers? The following example is perhaps typical of how many women discuss their experience in male dominated workplaces.

A female engineer who is a manager found herself in a totally male work culture. She says, "as the only woman there are advantages and disadvantages . . . everyone automatically assumes that you are intelligent as a female engineer . . . no one knew what to expect of you and so there weren't any rules, say about how you dressed and your style of doing things . . . there were times when I wondered if the lack of rules left me more vulnerable, people appeared to believe anything about me!" (Roberts, 1992). In this case, it felt as if the male discourse was the only one available and the woman had to find her way in with no rules and no space for any other kind of discourse. She was left feeling isolated and needing to meet the men on their own terms in order to gain acceptance. Yet their terms could not be hers and this alienated her as she was only perceived through the perspective of the dominant discourse.

Is this an example where the symbolic position is of a single gendered discourse with some who can, and some who cannot take up the position of subject or agent in the discourse? This would make corporate management discourse a subset of the gender discourse discussed above. It has been argued, for example, that the higher up the organizational hierarchy, the less important are gender differences and the more important are issues of politics and authority per se, so that it is difficult to separate gender from power (Kanter, 1977a). In fact, the issue of authority or legitimate power has been so enmeshed with gender that it is difficult for us to think of female leaders/authorities without either considering them as "masculinized" or "neuroticized" (Long, 1992b) or to believe that there is really a male in charge, de facto. The question remains as to whether or not the feminine subject is able to take up the (subject/agent) role of senior manager/corporate leader. It is argued here that in modern corporate discourse (meaning the discourse that shapes social relations in our large and powerful corporations) the language of power and authority is gendered, is male, and excludes the feminine in both females and males. That this is the case does not discount the presence of the feminine in the role of good mother-nurturer, nor in the role of seducer, medusa, witch, or other such archetypes. These are open to be taken up along with the male archetypes of idealized or evil leader-magicians. They enter corporate life, as they do any other institution, by the back door. But it is the discursive object of modern corporate leadership, the "tycoon," the "leader-warrior," the "corporate cowboy" or "corporate raider," the "visionary," the "self-made industrialist," or the "hard-nosed businessman"—all images of 20th century business life—that stand in contradistinction to the feminine. Neither does this mean that the discourse cannot be changed or that it is in some way essential. Nor that *women* cannot become subjects in or agents of the discourse. Clearly some do, and often at a great cost to their femininity; that is, the women are in many ways transformed.

An interesting question, then, lies around whether men and women have their own separate corporate discourses within organizations. Do they not only converse differently, have different linguistic subcultures, and different images of authority, but also create their own organizational objects in different ways? For example, does the term *manager* mean quite a different thing to a man and to a woman? In feminine discourse a manager may not be a distinctive individualized role but a function arising out of working relations between people, who may be called "managers," or "subordinates" (perhaps male terms in themselves). If this is so, then in our organizations feminine leadership within a feminine discourse may place us in a less defined, more vulnerable state. It may mean a leadership that does not direct others, but one that invites others to explore the emergence of something new through a working relationship that lets go of past definitions and certainties, like Gilligan's 4-year-old female subject who created the new game of "pirate next door" when faced with her own desire to play "next door neighbours" and her male companion's desire to play "pirates" (Gilligan, 1988). Kanter (1977a) examines the development of a management "class" that forms as an organizational defense against uncertainty. Through managerial orderliness, chaos might be averted! Although she sees this as primarily a class structure which engages men and women differentially, in the present analysis it may be seen as a defense emergent from male discourse. Females may have quite different organizational defenses.

Because it produces its own objects, its own concepts, its own strategies for development and usage and has its own authority, a discourse does provide for a social bond through its use and its products. This links all those who enter the discourse in defined social relations. If our organizations and institutions have historically developed from traditional patriarchal modes of organization, then this is the discourse that males are encouraged to enter as agents from their beginnings, with females being predominantly the recipients of the discourse—the *other* for the male. However, throughout their education and work lives, women, through the overt cultural practices of seeking equality, tend to take up the position of agent in this discourse also. They may have to work for their agency, as may men from minority groups; and they may have to do so with persistence and through showing great expertise. Yet the discourse is essentially masculine if not male. As women move into leadership must they be transformed to fit this masculine discourse?

Interestingly, the legislation of the early to mideighties to provide the possibility of equal opportunity and freedom from sexual harassment, which has enabled women to move more fully toward taking up agency or authority within this discourse, has simply provided an easier access for women to take up agency within the male discourse. It may be that a lot more has to be done in this direction, but it is also possible that the direction itself does not take women toward an understanding of what might be the feminine discourse, nor aid them in assuming agency in such a discourse at work.

The possibility is that our organizations themselves become transformed and that feminine discourse and leadership styles may find a place. This may be the sort of social change that feminist writers such as Sayers (1986) are looking for.

The next sections will first examine the ways in which male and female cultures interact in the workplace, shaping both the transformation of women leaders and their resistance to such transformation, and second will introduce Lacan's ideas on the four major discourses within our wider culture. From considering the transformations between discourses, a possible entry of the feminine into corporate discourse is discussed.

## THE DOMINANT AND SUBMERGED CULTURES

If, as suggested, corporate discourse is a subdiscourse of gender discourse, what currently occurs to the feminine in modern corporations?

This question may be understood in terms of relations between a dominant culture (in this case the male culture) and the culture that is submerged by this dominance. Such intercultural relations may range between friendly coexistence, as in multiculturalist societies, through hostile separateness, as in occupation, to a situation where the peoples of the submerged culture are abused and the culture deteriorates, as in colonization. Fanon (1961) describes the French colonization of Algeria and the consequent loss of identity and sometimes sanity of the Algerian people. The French came to regard the Algerians as intellectually, morally, and emotionally inferior, and Fanon demonstrates how the process of colonization brought about behaviors in the Algerians that on the surface seemed to support such judgments. One can only reflect on the way that women have also been judged in these ways throughout history. The psychodynamics of such relations reflect subjugation, identification with an impoverished image, and identification with the aggressor in relation to peers.

Even where the cultural relations are those of friendly coexistence, the dominant culture requests or demands that people of the submerged culture play a role within its cultural rules. In the dominant male culture women are to play a role—perhaps that of the"other half," or man's shadow; his anima or his fantasy. Women may play this role, or they may even strive to take the male's position in that culture and are hence perceived as masculinized. In this sense they are subject to the "conceptual trap" of patriarchy. Such a trap equates the universal with maleness.

On the other hand, the submerged culture is left to its own devices, mostly out of the consciousness of those of the dominant culture. In this case, there is the submerged female culture, played out in relative isolation, hidden and somewhat illegitimate.

At a gender relations experiential working conference held in Melbourne, Australia (August 1992) members attempted to understand gender issues at work in the context of an all female staff who were the authority figures. Exploring below the surface led to the formulation of several hypotheses about female leadership and its effects on both women and men. In this situation, when in single-gender member groups many of the men found themselves able to move away from their more competitive and aggressive posturing toward a more sharing interpersonal style. They did, however, tend to compete for the attention of the more powerful females (whether these were females with authority or females with other sources of power). Many of the women, by contrast, felt abandoned by the staff and less able to relate to one another in supportive ways. They were more able to be supportive toward the men in mixed groups, and some seemed to keenly miss the presence of males in authority. Without male authority figures, the women had to turn from their roles within the male culture and face the possibility of their own competitiveness and relatedness with each other and to deal with this. This was extremely difficult as they had few tools for so doing. It could be hypothesized that they themselves found it difficult to work with their own submerged culture. They were more accustomed to finding a role in the dominant culture.

On the whole the female authority was felt to be freeing, sometimes abandoning, on the surface at times weak, yet strongly present and hungered for. The images that emerged were at first of nuns (asexual or with sublimited sexuality and thus less threatening, yet powerful?), then of mothers (both good and bad) and finally figures of more primitive power, mystery, and seductiveness (e.g., the image of the Medusa was present in the final follow-up plenary, some six weeks after the conference proper). With such images around, it is not surprising that the type of leadership traditionally offered by males is invoked to "master" the situation. The father is felt to be missing, and in his absence there is

a threat of one being overwhelmed by forces not really understood. And we don't really understand the culture of women because it is submerged and regarded as not legitimate in the wider
scheme of things by both men and women.

## THE FOUR DISCOURSES

In 1969 Lacan introduced the idea of "four discourses" which
he believes are central to understanding relations between the
human subject, as described in his version of psychoanalytic theory, and the social order (Lacan, 1992). Now, we can say, following Lacan, that a discourse has an *agent* from whom it is
enunciated or spoken, and an *other* to whom it is addressed. Any
person or subject may take up the position of agent in the discourse, provided that they are legitimated by the discourse as
agent (Grigg, 1992; Rodriguez, 1992).

When discourse is engaged there is a *product,* and underlying
the discourse is a *truth.* The *truth* of the discourse is not always
self-evident, but it is basic to it and drives the agent in the discursive act. We could say the agent suffers the *truth* of the discourse
in which he or she engages. We may see the *truth* of the modern
corporate discourse, a version of a discourse which Lacan names
the "Discourse of the Master" as lying in the "split" or disharmonious nature of the human subject. Disharmonious because the
culture that we enter as children requires the subjugation of "natural" desire, to the Law. In becoming civilized, we become alienated from our nature and hence, divided. (In analytic theory this
is seen as the process of the Oedipus complex, occurring in the
face of the law derived from the incest taboo. This law centers
around the importance of the father and the phallic function, at
least in phallocentric, patriarchical cultures.)

Lacan regards the Discourse of the Master as the central
discourse of at least Western, if not of all cultures. He is influenced also by Hegel's view of the master/slave dialectic. The *agent*
of this discourse is the master who engages through interdicts and
commands. He addresses the slave *(other)* who does his will. The
*product* of the discourse is the labor of the slave and the pleasure

of the master. The surplus product is acquired by the master; his is a psychology of acquisitiveness, appropriation, and ownership. The discourse legitimates and empowers ownership, first of others and then of material goods. In fact the discourse creates a world filled with material objects: insurance companies that sell "products" rather than rendering services; workers who are remunerated according to "productivity" rather than because of their skills (as in the older artisan idea of the worker). But with the production comes the *loss* of the slave's freedom. This is an essential other for the master. The *truth* of the discourse is, ironically, that the master is driven by his own disharmony and his own lack of self-knowledge. As *agent* of this discourse he is split off from his own natural desire and comes to serve his false acquisitions. This is recognized in the myths of King Midas and tales of Mammon, as well as in the theories of Marx, the tenets of Christianity, and the modern myth of the workaholic corporate high flyers (Lewis, 1989).

I am describing the discourse of the master in terms of the masculine gender. Controversial or not, this seems to describe the discourse of phallocentric, patriarchical cultures. This is so, notwithstanding that many masters are benign, even loving, and, notwithstanding that women may be agents in this discourse also, enslaving men and (perhaps mostly) women. Fanon (1961) did point out how in colonized cultures the members of what I have called the submerged culture aggressed more against each other than against members of the dominant culture.

Lacan (1992) names also the "Discourse of the Hysteric," presupposing the discourse of the master. The agent here is the disharmonious divided subject. She addresses herself to the master, her *other*, in order to evoke a response. She questions the master, as *other*, about her estranged desire. She tries to know who she is through engaging him, so that he as "expert" might tell her her nature. Here, quite obviously I am using the female gender in my description, although the *agent* of this discourse may be a man and he may address a woman. Still, one is reminded of the research quoted earlier in this paper where the woman is seen to use questions to evoke responses and to engage dialogue more than to command attention (as the master does).

In this discourse, the *product* or outcome is "knowledge" of the self. The divided, estranged subject comes to know his or her nature through the eyes of others. So with this product comes a *loss*. It is the loss of her own desire which recedes more fully as the subject comes more and more to live out what the *other* desires, to be what the other wants her to be. The truth of the discourse, according to Lacan, is that in the discourse of the hysteric, the idea of *woman* is a (masculine) phantasy. She is what the *other* wants her to be. To find her own desire, the subject must move out of the discourse, no longer its agent. For within the discourse both genders are subjected to definition from the outside alone. This is the position of the member of the submerged culture who attempts to find herself through the rules imposed by the dominant culture.

Lacan offers the Discourse of the Analyst and the Discourse of the University as the other two in his significant four discourses. Briefly, they are as follows: The discourse of the university has impersonal knowledge in the place of the *agent*. In this way all is subjected to requirements of understanding, logic, and reason. When someone enters this discourse in the place of the *agent* he or she is speaking from the position of impersonal knowledge to the desiring other who wishes to learn. The *product*, however, of such knowledge is the divided subject, because the underlying *truth* of the discourse is that it is a cover for the blind authority of the master's discourse. All seemingly objective knowledge is ultimately in the service of the master's ideology, good or bad as this may be. This discourse legitimates and rationalizes the social, political, and cultural practices surrounding it. So, the subject is divided from his or her desire by the cultural practices of the master. This also is the discourse of bureaucracy.

The discourse of the analyst, on the other hand, has the analyst in the place of the *agent*. From this place, the analyst creates in the *other* (the analysand) the desire to know and construct the significant meanings of his other life. The work of analysis *produces* knowledge of a different kind to that produced in the university or in the hysteric or in the master's discourse. It is a knowledge of the subject and his or her important meanings. It is produced rather than being preexistent. The underlying *truth* is the unconscious desire of the subject which in the discourse becomes integrated back into the subject's total life.

Having named these discourses, how can we use the work of Lacan to further our understanding of the discourses of the genders? As mentioned earlier, if the discourse of the master and the derivative discourse of the university which are basic to our culture, are also the bases of traditional patriarchal modes of organization, then this is the discourse that males are encouraged to enter as *agents* from their beginnings, with females (first mother and then others) being predominantly in the place of *other;* that is being the recipients of the discourse. The very nature of the male's identification with other males requires him to move away from an identification with the mother and hence to stand in opposition to her (Chodorow, 1978).

Following Lacan and several feminist writers the discourse of the hysteric is seen to provide the predominant agency for the female. Here she (the female as *agent*) takes up the place of the enquirer who promotes and activates the other's knowledge of herself. In psychoanalytic terms the precursor of the discourse is an inquiry into the mother's or female's body; this being the initial provocation to developing knowledge of any sort. What is at stake in this discourse is possession of the female body. The discourse invites the other to its appropriation. Clearly it has been well appropriated by the advertisers. And, we cannot help being reminded here of the central issue of abortion in the feminist debates and the slogans about women wanting to take control of their own bodies rather than give them over to the establishment—the doctors and the medical establishment in general.

A parallel in the workplace is around the issue of sexual harassment. Recent work with a large sample of schoolgirls has highlighted the way in which this issue is felt to be important and part of a whole cultural approach. For example, teasing about their bodies by boys and male teachers was felt as harassment (Spender, 1992). Do we think of teasing as a natural part of social life or is it a result of the operation of the opposing yet linked discourses of the master and the hysteric? Of course males may suffer the same from the other if and when they enter the discourse of the hysteric as agents.

But it is from the discourse of the hysteric that one may enter the discourse of the analyst. The hystericized subject is the *other* that analysis is able to address. It is not surprising that women are often more amenable to psychological and "soft" interpretations of events, whilst men tend to retain their position in "harder" approaches. Girls tend to focus on relationships, boys on mechanics. On the whole, women, more often than men, are positioned to receive labels such as "not being able to cope with conflict," or "not being able to make the hard decisions." They also tend to be seen as "more understanding," "more open and approachable"; god help them when they're not! Then they're "hard, uncaring bitches"! But, men are also "hystericized"; men also suffer anxiety, indecisiveness, and ambivalence. They may in fact be caring, open, and soft. However, the discourses of the genders rarely allow for this. Registration at the level of the symbolic discourse outweighs many actual interpersonal relations.

However, if the discourse of the analyst is entered via the "hystericization" of the *other*, then it may be important that in our organizations we pay more attention to the discourse of the hysteric, how we enter it, and how we work from it toward a discourse that allows for a fuller understanding of our relations to our social worlds. A social world not based on master/slave relations, but on an openness for us each to find our own freedoms, our own bodies, and our own desire. This may require organizations to move away from the predominant master's discourse, including its exploitative premises and major focus on, e.g., economic rationalism, toward others. The discourse of the hysteric does have a socialized or symbolically castrated agent (Lacan, 1977) which renders its agents some possibility of collaborative teamwork. That is, unlike the master, its agents do not have an overarching belief in their omnipotence, but have some internalized recognition that they have limitations—the true basis for collaboration.

Even with the above, we are still left with the question of a submerged feminine discourse not named nor explored by Lacan. Not the discourse of the hysteric, it may be one where *agency* is transformed by relations with the *other* as Gilligan argues. This in itself is unsettling, more so because we may feel that in our organizations a feminine leadership within such a discourse may place us in a less defined, more vulnerable state. It may mean a leadership that does not direct others, but one that invites others to explore the emergence of something new through a working relationship that lets go of past definitions and certainties (Jones & Lawrie, 1994). Certainly many authors have outlined what might be considered feminine values (Gilligan, 1988; Marshall, 1994; Sayers, 1986). They include cooperation, consultation, containment, intuition, synthesis, openness, receptivity, attachment, transition, and compromise. Certainly they include the idea of relationship. Hirschhorn, Gilmore, and Newell (1989) point to the need for management training to focus on the acquisition of new roles and relationships rather than on fixed skills. The rapidly changing postindustrial world requires this because the challenge is one of dealing with new and complex unknowns rather than learning fixed solutions to easily diagnosed problems. Men and women need together to explore the territory of a new discourse, which although described as feminine and contained largely by women in society, is available to both sexes. And this not to replace those discourses already with us, but to transform them for the work we need to do together.

## PROMOTING A SHIFT TO FEMININE LEADERSHIP

It is worth noting some practical considerations to guide those wishing to promote the development of more feminine ways of leading and managing (Cargill & Long, 1992; Marshall, 1994). This will only occur when the basic discourse is shifted at the symbolic level. However, to use a cliche, "life is in the detail" and shifts at the imaginary level, when focused and massive, have an effect. How else might social change occur? Developing and maintaining different ways of leading requires efforts at the whole organization level, or at least through substantially sized groups within an organization, to develop what might be considered a critical mass. This is not an easy thing to do even in those corporations where the senior management professes an interest in promoting women.

## Normalize the Strengths of Feminine Leadership Through Networks and by Using Female Role Models

It is important to consider the particular strengths of feminine leadership which derive from feminine culture. These may involve different ways of communicating, of defining morality, and of assuming authority. These strengths, instead of being submerged or seen only as "soft" alternatives, should be normalized and seen as an important part of experience. Indeed, they are a part of experience in women's culture, and children of both genders are exposed to this culture and to these styles. It is only in their delegitimation in our organizational life that they become submerged or signified as less powerful or effective. Perhaps this is so because they signify much that is still incomprehensible, deeply unconscious, and frightening about our infant and childhood relations with powerful mothers (Dinnerstein, 1976) or because they are constantly and defensively equated with passivity (Sayers, 1986).

To reverse this delegitimation, the women in organizations (and it will be the women predominantly, but with the help of men) need to support and promote female role models in leadership positions and together legitimate and normalize the strengths of their feminine culture. This cannot be done in isolation but only through networking and building numbers by means of positive discrimination. There are several difficulties that women face in doing this. First, where women are promoted within a masculine culture, as argued in this paper, they themselves have often had to collude with that culture or have found themselves "masculinized" in their management practices. This leaves them conflicted in their roles as mentors toward younger women who may represent the femininity that they have had to leave behind, or at least leave outside their corporate roles. From such a conflicted stance they are unable to present unequivocally the feminine values of the submerged female culture. Unsurprisingly, the support of women by women may not always proceed smoothly. Any research in this area should at least ascertain in which discourse both mentor and mentee act as agents.

Another difficulty is that women tend to drop out of corporate culture when they encounter glass ceilings or destructive competition at senior levels. In Australia, the number of small businesses established by women since 1990 has been three times the number established by men during the same time period. Moreover, more than 50% of employees work for businesses employing less than 20 people. It is apparent where the women go when they know that the large corporations will not satisfy their work ambitions. Small entrepreneurial enterprise seems to benefit from feminine management practices, as evidenced, at least in Australia, by the number of such businesses currently flourishing. This may be due to the more flexible boundaries established by small business with their environments—suppliers, clients, competitors, and regulators. This flexibility is hard to achieve in the large corporations whose cultures are often more conservative. So if women drop out at the senior level, it is a difficult task to maintain female role models.

Finally, the complexity of women's family and career aspirations acts as a barrier to the adult developmental task of finding mentors when in their 20s and 30s as men tend to do. Roberts and Newton (1987) report on the difficulty of young women being able to find mentors of either sex. They note that the process of forming an occupation generally extends well into middle age for women. In reviewing three major studies in this area they state "in comparison to men of their own age, these women had a 10–20 year disadvantage and little hope of finding mentors to support their newly formed occupational dreams" (p. 159). Clearly the question of finding and working with good female role models is complex and not without difficulty. Nonetheless, these difficulties must be faced to enable the mentoring of women by women to occur in a creative manner.

## Shift the Dominant Culture Through Promoting Cohorts of Women Rather Than Promoting Individuals

To normalize feminine strengths in leadership requires that the dominant organizational culture is changed. As stated above, this

cannot be done by women in isolation. Promoting women singly
and in isolation subjects them to the pressure of a dominant,
traditional male culture and cuts them off from the needed networking and support potentially available from other women at
similar organizational levels and in similar roles. This was seen in
the example of the female engineer discussed earlier. Yet too
often affirmative action programs promote women in token
gestures. Moreover, the isolated position provides yet another
stimulus for women to leave the corporation and move to small
business.

It may be argued that it is not possible to promote several
women at once. This was done by a senior manager (a male) at
a recent conference ("Beyond Beginnings: Women's Education,
Employment and Training," Melbourne, 1992) who argued
against the possibility of promoting any groups in present low
economic growth conditions. However, it is possible for organizations to strategically plan the promotion of women over a period
of time. Each is then able to draw on support from a legitimized
plan and is able to plan a career path that does not have a glass
ceiling effect built in.

However, organizational culture is not changed easily, least
of all those attitudes and assumptions that are supported by the
general culture. There is a strong push once again amongst some
of our right-wing politicians for women to stay at home in order
to promote family values; the assumption being that the family
requires the financial and social subjugation of women. Few
voices call for the better integration of work and family needs; a
process that might emphasize equal responsibilities for both
sexes. Those women who do pursue both family and career paths
end up with the often socially dubious task of fighting for child
care facilities, and feel internally divided between their needs to
provide stable environments for their children and to develop
themselves in the world of work. It's the woman's problem and
she too feels it is!

The International Year of the Family (1994) did perhaps
bring to light issues of the work/family interface. However, at the
same time, organizations are "downsizing" and demanding more
and more from those remaining. For those with jobs there is less

time for the family. For those without, the family easily becomes a place of despair. In such a climate, organizational experimentation and planned cultural change not immediately and apparently leading to increased productivity are shunned. The arguments, such as those put forward by the speaker two paragraphs above, become those of: "It's a good idea to promote women but we can't. Not just now." Practice lags behind rhetoric and one suspects that the latter is simply a defensive maneuver.

## Shift Stereotyped Division of the Emotional Roles of the Genders

Both women and men collude in living with the traditional emotional roles of the genders. Women are likely to introject and contain (Bion, 1962) an emotional or "hystericized" position, whilst men tend to move away from this and to take up the rational or pseudorational position (Kanter, 1977b). This is a simple way of saying that the genders readily take up agency in their traditional discourses. And, it becomes a mutual protection racket in the face of anxieties. Shifts in this structuring can only come with efforts to provide an organizational environment where men can safely explore their "feminine" side and women their "masculine" side and where the hidden feminine discourse can emerge.

Shifting these emotional positions may be one of the most difficult transitions to effect, particularly as they are closely tied to the expression of sexuality and the defenses against this expression in the workplace. The argument here, which broadly takes the genders as classes rather than as individual instances, should be explained. Women readily are given and take on the position as instigators of desire. To defend against their desire (probably ambivalently held) men may split off and project "sexuality" as well as "emotionality" onto women as a class. Such a dynamic partially explains the denigrated position of women in the workplace. This is because after projecting their sexual desire into women, men may then express toward those women the disgust that they would otherwise have had to feel toward themselves as part of their ambivalence. Nathaniel Hawthorne's novel *The Scarlet Letter* (1935/1850) explicitly addresses this dynamic of the woman being publicly shamed and denigrated as a social defense against openly admitting the (uncontrolled) sexuality of the male. Such denigration may be structurally expressed in the organization by keeping women in the more lowly positions. The question of women's collusion in this dynamic is partially explained by projective identification (see the explanation above with regard to Fanon's work) and partially explained by women's denial of their own feminine sexuality (Irigaray, 1974). It is, nonetheless, arguably encoded in the symbolic discourse of sexuality.

Each of the above issues is important if we are to effect the organizational changes that might allow more feminine forms of corporate leadership to occur. The entrenched values and practices that are lined up against such changes are formidable and are supported by both men and women at conscious and unconscious levels. Nonetheless, men and women do move from and through different linguistic and discursive cultures and it will only be when they both share authority and the freedom that it brings that our corporations will be able to use the diversity implied by this. Whether or not our corporations can be transformed by the feminine depends very much on how we can address the deep cultural issues surrounding gender and sexuality currently encoded in the symbolic register of experience.

## REFERENCES

Armstrong, D. (1995, July). *The analytic object in organizational work.* Paper presented at the International Society for the Psychoanalytic Study of Organizations: Symposium on the Distinctive Relevance of Psychoanalytic Understanding to Organizations, London.

Bayes, M., & Newton, P. M. (1985). Women in authority: a sociopsychological analysis. In D. Coleman & M. Geller (Eds.), *Group relations reader* (Vol. 2, pp. 309–322). Washington: A. K. Rice Institute. (Original work published 1978)

Bion, W. R. (1962). *Learning from experience.* London: Marlesfield Library.

Cargill, B., & Long, S. D. (1992). Women and leadership. In A. Spencer (Ed.), *Beyond beginnings: Women's education, employment and training.* Swinburne University, Melbourne: Symposium Papers, National Centre for Women.

Chattopadhyay, G. (1995). Hierarchy and modern organization: Strange bedfellows. In S. Long (Ed.), *International perspectives on organizations in times of turbulence* (pp. 13–21). Melbourne: Swinburne University Press.

Chodorow, N. (1978). *The reproduction of mothering: Psychoanalysis and the sociology of gender.* Berkeley: University of California Press.

Chomsky, N. (1965). *Aspects of the theory of syntax.* The Hague: Mouton.

Dinnerstein, D. (1976). *The rocking of the cradle and the ruling of the world.* New York: Harper & Row.

Fanon, F. (1967). *The wretched of the earth.* Ringwood, Australia: Penguin Books. (Original work published 1961)

Foucault, M. (1972). *The archaeology of knowledge.* London: Tavistock.

Freud, S. (1961a). Female sexuality. In J. Strachey (Ed. and Trans.), *The standard edition of the complete psychological works of Sigmund Freud* (Vol. 21, pp. 221–243). London: Hogarth Press. (Original work published 1931)

Freud, S. (1961b). Some psychical consequences of the anatomical distinction between the sexes. In J. Strachey (Ed. and Trans.), *The standard edition of the complete psychological works of Sigmund Freud* (Vol. 19, pp. 241–258). London: Hogarth Press. (Original work published 1925)

Gilligan, C. (1988). Re-mapping the moral domain: New images of self in relationship. In C. Gilligan, J. Ward, & J. Taylor (Eds.), *Mapping the moral domain: A contribution of women's thinking to psychological theory and education* (pp. 3–19). Cambridge, MA: Harvard University Press.

Grigg, R. (1992, August). *Lacan's four discourses.* Paper presented at the sixth annual conference of the Centre for Psychoanalytic Research.

Hawthorne, N. (1935). *The scarlet letter.* New York: Heritage. (Original work published 1850)

Henriques, I., Holloway, W., Urwin, C., Venn, C., & Walkerdine, V. (1990). *Changing the subject: Psychology, social regulation and subjectivity.* London: Methuen.

Hirschhorn, L., Gilmore, T., & Newell, T. (1989). Training and learning in a post-industrial world. In H. Leymann & H. Kornbluh (Eds.), *Socialisation and learning at work: A new approach to the learning process in the workplace* (pp. 185–200). New York: Avebury.

Irigaray, L. (1985). *Speculum of the other woman.* Syracuse, NY: Cornell University Press. (Original work published 1974)

Jones, P. & Lawrie, G. (1994). Encouraging unplanning: How organizations can cope with uncertainty. In R. Casemore, G. Dyos, A. Eden, K. Kellner, J. McCauley, & S. Moss (Eds.), *What makes consultancy work: Understanding the dynamics* (pp. 66–75). London: Southbank University Press.

Kanter, R. M. (1977a). *Men and women of the corporation.* London: Basic Books.

Kanter, R. M. (1977b). Women in organizations: Change agent skills. In A. H. Burke (Ed.), *Current issues and strategies in organizational development* (pp. 108–130). New York: Human Sciences Press.

Kuhn, T. S. (1962). *The structure of scientific revolutions.* Chicago: University of Chicago Press.

Lacan, J. (1977). *Ecrits.* London: Tavistock.

Lacan, J. (1992). *Le semine de Jacques Lacan, livre 17, L'Envers de la psychanalyse.* Paris: Seuil.

Lewis, M. (1989). *Liar's poker: Two cities, true greed.* London: Hodder & Stoughton.

Long, S. D. (1991). The signifier and the group. *Human Relations 44* (4), 389–401.

Long, S. D. (1992a). Working with potential space: Individuals, groups and organisations. *Australian Journal of Psychotherapy 11*(2), 64–78.

Long, S. D. (1992b). *A structural analysis of small groups.* London: Routledge.

Long, S. D. (1995). Teaching organisational behiour to Eastern European managers. In J. Witt (Ed.), *Central and Eastern Europe and the CIS* (pp. 77–91). New York: Haworth Press.

Maltz, D., & Borker, R. (1982). A cultural approach to male-female miscommunication. In J. Gumpertz (Ed.), *Language and social identity* (pp. 196–216). Cambridge, U.K.: Cambridge University Press.

Marshall, J. (1994). Re-visioning organizations by developing female values. In R. Boot, J. Lawrence, & J. Morris (Eds.), *Managing the unknown by creating new futures* (pp. 165–183). Maidenhead, U.K.: McGraw-Hill.

Mitchell, J., & Rose, J. (1982). *Feminine sexuality: Jacques Lacan and the Ecole Freudienne.* London: Macmillan.

Roberts, P. (1992). Personal perspectives of women in non-traditional areas. In A. Spencer (Ed.), *Beyond beginnings: Women's education, employment and training.* Swinburne University, Melbourne: Symposium Papers, National Centre for Women.

Roberts, P., & Newton, P. M. (1987). Levinsonian studies of women's adult development. *Psychology and Ageing, 2*(2), 154–163.

Rodriguez, L. (1992, August). *The discourse of the analyst.* Paper presented at the sixth annual conference of the Centre for Psychoanalytic Research.

Rosenthal, J., & Jacobsen, L. F. (1968). *Pygmalion in the classroom: Teacher expectations and pupil's intellectual development.* New York: Holt, Rinehart & Winston.

Sayers, J. (1986). *Sexual contradictions: Psychology, psychoanalysis and feminism.* London: Tavistock.

Sinclair, A. (1995). Sex and the MBA. *Organization, 2*(2), 295–317.

Spender, D. (1992). The current position of women: Educational perspective. In A. Spencer (Ed.), *Beyond beginnings: Women's education, employment and training.* Swinburne University, Melbourne: Symposium Papers, National Centre for Women.

Tannen, D. (1991). *You just don't understand: Women and men in communication.* Sydney, Australia: Random House.

# 10

# Women's Exercise of Power and Authority in the Legal Profession

*Barbara B. Winderman, J.D.*
*and Margaret D. Sheely, M.S.W.*

This article began 16 years ago with our coming together around our interest in the difficulties that women encounter in the exercise of their personal and delegated power. Through the years, we have consulted to many different groups of professionals and have been impressed with the psychosocial dilemmas that confront women in law. Much is being done to facilitate women attorneys in taking up their roles. Creating and implementing

*Acknowledgments.* Portions of this paper were presented at the meeting of the 12th Annual Women and the Law Section of the State Bar of Texas, April, 1995, Houston, Texas.

We thank Phil Camus, Charla Hayden, Debra Noumair and Lee Winderman for critiquing our work and for their loyal support. We also thank Faith Gabelnick from whose writings and presence we have drawn inspiration.

legislation or other policy that renders gender discrimination in the judicial system illegal is critical to the process. Similarly, conferences focusing on the contributions of women to the theory and practice of law, such as those sponsored by the American and state bar associations, offer women knowledge and support in dealing with the difficulties of being a female attorney. In this chapter, we draw from clinical studies and our own experiences to illuminate issues of power as they confront professional women. We will then offer a paradigm, referred to as group relations theory, which we have found to be a key resource in helping women better understand, identify, and change their struggles with power and authority issues in the workplace.

## DEFINING POWER AND AUTHORITY

Webster (1993) defines "power" as a *position of ascendancy; ability to compel obedience; control; dominion.* Synonyms for the word *power* include *authority* and *command.* Power connotes the ability to produce a change. The distinction between power over, and power to, is critical to our discussion. It draws attention to the individual's experience where power is being exerted: oppression by the powerful, the experience of helplessness, and the desire to have influence.

Power can be analyzed at many different levels of human interaction—societal, organizational, interpersonal, and individual. Within these levels of analysis it is helpful to understand behavior as functioning like a system: in other words, all events in one part of the system affect, to a greater or lesser degree, all the other parts of the system. Likewise, all events and processes related to power are not only interconnected, but interdependent. For example, a discussion of women and power would be overly simplistic unless we recognize (1) that power is never independent of gender, race, ethnicity, class, sexuality, and other social differences; and (2) that different subgroups of women have different experiences of power and are usually responded to based on their gender and these other social differences.

The words *power* and *authority* are often used interchangeably. However, the distinction between personal power and authority and delegated power and authority is worth examining. For example, to exercise personal power and authority is a freedom that we as individuals always have available to us whenever we wish to speak or take action based on an inherent sense of what we want to do. Notwithstanding the possible consequences of exercising personal authority, we nevertheless have the freedom to do so. Delegated authority is considerably different in that one's authority is derived from an individual, group, or organization. Delegated authority may have specific restraints on it or may be carte blanche. For example, when handling a client's litigation matter, an attorney may have the authority to settle a claim for a specific value. In this situation the extent of the attorney's authority is limited and specific and requires the attorney to check back with her client prior to varying the amount, regardless of circumstance. In contrast, when handling the matter at trial, the attorney may be given wide latitude to speak or act within the framework of a known and agreed upon policy. While she may be given broad limits beyond which she cannot go, the attorney can commit the client's resources, point of view, or course of action.

## WHAT IS HAPPENING TO WOMEN'S EXERCISE OF POWER?

### "Becoming Gentlemen"—Cultural Pressures

Much has been written about the difficulties encountered by women professionals in fields historically dominated by men, where men dictate the culture, customs, and practices "of the game," and where a patriarchal system often defines success or failure. The authors have listened to the stories of many female attorneys who reported feeling disillusioned and frustrated in their law practices. These feelings, sometimes verging on despair, start long before the female attorney enters the marketplace of law.

It has been noted that for many women, learning to think like a lawyer is tantamount to learning to think and act like a gentleman in the sense that women should be neutral, unemotional, but courteous advocates for a client's interest (Guinier, Fine, Balin, Bartow, & Stachel, 1994). From the time of their entrance into law school, "becoming gentlemen" exacts an extraordinary cost, personally and professionally, from these women. In a recent study of law students at the University of Pennsylvania, the researchers found that men were three times more likely than women to be in the top 10% of their law school class by the end of the first year. This was true even though the two groups entered with virtually identical stellar credentials. Although the gap later narrowed (men were only twice as likely to graduate in the top 10th), it never closed, in part because first-year grades skewed important precursors of later success, such as law review, summer jobs, and judicial clerkships. As a result, women graduated with less competitive academic credentials, were not represented equally within the school's academic and social hierarchies, and were less competitive in obtaining desirable jobs after graduation.

As significant as the loss of academic standing for women is the study's finding that while there existed strong attitudinal differences between women and men in the freshman year, striking homogenization occurred by year 3 (Guinier et al., 1994). For instance, a disproportionate number of women entering law school evidenced a commitment to public interest law or other such altruistic areas of study. Their 3rd-year female counterparts had given up their benevolent aspirations and graduated with corporate ambitions. The researchers said the disparity in grades and the marked change in attitudinal differences were closely correlated to findings drawn from hundreds of questionnaires and student interviews which depicted a 3-year experience systematically alienating to both men and women and effectively hostile to women.

The experiences of these female law students are not unique to Penn Law School. For example, in 1994, the Texas Gender Bias Task Force confirmed the existence of gender bias in the Texas judicial system (Garcia, 1995). The task force noted that many women experienced hostile, demeaning, or condescending treatment by attorneys and judges; many thought they were held to higher standards than their male counterparts. Biased behaviors toward women were found to affect their credibility, if not to impact the litigation process and case outcome. Thus, the experiences described at Penn Law School, and the price exacted upon female law students, portrays law school as a "boot camp" for what lies ahead for the female attorney.

In our consultations with female attorneys, many reported feeling disillusioned and diminished in their law practices. Most felt too dazed, too overwhelmed, or too busy with their day-to-day responsibilities to understand what had happened to them. In essence, they had experienced small traumatic events, often so subtle that they could not articulate the discrete incidents that accumulated over time, leaving them with the psychological and physiological effects of trauma. These women were depressed, angry, irritable, and demoralized. People readily remember major traumas. However, small traumatic experiences over time become cumulative in nature and ultimately may have the same impact on the psychology and physiology of the recipient as a major trauma, without the benefit of understanding the source (West & Sheldon-Keller, 1994).

The depiction of the female students' experience at law school aptly demonstrates the impact of cumulative trauma on the confidence and competence levels of these women. In the researchers' words, "[M]any students, especially many women, have simply not been socialized to thrive in the type of ritualized combat that comprises much of the legal education method" (Guinier et al., 1994, p. 62). They felt alienated by the Socratic teaching style, the dominant, competitive hierarchical method for all freshman classes. Many women said they were intimidated and condescended to by male professors and classmates. Male law students discouraged women's participation by linking it inversely to female sexuality or by making disparaging comments. For example, loquacious women were referred to as "man-hating lesbians" or "feminazi dykes," while loquacious men were simply designated "assholes." Women students noted concern that faculty did not intervene. One said, "[W]hatever ideals we came in with, they get bashed out of us" (p. 43). Tragically, "[F]or these women, the moment they speak out to challenge what they perceive as sexist assumptions or offensive language, they diminish the level at which they are taken seriously" (p. 66).

Female attorneys, like their law student counterparts, often feel caught in a double bind. If they speak quietly, the determination in their voices may be lost, they are seen as weak, and not partner material. If they speak loudly and aggressively, counterpunch like the boys, then they risk being seen as masculine, disruptive, and perhaps reputed to need to act like a man to get their point across. In a very brief period of time, they, too, could be seen as "man-hating lesbians or feminazi dykes." Many junior female attorneys indicate they are held to a higher standard than their male counterparts when learning new skills, and that the mistakes of young female attorneys are not readily forgotten. Women lawyers relate that the very essence of their person is altered in taking up the role of attorney, whether in the law firm, the courtroom, or in the community. They are told that they are not measuring up because of their particular style of exercising authority. Senior male partners counsel females to speak louder and sterner. They are unable to see that the female way of practicing law actually encompasses a broad range of behaviors and that a woman's gentle, steady approach is effective in a variety of contexts.

The now familiar adage that a woman's expression of feelings evidences weakness, not strength, hits hard in legal arenas. When watching the O. J. Simpson trial, we flinched when Deputy District Attorney Marcia Clark showed her emotions, anger, irritation, frustration. Even though we were well aware of our capacity to both feel intense emotions and function competently at the same time, we found ourselves counseling Ms. Clark, "do not show your emotions, do not get upset or outraged"; or, "if you must be emotional, be emotional like the men." These thoughts were evoked out of a fear that people would not take her seriously or that her style of being emotional would be seen as weak and ineffectual. Be more like a man—that is the culture of the courtroom. How appalling! We wanted this woman to not be a woman, to split off the emotional aspects of herself such that she either act asexual or like a gentleman. It was all right for Johnnie Cochran to speak with bravado and Robert Shapiro or F. Lee Bailey to speak with arrogance, for that is "the male way"; the same latitude, however, was not afforded Ms. Clark—by us.

In 1992, the American Bar Association (MacCrate, 1992) formulated a list of skills and values which it considered fundamental for the professional lawyer. In addition to providing competent representation, primary values included: striving to promote justice, fairness, and morality; striving to rid the profession of bias based on personal characteristics such as race and gender; and selecting employment that will allow the lawyer to pursue her professional and personal goals. Of the 10 skills listed, only two pertain to legal analysis or litigation. The remainder included proficiency in problem solving, research, factual investigation, communication, counseling, negotiation, and resolving ethical dilemmas. Most, if not all of these values and skills are inherently synchronistic with a woman's relational style of working; that is, a style which is more person-directed, more empathic. Thus, the pitiful irony of a woman becoming a gentleman to succeed at law is that by doing so, she forsakes her benevolent professional aspirations, and she undermines her competence and her relational leadership advantage at a time when the legal profession is under public attack for its social destructiveness. She forsakes these aspirations at a time when her contribution is most needed to counteract the ruthless competitiveness of the legal profession. In becoming a gentleman, she tragically alienates herself from the relational components of her self, her life, and her work.

## Assigning Priorities: The Delicate Balance of Work and Home Life

Another issue that bears on a woman's sense of power and competence has to do with the assignment of priorities, especially regarding the balancing of work and home life. Women are very committed to the importance of their relationships. As Gilligan states: "The elusive mystery of women's development lies in its recognition of the continuing importance of attachment in the human life cycle" (1982, p. 23). As a result, the emotional bonding with those at home tends to take more of a toll on women than men. Women often develop a precarious balance between their home and work life. If the balance is threatened by either more demands at work, or more demands at home, women experience enormous anxiety (Stiver, 1991).

Female attorneys who do attempt to return to work on a part-time or "flextime" basis often feel diminished. In our culture we take advantage of a woman's commitment to relationships and her role as primary caregiver by giving her lower status and dead-end positions in our organizations (Acker, 1992). While men are expected to use family time to continue to meet their work responsibilities, women are required to adjust their involvement in paid work to meet responsibilities at home (Sheppard, 1992). Burdened with the primary responsibility for home and family, women may not be able, or care to live up to the impossible expectations we often place on the "ideal attorney": the attorney with no body, no feelings, and no gender.

Many women attorneys have elected to make radical career changes, to retire altogether, or to take prolonged leaves of absence from their legal practice, because they have found the balance between home and work impossible to negotiate. For some women, this decision reflects a process of stagnation, of constriction and alienation from the world and from the self. For other women, this decision reflects a developmental transition through which her life becomes rejuvenated (Levinson, Darrow, Klein, Levinson, & McKee, 1978).

During her early 40s, one of the authors (B. B. W.) who enjoyed a successful legal career, gave birth to her third daughter. Sensing in a profound way the preciousness of life, in part through the development process of middle adulthood, in part through the mothering of this new life, she came to reflect on the meaning and value of her success and of its limitations. Intuitively knowing that it was time for a career change, yet fearing the consequences of giving up the power and security it afforded, she left her legal practice, opening herself up for a fuller, more diverse life not yet dreamed of. Leaving her law practice precipitated the concomitant feelings of grief associated with the giving up of her professional work world on the one hand, and embracing the joys and fears of reaching for the dream not yet obtained on the other.

Whether representative of stagnation and decline or reflective of rejuvenation and generativity, the journey to the decision to leave is a painful one. Judith Duerk captures it well in *Circle of Stones* when she says,

> She must leave the safe role of remaining a faithful daughter of the collectives around her and descend to her individual feeling values. It will be her task to experience her pain . . . the pain of her own unique feeling values calling to her, pressing to emerge. (1989, p. 21)

It takes great courage for a woman to tolerate the aloneness engendered by a decision seen not as admirable, but rather misunderstood as weak by her contemporaries.

## Women as Managers

Women are often perceived, and perceive themselves, as unsuited for positions of authority; many capable women do not aspire to high-level management positions. The reluctance of both men and women to be subordinate to a woman manager is well documented. When a woman becomes a manager, she and her staff may behave in ways that deskill her, deny her authority, and undermine the work task (Bayes & Newton, 1985). It has been hypothesized that "because of the fantasy and fear of women's power, both men and women are socialized to accept a strongly held stereotype of women as possessing legitimate authority only to nurture" (p. 321). Thus, she may have difficulty exercising authority in those areas in which she has received little early training, and she may unknowingly stimulate and collude in the maintenance of dependency in her staff.

One author (M. D. S.) consulted with an organization (composed of two females and four males) because the senior female partner was considering leaving the group. In reviewing its history, the consultant learned that each member had joined at a different time and that the original partners were no longer with the organization. The most senior person was a woman who joined the organization 25 years prior when the group was composed of five white males. She said that initially upon joining the organization, she expressed her thoughts and feelings openly about a variety of issues that seemed to be deterring the group from getting on with its task. She involved herself in the management of the organization with enthusiasm, thinking that her contributions would be found valuable and collaborative with the goals of the group.

In time, she realized that there was a significant resistance to her suggestions; and that the same suggestions, if made by one of the men, were seen as helpful. She felt "spun around" by the covert processes that devalued and undermined her personal power and authority. She felt humiliated when she made procedural suggestions. Consistently leaving partnership meetings with a terrible sense of shame, she began to "pretend" and "go along with" in order to appease this all male environment. At a luncheon meeting with one of the male partners, she was told that the senior men were working out unconsciously which one would "get to f——— her"; that this was the basic issue confronting the group. From that point forth, she withdrew from the group interaction and, in retrospect, realized that the comment had traumatized her.

Twenty-five years later, this female manager strongly contemplated leaving because of the processes within the group that had taken place over a 6-year period of time, such as the rigidification of the alliances and coalitions. Upon talking with the younger partners and observing the partnership meetings, it became clear that the power of this senior woman was being held in check by the social fabric of the partnership. Fearing that she might abandon them and, at the same time, fearful of her power, the partnership unwittingly engaged in behavior provoking her to react. In this double-bind situation, she was subtly ignored when she spoke directly to what was occurring. When she finally had enough and spoke with anger, this formidable coalition reacted as if the expression of strong feelings was inappropriate. The intensity of their reaction was in direct proportion to their fear that she would leave. Her desire to leave began to emerge in a stronger sense as time passed.

Even though her partners acknowledged their respect for her in individual meetings, an entirely different experience occurred when the partnership group met as a whole: it was as if the group had a mind of its own. She tried a variety of ways of intervening, and finally found herself enraged at what seemed an impermeable boundary between herself and the other partners. One would have expected a strong alliance to develop between the two females in the organization. This was true in the informal activities of the organization. However, in partnership meetings, the younger woman, acting coy and seductive, betrayed her senior colleague when she turned like a chameleon, joining and supporting the male partners to hold in check the power of this senior woman.

Feeling unheard and not valued, the senior woman continued to detach from the situation, which was manifested by coming late to the meetings, engaging in work while at the meetings, or not going to the meetings at all. Concomitant with feeling alienated from the group, she felt a high level of stagnation in her work which accentuated her disengagement. The distancing maneuvers evoked an escalatory phenomenon; the more she distanced, the more the group would react with hostility. When questioned why she was unable to address these issues in an explicit way, she reported feeling exhausted from her extensive prior attempts at doing so. She continued to experience painful isolation and feelings of alienation, increasing her interest in leaving.

This woman's struggle to take up a leadership role in an organization is oftentimes the rule rather than the exception. That is, women in management positions, skilled and competent in their profession, often desire to move away from the competitive world of men and women because the work environment becomes too toxic. It is not unusual to hear of female attorneys moving from law firm to law firm and finally to a solo practice because they are exhausted and demoralized from being confronted day after day with ruthless competitiveness between men and men, men and women, and women and women.

There was remarkable irony in the timing of this consultation for the consultant, for she, too, was feeling a sense of dissatisfaction in her work world which seemed lacking in creative opportunities. She noted many of the same feelings—stagnation, despair, alienation, and a sense of "not having a place." She felt a pervasive aloneness that comes with "seniority" and "having arrived," an aloneness that emerges out of aging and the evolution of wisdom that comes from living. While on the one hand she was proud of her seniority and accomplishments, being "senior" left her with a lack of synchrony with those around her. Aware of the pain of this aloneness, she found herself searching for a partnership in which to work. Like a spiral, she experienced periods of both despair and exhilaration, creativity and stagnation, connection and aloneness. Embracing the aloneness with less despair seemed to foster the reemergence of her creativity and the amelioration of her sense of stagnation; it allowed for a heightened sense of appreciation for her contributions and an increased tolerance of what she observed. Levinson et al. (1978) describe such transitional intervals of adult development, abundant with paradox and deeply conflicted feeling states, as phases through which one emerges once again from the state of "disillusionment" to a state of "deillusionment."

## "BECOMING A LADY"—CULTURAL PRESSURES

In a culture where we as women most often look to the male gender to blame for and rectify our travails, we fail to adequately discover crippling issues which rest within ourselves. Two such issues have to do with: (1) women's reluctance to take power positions in overt ways, and (2) women's difficulties in working with other women in a collaborative manner. Baker Miller (1991) notes that confronting power issues is extremely difficult for women. When women think about acting powerful, they fear the possibility of putting down another person; they fear admitting the need or desire to increase their own powers; they fear the possibility of isolation and abandonment that the use of power may bring. Though external conditions block advancement for women or render them impotent, it is the internalized forces in a woman such as self-criticism and self-blame which replicate external conditions and create even more disadvantageous circumstances (Stiver, 1991).

## The Exercise of Covert Power

There is what seems a polarization in how women approach power. Women may steer clear of being overtly powerful, not wanting, or fearing, the official delegation which brings with it title, status, and recognition. Instead, they use a more traditional female way to achieve power, referred to as the "instrumental" achieving style, which, until recently, has been labeled and perceived as unsavory or manipulative. Instrumental behavioral styles reference the self and others as instruments for accomplishment and involve using such aspects as skill, wit, charm, family background, and previous success (Lipman-Blumen, 1992). This type of power attainment, used by both men and women from pre-Biblical days, serves an important survival function.

Some women exercise covert power primarily by pairing with men; "the woman behind the throne" metaphor aptly describes these women who desire power but who are reluctant to seek it overtly. The collusive pact between men and women in this scenario requires the woman to make the man feel strong and powerful in exchange for the man protecting the woman from the envy and aggression from men and other women. Sometimes this collusion is entered into within the context of a sexual relationship. At other times the woman need only enhance the male ego by deferring to the "male brilliance and wisdom," by agreeing with her male partner without much contribution of ideas, or by being coy and seductive. In return, she experiences the fruits of this quid pro quo, such as promotions, salary increases, bonuses, or travel opportunities, without the need to take a direct stand to get them.

Although the exercise of instrumental styles of behavior serves a protective function, it can become a weapon of destruction to both the self and to other women. For example, some junior women attorneys unwittingly engage in an illicit sexual liaison with their male mentor in an attempt to achieve power and protection. The sexual relationship confounds and complicates their life as they attempt to develop professionally, preserve their integrity in the face of lowered self-esteem, and maintain their secret collusive pact. Additionally, being the Special Woman to a powerful male brings with it the fears of replacement, envy, and devaluation from other women. For men, this confirms their sexualized image of and use of women and acts as further evidence of female ineptness.

## The Overt Ascension of Women to Power Positions

Women who focus on men as being the primary deterrent to a woman's ascent to power often fail to see that collaborative endeavors amongst women raise tremendous fears regarding issues of competition and envy. Women have great difficulty owning their ambivalent feelings about women or talking about troubling issues which arise amongst themselves because of the preciousness of the relationships between women on the one hand, and because of the primitive fear of powerful women and of being powerful, on the other. Often what appears on the outside to be authentic communication between women is actually a primitive dynamic of pseudomutuality. J. Baker Miller (1991) advanced the notion that most women would probably be most comfortable in a world in which we feel we are not limiting, but rather are enhancing, the power of other people while simultaneously increasing our own power. While this, indeed, may be a goal worth striving for, it seems idealistic when coupled with the painful reality that women participate as vigorously in their own deprecation as do men by harboring an unconscious attitude that their gender is not as valuable as the male gender (Lerner, 1974).

We gratefully recognize those women who have pressed ahead under tremendous societal burdens to make the world a better place for women. However, many self-defined feminists operate out of a reaction formation, a psychological defense whereby one acts the opposite of what one really feels and thinks.

For example, as discussed above, the woman who seems supportive of her female counterparts, always collaborative, may be the
same woman who turns into a chameleon when males are present.
Acting coy and seductive in the process of dealing with men,
she attempts to exclude her female colleagues while all the time
denying her unconscious intent to cause harm or her wish to be
the Special Woman to the male power broker. These women,
believing they are feminists, manifest an unconscious ambivalence
toward women who seek power positions; they speak to the rights
of women, yet cannot acknowledge their disdain or fear of women
in power.

A number of years ago, a group of women came together to
examine the particular difficulties that women might experience
around issues of leadership, authority, and power in same sex
groups. They planned an experiential group relations conference
designed to explore the issues of women working with other
women (Taylor et al., 1979). They anticipated it would be a wonderful, collaborative endeavor. Contrary to their initial beliefs
and assumptions, the women in this conference who attempted
to assume leadership roles were, in the main, confronted not by
support and collaboration, but rather with envy and aggression
from their female colleagues. As the authors noted, "[T]he sight
of a woman so overtly differentiated (even spatially) from other
women was intolerable: she must be returned to the undifferenti-
ated circle" (p. 127). Thus, in order to deal with a woman in
power, the other women in the group attempted to "fuse her
back into the homogeneous mass" (p. 127). A woman who dared
to differentiate herself on the basis of her attributes of competence, leadership abilities, and the power assumed with an authority role, became the subject of great envy. She, in turn,
experienced a nonrational primitive fear of being ripped apart
by the other women on the one hand or rendered incompetent
on the other.

For many women, the experiences at this conference were
painful and raised difficult questions. It brought into bold relief
their ambivalent feelings toward other women in power positions,
their envy, and the deadliness of their response to the ascension
of power in others. They were shocked to see their own primitive

responses to the fear of being destroyed or wanting to destroy other women. The far-reaching ramifications of this conference's experience highlight the nonrational forces that operate intensely between women. Despite our wish for a sisterhood characterized solely by mutual support and collaboration, we must also acknowledge our dark side. We must recognize the primitive responses we have toward ourselves and toward other women in power positions. Once we shift our focus from the inherent dilemmas of dealing with male authority, we can deal with the far more difficult issues of how women can truly collaborate with one another, holding in check the envy, the aggression, and the fears that arise in such a collaboration.

Clarissa Pinkola Estes (1992) sums it up well in *Women Who Run With the Wolves:*

> A good deal of literature on the subject of women's power states that men are afraid of women's power. I always want to exclaim, "Mother of God! So many women themselves are afraid of women's power" . . . If men are going to ever learn to stand it, then without a doubt women have to learn to stand it. (1992, p. 93)

This brings us face to face with our own reluctance as women to take positions of power, and our own ambivalence in allowing other women to take those positions. What then does the future hold for those of us still wishing to forge ahead to establish ourselves as leaders in the legal profession?

## PROSPECTS FOR CHANGE

### Connective Leadership for the Millennium: Myth or Reality?

As we move toward the millennium, women find themselves working in organizations characterized by global interdependence externally and by a highly diverse workforce internally. To succeed, the workplace and organizational and political leadership must change to reflect the interdependent diverse qualities of this new world order. Jean Lipman-Blumen (1992) asserts that global interdependence calls for "connective leadership," a leadership style that integrates ideas and behaviors previously associated exclusively with either males or females. In her words,

> "Connective leadership" derives its label from its character of connecting individuals not only to their own tasks and ego drives, but also to those of the group and community that depend upon the accomplishment of mutual goals. It is leadership that connects individuals to others and *others'* goals, using a broad spectrum of behavioral strategies. It is leadership that "proceeds(s) from a premise of connection" (Gilligan, 1982: 38) and a recognition of networks of relationships that bind society in a web of mutual responsibilities. It shares responsibility, takes unthreatened pride in the accomplishments of colleagues and protegés, and experiences success without the compulsion to outdo others. . . . (p. 184)

This type of leadership style requires values and skills in keeping with those identified by the bar associations and discussed previously; for example, values to promote justice, fairness, and morality, and skills in areas of problem solving, communication, counseling, and negotiation. Women attorneys are known to naturally excel at most, if not all, of these skills.

Do these values and skills, espoused by the bar associations, fit the actual values and skills of the professional lawyer? Is an integrated leadership style or work environment possible? We would hope that it is possible. But some of it sounds idealistic, too simplistic, out of touch with the reality of the primitive nature of people. The embeddedness of sexism in our culture's social structures beyond a particular organization continues to profoundly shape the reality of the individual workplace (Faludi, 1991; Sheppard, 1992).

Connective leadership denies the primitive process within women who not only sabotage their own power-hungry stances, but undermine other women's achievements as well because of their lack of awareness of the painful internal conflicts which arise when they are confronted with these issues (Baker Miller, 1991). Connective leadership? William Simon, a prominent sociologist, said in a discussion of these issues at a meeting held in Houston, Texas, in 1993, that it will never happen in our lifetime.

## Group Relations Theory: An Introduction

We draw from a model called group relations theory which was developed primarily by Dr. A. Kenneth Rice at the Tavistock Institute for Human Relations in London (Rioch, 1975). Internationally known, the "Tavistock" model was brought to the United States by Margaret Rioch in 1965 and further developed by the A. K. Rice Institute. It involves a paradigm shift that focuses on the group as the first subject of study and on the individual as secondary to the group. In other words, the individual's behavior is examined in the context in which it occurs; the focus shifts to the organization as a whole rather than to examining only the characteristics of the individual. Any understanding of what might be taking place regarding an individual's behavior must be understood by examining the group or organization in which that individual belongs.

Essential then to the Tavistock approach is the belief that when an aggregate becomes a group, the group behaves as a system—an entity that is greater or lesser than the sum of its parts. There are no victims or villains in this paradigm; all that occurs in the group context is viewed as a collusive enterprise of entanglements. Group relations theory invites us to understand the groups we are a part of and to consider our own participation in the group processes that are obstructive to our professional development. It offers a paradigm of shared responsibility—an understanding of how women are part of a greater whole and how it is that empowerment of each of us as individuals is related directly to the empowerment of women as a community.

## Theoretical Constructs

Using evolving theories from dynamic psychology and open systems, group relations theory aims to promote the understanding of processes that influence how we take up our roles in groups, how we exercise our authority on behalf of the task of the organization, and how we experience the organization as a whole. The quintessential element of the theory is this: Belonging to groups and organizations creates an underlying anxiety; to be a member of a group confronts us with the universal conflict of how one can maintain autonomy and one's individual striving while still remaining loyal and a part of the group. To cope with this anxiety, a variety of processes occur which we delineate here:

1. Every organization has a primary task around which the work of the organization revolves. Each organization has an external boundary which surrounds the organization. Generally when a person with a role provides services for individuals or groups, this person in role acts on behalf of the task of the organization. For example, lawyers in law firms act on behalf of the law firm to foster the primary task of providing competent, efficient, legal services to clients.

2. Organizations contain two levels of group processes: the overt level which is central to the implementation of the primary task, and the covert level which deals with the subjective experiences and processes within the organization. The overt refers to what is actually taking place, what is observable, the content of what is being communicated. The covert refers to what is taking place under the surface, what is implied and not stated, the process of what is being communicated. Oftentimes it is the covert, rather than the overt processes of board meetings or staff meetings which are the most riveting dynamics to watch and which impact, if not predict, the final outcome. Group relations theory attempts to understand these covert forces, in particular as they enhance or impede an individual's effectiveness and the primary task of the group.

3. The manner in which a person takes up work roles and performs primary tasks within organizations is influenced by how one experiences authority in the first group to which one belongs—that is, the nuclear family. As children, we learn and internalize representations of how parental authority is exercised. We observe the division of authority between our parents and began to build assumptions, expectations, and models of authority which we later import into our work setting. The assumptions, expectations, and models are internalized, that is, taken into our view of authority systems. They operate both on a conscious as

well as an unconscious level. From within this early family experience then, we come to understand how we are expected to act as women in authority, how we view other women and men in positions of authority.

4. Nonrational forces impact organizations. (In this chapter the authors chose to use the word *nonrational* rather than *irrational* because of the pejorative connotation of the latter.) As much as we would like to think that as individuals we operate rationally, logically, and objectively at all times, many of our behavioral responses are subjectively colored and nonrational in nature. The same is true for the groups of which we are members and the organizations in which we work. It is disquieting to think that the decisions we make in the workplace are based on both nonrational and rational processes. Yet, we participate in perpetuating these nonrational forces and are influenced by them out of a lack of understanding about them, by our inability to see them operating, or by our fears about changing them.

5. In our work setting, work is influenced by personal identities which include gender, race, ethnicity, and class, as well as our own individual history, needs, and behavior styles. "[T]he individual is a creature of a group, the group of the individual. Each, according to his capacity and his experience, carries within him the groups of which he has been and is a member" (Miller & Rice, 1975, p. 55). Personal identities influence the manner in which work is accomplished and the way in which stereotypical beliefs emerge about the gender, race, ethnicity, and class of others.

6. Within any group or organization, there are alliances and coalitions. For example, within a functional family group, parents form an alliance around which there is a permeable boundary in order to manage family life; the siblings form a coalition vis-à-vis the alliance of the parents. In dysfunctional family systems, the loyalties often cross generational lines, for example, where a parent is more aligned emotionally with one of the children than with their spouse (Minuchin, 1974).

Within functional groups, alliances form and change in support of the task of the group. However, working in groups and organizations challenges our individual autonomy and identity.

On a nonrational level women in their work worlds may fear being excluded from the group, not being connected with the power base of a group, being scapegoated, or being captured by the group. If unacknowledged, these fears may dictate their choices about which group to join. For example, members of an organization may vie for alliances and coalitions with individuals based on sentient connections, that is, based on relational needs, or with individuals perceived to have the power or the ability to enhance the "rise to power," such as in the example of the "woman behind the throne." Based on concerns of being either engulfed or abandoned, rejected or accepted, women may be drawn to the individuals or groups which feel protective, rather than to the individuals or groups with which the work task might best be accomplished.

7. To cope with the anxiety experienced in groups, group members use defense mechanisms, such as scapegoating, splitting, and projective identification. For purposes here, we will define "splitting" as the defense mechanism wherein a group member divides the world into all good and all bad; for example, that one member or subgroup within an organization contains all that is wrong within the group or organization, and one member or subgroup contains all that is good. We see this dichotomy in literature, movies, and other art forms. The more anxiety there is within an organization, the more the tendency to see people, groups, organizations, nations, in this light—either they are good or they are bad, there is no in between. Projective identification refers to a highly complicated process by which individuals and groups unconsciously deposit the split-off, unacceptable parts of themselves into other individuals in the group; and, within this unconscious collusion, the other individuals accept the projected attribute and act it out within the group.

How one uses and is used via projective identification relates directly to one's individual demographics, history, needs, and experiences. To the extent we unwittingly disown unwanted aspects of ourselves and take on unwanted aspects of others, we tacitly participate in a collusive process. This process serves to connect and, simultaneously, govern relations among those who comprise the group system.

For example, women are frequently scapegoated by becoming the group's "cute young thing," its "mother," its "cold bitch," or its "slut." Women may find themselves sitting dumbfounded, feeling competence and power ebb from their bodies as the "man" in the group, or the "gray-haired" person, or the "doctor," magically rises to stardom and becomes the group's leader—all-knowing and all-powerful. These are the experiences of scapegoating, splitting, and projective identification, and denote the inherent primitive wish to be taken care of.

An issue insufficiently engaged by women is that we do not readily accept our own participation in becoming victims. We sometimes collude in allowing ourselves to be scapegoated or by participating in scapegoating others, including other women, oftentimes having no conscious awareness of such. We do not acknowledge how we destructively edge out other women, our competitiveness, our wish to dominate and not collaborate.

8. Understanding power and authority issues within the organizations in which we work influences directly the manner in which we exercise our personal power and authority. Knowledge of these theoretical constructs makes us stronger and more aware, and gives us the ability to make previously unavailable choices about our identity and function in the workplace. Without this understanding we act in collusion to perpetuate the very patterns that we wish to change.

In summary, individuals bring to organizational life their character and identities, their individual perceptions of authority based on experiences in their nuclear families. Our relationship with authority is oftentimes a recapitulation of our early experiences with parental authority. Organizations have both rational and nonrational forces operating at all times; the alliances and coalitions of organizations are influenced by the nonrational fears and anxieties of the individuals within them. Clearly, women's understanding of the power and authority issues and relationships and awareness of the nonrational forces within their organizations will influence directly whether they will succeed in empowering themselves or others.

## Applications

Two examples will highlight the significance of scapegoating, splitting, and projective identification. One of the authors (B. B. W.) was asked to consult to a group at a group relations conference in California. Group relations conferences are uniquely designed to provide opportunities to study unconscious processes of organizational life, in particular the projections and fantasies surrounding leaders. Inevitably issues related to authority, power, gender, race, and sexuality become topics of discussion during the course of the conference experience. Typically, little personal data is known about the consultants. Characteristics the group knew about the author included her gender, her race, her role at the conference, her credentials, and that she was from Texas.

When issues of power and race began to surface in the group she was consulting to, the group members became quite anxious, not wanting to recognize their own sexism or racism. At a nonrational level, the men and women in the group sought to manage this uncomfortable experience by dissociating themselves from it and then attempting to induce it in the consultant. The consultant, being a Southern white woman in a position of authority, was the natural target for these primitive feelings. Should she have taken in and then acted out these projections—again, at a nonrational level—the group could feel relieved to know that she was the sexualized racist and they were not, that she was Bad and they were Good. Thus they could discharge their anxiety, deflate her power, and create a scapegoat for unwanted feelings. While this example occurred in a conference setting and may seem removed from the "real world," consider for a moment what it would be like if such a process did indeed occur to a female attorney in a law firm. Consider having the experience of being perceived as a racist, sexualized object of contempt rather than a competent legal professional.

The Clarence Thomas/Anita Hill hearings provide another excellent opportunity to apply group relations theory to our understanding of how covert dynamics in groups and institutions affect the outcome of a particular event. The Hill–Thomas hearings drew enormous media coverage and public fascination. Yet, for many, in the end it seemed to be understood as a problem located in either Judge Thomas or Professor Hill or between the two of them.

Applying the group relations model to the hearings, Noumair, Fenichel, and Fleming (1992) concluded that at a covert level, Clarence Thomas, Anita Hill, and the Senate Judiciary Committee were put forward by the nation to work through issues that we as a nation could not otherwise consciously address, such as issues regarding authority, leadership, and power. The authors hypothesized that when President Bush put forth Clarence Thomas as Supreme Court nominee, a nominee whose qualifications were questioned by the American Bar Association, the Judiciary Committee was faced with a moral dilemma regarding the authority of Bush. This tension was solved when Anita Hill came forward and these authority issues could be buried in the struggle between the individuals, Anita Hill and Clarence Thomas. In effect, Anita Hill and the accusations she made were the vehicle to avoid the more covert issues of authority, power and leadership.

Organizations and institutions often use women and other visible racial or ethnic group members to obscure the need for shared responsibility (Fouad & Carter, 1992; Noumair et al., 1992). Accused of seeing only a limited piece of the picture (for example, limited to only a woman's point of view or a Black's point of view), these individuals are then undermined, thus guaranteeing maintenance of the status quo. Putting up Anita Hill and then undermining her was vital to serve the nation's purpose of avoiding having to address directly the issue of President Bush's choice and the power balance between the legislative and executive branches; thus, the status quo was maintained. The authors write:

> Taking the allegations seriously would have meant recognizing and acknowledging Professor Hill's power. Powerful women engender powerful feelings. . . . Because any talk or focus on power engenders deep and primitive fears of mother, the group went to great lengths to keep Clarence Thomas, the all-male Senate Judiciary Committee, and the overwhelmingly male Senate body in power in order to control Anita Hill's power. A man's corrupt power is

still more tolerable than a woman's power, corrupt or otherwise. (pp. 384–385)

For the nation to have supported Anita Hill's success, would have meant that we were empowering her to lead the challenge against the white patriarchal structure of our culture and the homeostatic balance of gender and racial inequity in our country (Noumair et al., 1992).

## MEETING THE CHALLENGE

The politics familiar to women are those of being in the disadvantaged or inferior position. Women are less familiar with the politics of being in power. The politics of being in power require skills learned from living in a patriarchal society; they involve being competitive, "being your own man," being concerned with individual pursuits. Being "female" implies being in relationship, making career and personal decisions based on empathic relationships with others. In consulting to women attorneys, we have found that for them, accepting suggestions regarding political moves or strategies about how one might succeed in a male-dominated profession flies in the face of being honest, of telling the truth. Lerner indicates that women have a terrible aversion to planning strategies and moving politically through the workplace (1993).

Hope comes in many forms. It comes in mentorship programs where women can learn from the wisdom of senior women who have survived and thrived in this culture. Hope comes in changing our legal education system, our laws, and our professional codes of conduct. It comes in support groups for female attorneys, and it evolves through knowledge and education from fields of study that are not standard fare in the law school curriculum.

The professional world of law challenges us as women to reconsider our prior assumptions and to take a proactive role in bringing our profession to a better place; a place which fosters the professional lives of all people, men and women alike while, at the same time, serves the interests of contemporary society. We have no ready solution, certainly no easy answers. We do, however, offer several points to consider. Mindful that the source of the difficulties women encounter are complex and multifaceted, we focus here on what women individually can do; in our view this individual focus, not adequately addressed by women, is at the heart of any real change.

## Support Systems

A pervasive and crippling theme in the stories we have heard and read about professional women is that of feeling acutely isolated, as if the dilemmas and struggles experienced are individual problems to be faced alone. As we have discussed, many women experience significant struggles in the workplace related to their gender. We have found that women become empowered by sharing their experience and hearing the experience of others, whether in a pair, or in a group setting. We encourage women to seek out colleagues, both senior and peer, to provide a context in which they can become acutely aware of the similarities of experiences of women in the legal profession. Knowing that primitive group processes profoundly influence support groups, like any other groups, women can use group relations concepts and skills to manage these groups more effectively.

## Intuitive Development

In our traditional role as women, we have learned to be finely attuned to the needs of others; we readily identify their needs and feel drawn to respond. As a result, women have, in many instances, lost touch with their own experiences and needs. To meet the challenges of the external world, to change the status quo, and to empower ourselves and other women, we need to develop and trust our intuitive self. Quoting Duerk:

> To discover who she is, a woman must trust the places of darkness where she can meet her own deepest nature and give it voice . . .

weaving the threads of her life into a fabric to be named and
given . . . sharing it with the women around her as she comes to a
true and certain sense of herself. (1989, p. 21)

Women need to celebrate their many special talents and gifts,
while they should also reflect internally, discover, and perhaps
reclaim parts of themselves which they may not wish to
claim—that is, their dark side—envy, jealousy, self-hate. For instance, it would be considerably difficult, though extraordinarily
empowering, for a woman to bring into awareness the envy she
might feel toward another woman and to notice the internal pull
to subtly discredit the other woman to enhance her own position.
Equally difficult for some women is to acknowledge their own
contributions and to tolerate the envy and threat of alienation
that comes from such recognition. The more aware we are of
our internal experiences, the more enabled we become to make
reasoned choices about our behavior.

## Cognitive Development

As important as intuitive development is cognitive development,
not only in areas of substantive law, but in feminist theory and
group process. To learn about group process, to understand the
systemic pulls that inhibit the expression of female power, is vital,
not only for survival, but to ease the stress from the confusion
that one feels working in the legal profession. An understanding
of group processes, such as those discussed here, is critical to
sustaining cooperative organizational systems. Becoming more
aware of the covert and non-rational forces which impact our
work on a daily basis will enable us to mobilize our resources in
more effective ways.

## Finding Our Voice

Realizing the process by which women are silenced is helpful in
understanding the unsettling feelings that one has but cannot

articulate. For example, women often feel silenced by the implication that anything that is spoken with emotion necessarily must be crazy, hysterical, or castrating. The myth that a woman's emotional style renders her incompetent or ineffectual is generated out of a patriarchal culture and is incongruous with the reality that women can be emotional and speak with great clarity at the same time.

Of course, it would be unwise to publicly address everything that one observes without regard to context or consequence. The importance of being instrumental, of being political, is imperative. Equally important is finding one's voice. As Duerk writes:

> To come, each one of us, to our own voice . . . our own feminine voice. It is an enigma that when a woman first expresses herself, even if it is a matter for which she cares deeply, it may emerge in a false-masculine voice. It may state her matter factually, but without the shadings and overtones from her own life . . . without the nuance of her womanly feeling values. Or, if she is ill at ease, she may hand her script over to the animus and let him play the role for her, not out of her feelings, her relatedness and vulnerability, but out of an abstracted, polished, harder side of herself that feels a pressure to have all the answers, that has lost touch with softness, uncertainty, and weakness. (1989, p. 64)

Walking the tightrope of integrating male behavior styles while remaining true to one's femininity is an arduous task. However, doing so is critical to the development of skills necessary to function effectively in the workplace. For example, we believe it essential for women to be aware that from a group relations theory standpoint, not to register opposition to a particular event is tantamount to ratifying it. Thus, when witnessing a female colleague being treated badly by one of the power holders, women should search their consciousness to see whether they might be feeling fortunate that it was someone else and not them, and that if they had spoken, they, too, might have been treated badly. By being aware of one's experience as well as the concept that to remain silent ratifies the injustice, one will have enhanced abilities to make a reasoned judgment on how, when, and with whom to respond.

## To Stay or to Go

We have learned that many women may have placed themselves in work situations that do not fit with their intrinsic skills or values. For example, women committed to serving the public interest coming into law school, may have changed to litigation because litigation enjoys greater status than public law. Yet once in a litigation career, these women may feel alienated and less competent in the highly competitive, aggressive culture frequently found in this area of the law. As Stiver points out, "[I]t is crucial to help women see how deeply they have internalized assumptions, attitudes, and stereotypes of what is better, worse, valued, and not valued, based on a masculine model of success" (1991, p. 236). At the same time, we need to discover and affirm our own qualities as women and pursue career interests which reflect these values, even at the risk of disappointing others. It is important, whether or not we ultimately decide to leave, to reconsider our career choice in light of our values rather than solely in the light of the assumption that we're afraid or unable to perform the skills required.

## CONCLUSION

Women have effected tremendous changes as they have made their way in the legal profession. Women have both created and discovered sufficient support to enable them to continue in a field dominated by men. The efforts of women to find their voice and proactively change the status quo are largely enhanced by the ability to discover their inner selves, the ability to embrace their talents, as well as to acknowledge their dark side. By becoming aware cognitively and intuitively of how the system works, and by owning their participation in the processes that are destructive to their professional goals, women will find their power as we move toward connective leadership within the 21st century.

## REFERENCES

Acker, J. (1992). Gendering organizational theory. In A. J. Mills & P. Tancred (Eds.), *Gendering organizational analysis* (pp. 248–260). Newbury Park, CA: Sage.

Baker Miller, J. (1991). Women and power. In J. V. Jordan, A. G. Kaplan, J. Baker Miller, I. P. Stiver, & J. L. Surray (Eds.), *Women's growth in connection* (pp. 197–205). New York: Guilford.

Bayes, M., & Newton, P. (1985). Women and authority: A sociopsychological analysis. In A. D. Colman & M. G. Geller (Eds.), *Group relations reader* (Vol. 2, pp. 309–322). Washington, DC: A. K. Rice Institute.

Duerk, J. (1989). *Circle of stones.* San Diego, CA: LuraMedia.

Estes, C. P. (1992). *Women who run with the wolves: Myths and stories of the wild woman archetype.* New York: Ballantine.

Faludi, S. (1991). *Backlash.* New York: Doubleday.

Fouad, N., & Carter, R. T. (1992). Gender and racial issues for new counseling psychologists in academia. *Counseling Psychologists, 20*(1), 123–140.

Garcia, R. (1995). Eliminating gender bias: Let's do our part. *Texas Bar Journal, 58*(3), 273.

Gilligan, C. (1982). *In a different voice: Psychological theory and women's development.* Cambridge, MA: Harvard University Press.

Guinier, L., Fine, M., & Balin, J., with Bartow, A., & Stachel, D. L. (1994). Becoming gentlemen: Women's experiences at one ivy league law school. *University of Pennsylvania Law Review, 143*(1), 1–110.

Lerner, H. (1974). Early origins of envy and devaluation of women. *Bulletin of the Menninger Clinic, 38*(6), 538–553.

Lerner, H. (1993). *The dance of deception: Pretending and truthtelling in women's lives.* New York: HarperCollins.

Levinson, D., with Darrow, C., Klein, E., Levinson, M., & McKee, B. (1978). *The seasons of a man's life.* New York: Alfred A. Knopf.

Lipman-Blumen, J. (1992). Connective leadership: Female leadership styles in the 21st century workplace. *Sociological Perspectives, 35*(1), 183–203.

MacCrate, R. (1992). *Legal education and professional development—An educational continuum.* American Bar Association Section of Legal

Education and Admissions to the Bar; Report of the Task Force on Law Schools and the Profession: Narrowing the Gap. Chicago: American Bar Association.

Miller, E. J., & Rice, A. K. (1967). Systems of organization: Task and sentient systems and their boundary control. London: Tavistock.

Minuchin, S. (1974). *Families and family therapy.* Cambridge, MA: Harvard University Press.

Noumair, D., Fenichel, A., & Fleming, J. (1992). Clarence Thomas, Anita Hill, and us: A group relations perspective. *Journal of Applied Behavioral Science, 28*(3), 388–393.

Rioch, M. J. (1975). "All we like sheep—" [Isaiah 53:6]: Followers and leaders. In A. D. Colman & W. H. Bexton (Eds.), *Group relations reader* (Vol. 1 pp. 159–177). Washington, DC: A. K. Rice Institute.

Sheppard, D. (1992). Women managers' perceptions of gender and organizational life. In A. J. Mills & P. Tancred (Eds.), *Gendering organizational analysis* (pp. 151–166). Newbury Park, CA: Sage.

Stiver, I. P. (1991). Work inhibitions in women. In J. V. Jordan, A. G. Kaplan, J. Baker Miller, I. P. Stiver, & J. L. Surray (Eds.), *Women's growth in connection* (pp. 223–236). New York: Guilford.

Taylor, S., Bogdamoff, M., Brown, D., Hillman, L., Kurash, C., Spain, J., Thatcher, B., & Weinstein, L. (1979). By women, for women: A group relations conference. In G. Lawrence (Ed.), *Exploring individual and organizational boundaries* (pp. 123–133). New York: Wiley.

*Webster's third new international dictionary* (1993). Springfield, MA: Merriam-Webster.

West, M. L., & Sheldon-Keller, A. E. (1994). *Patterns of relating: An adult attachment perspective.* New York: Guilford.

# 11

# The Organization Woman

## Reflections of Society in the Workplace

*Edward B. Klein, Ph.D., Ellen E. Kossek, Ph.D.,*
*Joseph H. Astrachan, Ph.D.,*
*and Claudia H. Fleming, M.A.*

There has been little systematic work investigating gender and level differences with senior managers. Much of the research has been conducted with students in laboratory settings. Consequently, the professional literature is marked by attitude surveys, university based simulations, rating scale research, and theoretical formulations primarily based on men. Rarely has there been an informed discussion of work dilemmas based on the actual

*Acknowledgments.* This study was supported by the Levinson Institute. We would like to thank Laurence J. Gould, Judith L. Kirkeby, and Marcia Slomowitz for their assistance, and Lorna Volk for her typing.

experiences of women and men in authority in major organizations.

This is an important issue since the increasing number of women in managerial positions has led to a growing interest in understanding how people respond to women in authority. The literature on women in organizations shows mixed results in part because the prevailing corporate social structure includes the presence of unconscious bias toward competent women middle managers (Rosen & Jerdee, 1974). Women are subject to a high level of sex-role incongruence because the prevailing image of the corporate executive is masculine. Further, the generally amorphous criteria for performance at this level of management stimulates stereotypical thinking. As Nieva and Gutek (1980) note, women are more likely to be subject to bias when the situation is ambiguous, the job requires behavior that is sex-role incongruent, and the women are highly competent.

To understand reactions to female authority one can examine women in the organization by level: individual, group, intergroup, and system. On an individual level, a woman manager may not be sure how to enact her role because the presence of females in the executive suite is a relatively recent phenomenon (Harrigan, 1981). On an intergroup level, women are a minority group embedded within the larger organization (Alderfer & Smith, 1982). On a systems level, women are less likely to be hired, promoted, or paid as well as men (Tsui & Gutek, 1984).

These gender distinctions can be understood by applying a social psychological approach to roles. Bakan (1966) suggests that gender differences can be divided into communal and agentic aspects. The communal dimension refers to a concern for others: caring, nurturing, interpersonal sensitivity, and emotional expressiveness. The agentic dimension includes self-assertion, independence, and personal efficacy (Eagly, 1987). In general, men tend to be viewed as agentic and women as communal (Williams & Best, 1982).

In a four-stage theory of career development based primarily on male subjects, Dalton, Thompson, and Price (1977) label the later stages as mentor (developing others) and sponsor (broadening the organizational perspective). These are more communal in nature than earlier action-oriented stages. Similarly, adult development theory suggests that men at midlife and beyond are more concerned with others (mentoring at work, family, and community) and not as achievement driven as when they were younger (Levinson, Darrow, Klein, Levinson, & McKee, 1978). Research in non-Western cultures suggests that women at midlife are more independent and assertive, while men are more responsive and nurturant (Gutmann, 1981).

As the preceding review suggests, there may be differences in the communal–agentic dimension between managerial women and men in their work roles. There may also be level differences—older male executives may be more communal both developmentally and in their work roles—while younger male managers are more agentic. On the other hand, older female executives may be more agentic while younger female managers are more communal.

One area of study is leadership training; with enhanced global competition organizations are strongly supporting management training. More than a third of the educational budget in Fortune 500 companies is spent on middle and upper level employees (Stephen, Mills, Pace, & Ralphs, 1988). Unfortunately, there is a lack of research on gender in these training programs—in part because upper management historically has been a male domain (Fagenson, 1990).

Given the increasing number of women in managerial positions we conducted empirical studies with men and women leaders in major private and public organizations. After participating in one-week leadership seminars, men managers reported more positive affective reactions than women managers; the most positive reactions were reported by female managers who had female group leaders (Klein, Kossek, & Astrachan, 1992). In an expanded sample more learning was reported in follow-up questionnaires by executives than managers and by women executives than women managers (Klein, Astrachan, & Kossek, 1996).

We used a combination of majority–minority membership, communal–agentic role, and executive–manager level to provide an understanding of the findings. Male managers being the majority group were relaxed and learned more than women managers who were minority members at work and in the seminar.

Women managers may have felt more supported and empowered with a woman group leader in a position of authority and therefore learned more than when in groups with men leaders. Older executives in communal roles appeared more open to learning about the psychological aspects of leadership than younger mangers in agentic roles. Senior women executives who are more self-confident and in less role conflict were more open to learning than younger women managers.

Like most investigations, these studies were based on questionnaire responses to researcher designed instruments. In this chapter we directly explore managers' work dilemmas as indicated in their own case material which may provide insight into these findings. It is our hope that case analyses will generate hypotheses to be tested in future empirical research. For instance, cases written by women managers should illustrate the dilemmas experienced by women in their minority group status. Case analysis may also help in understanding differences in the experiences of older women executives and younger women managers. This clinical approach should be particularly helpful as more women advance in major institutions. This study contributes to our knowledge of gender and level differences by examining the actual work experiences reported by women and men leaders.

## SAMPLE AND METHOD

Five hundred and fifty participants from major companies and public organizations attended 14 separate training seminars held between 1984 and 1988—six for executives (vice presidents and above) and eight for managers. There were 5 women and 202 male executives and 35 women and 250 male managers reflecting the gender distribution at this high level in major organizations. The training included lectures and discussion groups. Before attending this prestigious program, each applicant was asked to submit a two-page typed case involving unresolved organizational issues to be reviewed in the discussion group at the seminar.

Cases were reviewed for whether the problem was with a superior, peer, or subordinate. The writing style was noted for emotionality, psychological involvement, and control. We checked as to whether the specific problem involved authority, motivation, reorganization, psychological contract violation, conflict or legitimacy. We noted whether the reported managerial style differences were due to age, gender, and race.

To review gender differences, all 5 women executives' and 12 female managers' (one-third of the women managers in the sample) cases were selected. A sample of five men executives and 12 male managers, matched for attendance at the same seminar and age were chosen for comparison. The sample results showed little difference in age, but men were more often married, with more children, had been with the organization longer, and were less likely to be in human resources or the public sector, than women. These results may reflect differences in career opportunities and/or preferences between the genders at this level in major organizations, and suggest some of the familiar costs women paid for achievement in the mid-1980s.

Even with this small sample there were some differences. Men, more frequently than women, tended to experience problems with subordinates and focused on changes in authority, difficulties in motivating others, reorganization, and violation of the psychological contract. Women tended to report more problems with superiors, their own legitimacy, and issues of age and gender. Although these trends make sense, none were statistically significant. Therefore, the following is a qualitative clinical analysis of the case material.

## CASE RESULTS

The following discussion first highlights overall gender differences. Seven cases, selected for heuristic purposes, are presented by major themes. These themes are: legitimacy, gender, age, emotional distance, and control. Material from the cases of four women and three men, with appropriate changes to protect confidentiality, are provided. Second, briefer quotes from two female executives are presented in order to illuminate differences by level.

## Overview of Findings for Managers

Some fairly consistent differences occurred between male and female managers. Most noticeably, over half of the women discussed gender and/or age as important work issues, while few men mentioned either one. Women managers tended to discuss interpersonal issues and to mediate between conflicting parties, rarely focusing on systems issues. Their cases were marked by a lack of mentors and questions of legitimacy reflecting their minority group status.

In contrast, men were goal-directed, felt empowered, and provided an organizational context for their situations. However, male cases were marked by greater emotional distance.

### *Gender*

Ms. Sarah Jones a 40-year-old manager in the public sector directly described sexism:

> I feel that in over 15 years with the agency I have developed a good balance of being demanding and supportive. I have gained respect based on my many accomplishments. There are few women above me in this powerful agency.
>
> Mr. Mitchell, my boss, is a 45-year-old Ivy League graduate who is macho and puts people down. Mitchell is a man of contradictions. But we have a good relationship. Yet, he has questions about accepting me as a senior manager. I don't get the endorsement that he willingly gives an equally competent male. I have to work harder to get ahead because I do not fit naturally in the male organizational world. Mitchell is sensitive about gender issues and careful in what he says to me. But, when the pressure mounts, his real sexist feelings come out. Mitchell is powerful and important in my career. How do I directly address this issue with him now?

Ms. Jones was realistic about organizational life. She was aware of how gender issues are played out around her career concerns. Ms. Jones had a sense of how far she had come, as well as an awareness of the strong obstacles ahead. Of the women managers, she most directly discussed her own experiences with sexism.

## Age

The next two cases involve age as discussed by a male manager and a female executive.

Howard Dyer was a 35-year-old manager in a major insurance company.

My case is about a 60-year-old employee. His name is John McMicken. He works as a computer analyst on the West coast. His job involves interpretation of complex data and interaction with lots of clients. The job has changed greatly in the past few years and is likely to continue at an even faster pace.

In 1969 John was moved from the field to a Western city where he did well. In 1981 there was an economic downturn. This, coupled with technological changes, made his job obsolete. Others made the transition to the newer technology. Several took early retirement. John was in the middle—not old enough to retire, but not ambitious enough to make the change. Over the past 5 years, John has been given training to help make the transition. The results have been disappointing.

After John's 60th birthday, I offered him an enhanced retirement package. He said he was not ready to retire and would improve. His most recent performance rating was unsatisfactory. I asked his supervisor to set specific performance improvement objectives for John to be completed in the next 60 days. I reviewed John's performance. He had made a sincere effort, but fell short of the specific objectives.

Now I have three options. First, dismiss him due to poor performance. Second, place John back in the field. This is unrealistic due to his age and being out of the field for almost 20 years. Third, offer him an early retirement with good outplacement services. I cannot continue to accept John's inadequate performance, although I feel for his situation. A final decision will be made in the next 3 months.

Ms. Joanne Smith, a vice president in the private sector, in her midforties, took a different tack in her discussion of an aging peer.

Mr. Wellington is a 62-year-old task oriented manager with lots of energy, a parochial viewpoint, and strong autonomy needs. I have a global outlook, but we need to cooperate. The problem has existed for 9 years. We have avoided it since it is draining. It affects my ability to perform and takes the fun out of work. The current strategy disturbs him. Wellington likes to do things his way. The new reorganization requires him to coordinate more with both local plants and headquarters.

At the end of the case Ms. Smith noted:

Wellington has limited outside interests. He works very extensive hours. Retirement, which is 3 years off, must be an uncomfortable perspective. The flexibility to change may be there. Our company encourages creativity in problem solving, but will not tolerate lack of accomplishment of its objectives.

This is a clearly stated case of an aging peer with a different management style who was causing problems. Although superiors tolerated the situation, enhanced competitive pressures seemed to demand action of some type. Ms. Smith was sympathetic towards her peer regarding his age, preretirement stage, and the personal effects of the reorganization. She had difficulty proposing a clear plan of action for someone with whom she was disappointed for not changing with the times.

Joanne Smith was more sensitive to issues of age than Howard Dyer. Dyer was aware of McMicken's age; despite this, he will decide, one way or another, in 3 months. Smith was more communal in her concerns about Wellington's life and clearly saw age as a factor in his emotions and work.

## Emotional Distance

Bill Sunshine was a 39-year-old executive of an energy company. His case illustrated how emotional distance is maintained in the split between friendship and work.

Mark Johnson and I have been good friends for over 15 years. Our families get together several times every year. For 10 years we were peers. Five years ago, I was promoted to head the organization. At this point, Mark reported to me.

Mark reacted favorably to this new relationship. However, the business began to expand and the need for strong leadership was apparent. I decided that Mark could not manage a rapidly changing department. I told Mark that we were going to expand his department, but that he would no longer be reporting directly to me because we were bringing in someone new. Mark was now second in command of the larger department.

Mark accepted this situation reluctantly and while he didn't undercut, he certainly didn't go out of his way to help his new boss. After 2 years, the new boss left. I made it clear to Mark that we were going to bring in a second new person to head up this department. Mark began to push for a split of the department so that both he and the new person could report directly to me. He attempted to use our friendship in this process.

Mark has a lot of talent and experience. We would like to take advantage of this. His current job as second-in-command is ideal for him if he will accept it. Through this process, I would also like to maintain my friendship with Mark, if possible.

There was emotional distance in this story as Bill tried to split his work relationship and friendship with Mark. Sunshine was in control, the job was first, friendship with Johnson was second.

## *Control*

Debbie South, a midthirties manager in the public sector illustrates lack of control when she described a relationship dilemma with her female boss and male ex-boss, who had become her boss's superior.

Two years ago Mr. Thomas was promoted to officer status. I helped him with interpersonal relations and to move up the agency ladder. Ms. North was one of five candidates to take Mr. Thomas's old position. She was chosen without input from Mr. Thomas. Ms.

North is a personal friend, who is a workaholic. She is exciting to work for, but so demanding that it is always stressful. Ms. North and Mr. Thomas were peers and are very competitive. I am caught in the middle between two powerful superiors. Ms. North questions my loyalty because I have tried to be friendly with Mr. Thomas; this leaves me feeling ineffective.

For the first time ever, I do not feel in control of my destiny. Yet, I feel I should give feedback to my boss. Ms. North is seen by others as stubborn and not likely to be influenced. Should I try? I find myself highly stressed and unhappy. I have been with the agency for 12 years and Ms. North will influence my career progress. I would appreciate any ideas that would help in this situation.

Ms. South's case demonstrated a number of themes. The story was told with great emotional involvement and a sense of little control. She mediated between parties and provided feedback to a competitive boss, who questioned her loyalty. She ended on a pleasant note, inconsistent with the feeling that her boss did not listen to her and personalized situations.

David Eaton was a midlife financial manager in the private sector. His case also illustrated the control issue.

My case begins 20 years ago when I started with the company. At the time, my responsibility was to provide financial support services to all departments. However, one department was allowed to develop its own independent support organization. From the beginning, conflicts arose over the direction that this department was taking in contrast to the total company. An adversarial relationship developed between myself and Mr. Little, the person responsible for supporting the single department. This continued for the next 10 years until my transfer to corporate staff.

About 5 years ago a corporate reorganization placed Little under my direct supervision. The problem that I now face is supervising Mr. Little who has not agreed with me. In my view, Little's past success with this single department was because of his full-time attention. The new broader reorganized service cannot be implemented with his approach.

The conflict remains and Little has threatened to quit. Senior management feels I should resolve these differences and Little should be retained, if at all possible. Except for this issue, Little is a hard worker and a good employee.

I am caught between keeping Little and resolving the conflict or forcing a resignation. Little has to give up his strategy or resign. I have now given Little the responsibility to formulate an overall plan for adopting my strategy and determining how to bring his functions into this plan.

In contrast to the previous case, Debbie South, who had little control, David Eaton demonstrated strong control. He expected Mr. Little to follow his strategy and do it his way, now!

## Legitimacy

Mary Weston, a marketing manager in her late thirties, in the private sector, presented a case which raises questions about legitimacy.

I've been with the company 7 years and have had rapid career growth. I was hired by and worked for Harold Meyers for 6 years. We had a fine work relationship, I was then promoted out of his department. After Mr. Meyers was promoted to V.P., I was to return to my old department in Meyers' former role as department manager. Two women staff, hired by Meyers within the last year while I was out of the department, requested a meeting before I became the department head.

They viewed me as a peer. They seriously questioned the value that I would add to the department and to their personal development. It was a difficult, frank, and honest discussion. I felt that although the situation was less than optimal, it certainly was workable as long as everyone continued to communicate openly.

One of the women got excellent evaluations from Meyers, but her current performance is not up to standard. She blames the performance difference on my style. I want this uncooperative woman to work hard and succeed, and not affect her coworkers and the department negatively.

The case ended on this note:

I believe I need to continue to work on performance with her. I have handled the situation successfully so far, but would welcome any insight that an outsider would provide.

Ms. Weston's case was marked by attacks on her legitimacy and authority. She was inappropriately made into a peer by subordinates. She ended with a request for assistance as she tried to nurture a somewhat hostile subordinate.

Men felt empowered, in control, and discussed systems issues more than women, reflecting their more secure majority group membership. As a group, the women managers focused on age and gender, had less of a sense of legitimacy, and were more concerned about fitting in than men, reflecting their embedded minority group position.

## Level and Gender Interaction

So far we have been looking at gender differences mostly among managers. Differences may also be affected by level. Therefore two brief cases of women executives are included to explore how level and gender interact.

Roberta North, a marketing vice president in the private sector, presented an impasse with a peer.

> We both agreed to a schedule, then Accounting said it was pulling support out because their people were needed on other corporate projects. The Accounting V.P. and I have been fighting about this for months. I met with his and my subordinates to help them share in the decision making, understand both viewpoints, and compromise to meet the two divisions' needs. Both managers agreed. The next day the V.P. suddenly changed his mind. We need to work together to control costs. The two of us have to facilitate cooperation. Accounting has a history of ignoring Marketing. But the issue is broader than Marketing, this situation has increasingly occurred over the past 5 years. Other divisions' needs have been ignored; Accounting *must* function in a more supportive way. A compromise is necessary; I'm willing, he is not.

The intergroup conflict was noted and was long-standing. It recently had affected a number of divisions. The other V.P. was not held accountable in the past. Now Ms. North was using her managerial skills to get both divisions to cooperate and invoked her authority with the male V.P.

Sherry Jung, a 42-year-old vice president in a major company described a case of discrimination.

I'm concerned about three managers: a woman administrator, her male boss, and a senior male manager. A personality clash between the woman and her boss has become a serious personnel problem for our company. She has filed a discrimination complaint. I told the senior manager to step in to ensure that the boss is not harassing the administrator. The senior manager has relinquished his authority and allowed the boss to act on his own. The woman wants to be reassigned. I want the senior manager to deal with the boss, not just move the woman to avoid using his authority.

Jung ended on this note:

The next steps depend on the actions of the senior manager. I don't plan to wait for the results of the discrimination case before acting.

This was a clear, concise, businesslike case. Ms. Jung was in control. She wanted an appropriate response from the senior manager and responsible behavior from the boss. Jung would not allow discrimination in her domain within this nationally prominant company.

The cases of men and women executives were similar but men managers displayed more of a sense of legitimacy and control than did women managers.

## DISCUSSION

The following discussion examines gender differences among managers, contrasts differences between males and females overall, and concludes with career development and work implications and research directions for the future.

In general, male managers were more emotionally distant than female managers. Women managers being in a token (Kanter,

1977) position at this level in the organization, expressed lack of control; young male managers rarely did. Possibly the male managers took it for granted that in "their" agentic work world they had control.

The most striking differences were the lack of gender conflicts or clearly stated control issues in the men's cases as compared to those for women. Most likely, these results were due to the minority group status of women in the world of work. In addition, these findings may have been due to sample differences. Even though we balanced the genders by seminars and age, more women worked in human resources or the public sector than did men. Given the influence of cultural norms for each gender, individual preferences, training, and career opportunities, these sample differences reflect societal and organizational realities in the 1980s and today as well.

American culture stresses instrumental behavior for men and expressive behavior for women. Historically, the assumption is that autonomous men are individuated and mature, while women with relational skills are weak, as noted by Gilligan (1982). But these cases indicate that mature women executives were self-assertive and combined interpersonal skills with the ability to make difficult decisions. They were also able to collaborate. These women executives were both goal directed and caring.

As Erikson (1959) notes, one needs a firm sense of self to be intimate. While younger women managers appear to have more difficulty combining their masculine and feminine aspects in the agentic world of middle management, older female officers seem better able to bring the instrumental and expressive parts together. It might be that midlife women officers can combine their feminine and masculine traits into a new strength in the communal work world at higher levels in the organization without the martial stress found in the lives of younger professional women in their thirties (Roberts & Newton, 1987).

Taking the above findings into account, we speculate that women's concern about interpersonal relations may have helped both fellow employees and the organization as a whole to work more humanely and effectively. Men, demonstrating little emotional involvement, may have been less effective in their interpersonal relations at work. Indeed, some men may have been attending the training program to improve their interpersonal skills.

There are several implications from these case analyses. Organizations can make business less stereotypically male by assigning younger women to roles with line authority—for example, managing plants, stores, and offices—rather than to staff roles supporting these activities. Such agentic roles provide experience for future promotions, contacts, and legitimacy. Executives need to make sure that young women aren't put into limited-growth positions or compartmentalized in human resource and/or staff functions. Well-meaning senior managers also need to resist the pressure to promote women before they are qualified. Such guilt-induced "social promotions" ultimately lead to a dead end.

Providing mentors is critical since the predominately male environment present in early management positions is often hostile to women. Women need support for their autonomy from superiors in order to develop their managerial capabilities (see chapter 8). But spurious or premature autonomy can be just as destructive as patronizing overprotectiveness. Given these gender sensitivities, an appropriate balance must be continually renegotiated.

We advocate open acknowledgement of the underlying issue of gender in the workplace in both formal and informal dialogue. Such steps should provide for more humane and effective management for everyone, as well as enhance organizational performance. Certainly it would serve to facilitate cooperation and self-confidence and decrease stereotypical thinking. For instance, a retreat in the first author's department, stimulated by women faculty, revealed common concerns among men and women about not being heard, taken seriously, or valued by the larger educational system. The similarities were striking and led to greater understanding and collaboration. Over time some of these positive outcomes diminished suggesting the need to continually address major systems issues.

Based on the qualitative clinical analysis of the case material, future empirical research can address the greater acceptance of women as they become less of an embedded minority group in middle management. Senior women executives will be more valued in the future than in their current token status. Male executives will become better mentors to both younger men and women as the upper levels of management reflect the more diverse larger society. We think this will happen because adult development theory and research find that both men and women at midlife are better able to balance their competitive and collaborative aspects; be more attentive and successfully mentor younger managers, even with the cross-gender problems noted by Kram (1983). Finally, one can study how midlife executives sponsor new organizational directions which address educational and psychological issues as well as economic and technological concerns.

## REFERENCES

Alderfer, C. P., & Smith, K. K. (1982). Studying intergroup relations embedded in organizations. *Administrative Science Quarterly, 27,* 35–65.

Bakan, D. (1966). *The duality of human existence: Isolation and communion in western man.* Boston: Rand-McNally.

Dalton, G. W., & Thompson, P. H., & Price, R. L. (1977). The four stages of professional careers: A new look at performance by professionals. *Organizational Dynamics, 6*(1), 19–42.

Eagly, A. H. (1987). *Sex differences in social behavior: A social-role interpretation.* Hillsdale, NJ: Erlbaum.

Erikson, E. (1959). *Identity and the life cycle.* Psychological Issues, 1, 1–171. New York: International Universities Press.

Fagenson, E. (1990). Perceived masculine and feminine attributes examined as a function of individuals' sex and level in the organizational power hierarchy: A test of four theoretical perspectives. *Journal of Applied Psychology, 72,* 204–211.

Gilligan, C. (1982). *In a different voice: Psychological theory and women's development.* Cambridge, MA: Harvard University Press.

Gutmann, D. L. (1981). Psychoanalysis and aging: A developmental view. In S. I. Greenspan & G. H. Pollack (Eds.), *The course of life: Adulthood and the aging process,* DHHS Publication No. (ADM) 81–1000. Washington, DC: U.S. Government Printing Office.

Harrigan, K. R. (1981). Number and positions of women elected to the corporate board. *Academy of Management Journal, 24,* 619–625.

Kanter, R. (1977). *Men and women of the corporation.* New York: Basic.

Klein, E. B., Astrachan, J. H., & Kossek, E. E. (1996). Leadership education: The impact of managerial level and gender on learning. *Journal of Managerial Psychology, 11,* 31–40.

Klein, E. B., Kossek, E. E., & Astrachan, J. H. (1992). Affective reactions to leadership education: An exploration of the same-gender effect. *Journal of Applied Behavioral Science, 28,* 102–117.

Kram, K. F. (1983). Phases of the mentor relationship. *Academy of Management Journal, 26,* 608–625.

Levinson, D. J., Darrow, D., Klein, E. B., Levinson, M. H., & McKee, B. (1978). *The seasons of a man's life.* New York: Knopf.

Nieva, V. A., & Gutek, B. A. (1980). Sex effects on evaluation. *Academy of Management Review, 5,* 267–276.

Roberts, P., & Newton, P. M. (1987). Levinsonian studies of women's adult development. *Psychology and Aging, 2,* 154–163.

Rosen, B., & Jerdee, J. H. (1974). Sex stereotyping in the executive suite. *Harvard Business Review, 52,* 45–58.

Stephen, E., Mills, G. E., Pace, R. W., & Ralphs, L. (1988). HRD in the Fortune 500. *Training and Development Journal, 42,* 26–32.

Tsui, A. S., & Gutek, B. A. (1984). A role set analysis of gender differences in performance, affective relations, and career success of industrial middle managers. *Academy of Management Journal, 27,* 619–635.

Williams, J. E., & Best, D. L. (1982). *Measuring sex stereotypes: A thirty-nation study,* Beverly Hills, CA: Sage.

# 12

## Feeling the Work in One's Bones

### Self-Authorization and Group Dynamics from a Woman's Perspective

*Vivian Gold, Ph.D.*

The study of women and authority raises questions about why leadership in politics, business, literature, science and written history has generally been by men. Is there something inherent in women's psychology and biology which has led them to choose not to compete for leadership positions or to define social reality? Is it a social systems issue, in which opportunity is not provided by tradition and practice, and punishment is the consequence of nonconformity to a patriarchal social order? A strength of the Tavistock approach to group relations is that the focus is on both the group as a whole, with its interconnectedness of roles, and the personal experiences and responsibilities of the individuals who comprise the group. This chapter, focusing on the self-authorization of women within social systems, explores the interconnections between the experiences of women in their bones, a metaphor for the deepest internal space, and the social systems in which women seek authorization for leadership.

Consultants at the Tavistock Institute developed an approach to groups and organizations which emphasized social systems theory, analysis of the "group as a whole," and a probing of unconscious aspects, which will be described here with the metaphor of "deep-sea diving" into group dynamics. These professionals were mostly men, with some women learning group relations from men and transmitting it to the general public. Group relations conferences provide a microcosm of social learning experiments in which dynamics and authority relationships in groups and organizations can be examined.

This paper explores the roles of women in the work, not only in the mentoring and the induction of women into the organization, but also in changing what is learned about the dynamics of institutions. It offers some observations about the process of women entering the work, how they have been chosen and mentored, and what these factors imply. The process of women authorizing themselves within the microcosm of group relations work parallels the process of women being authorized by the self and by institutions in the macrocosm of larger organizations and politics. The foundation for this paper is my experience as a consultant to various organizations, as well as my work experiences in the A. K. Rice Institute (AKRI) in America and in group relations conferences in various countries.

Many women, as well as men, have a proclivity for doing group relations work, for deep-sea diving into the unconscious aspects of groups and social organizations. However, mentoring, authorization, and generative issues have been experientially linked to gender and sexual politics. What will happen as women use their own perspectives to define and to understand group dynamics? Is the work experienced differently once women are self-authorized? Will this change the work itself? Will there be development of different theories and approaches to how one conceives of the work? Until the time that women are both fully authorized by the organization and self-authorized, they cannot transform the work in major ways. Once one owns the work fully, feels it in one's bones, then the quality of the work may shift. In reaching these conclusions I have been influenced by women's literature and thinking, as well as by formulations from within the Tavistock and analytic communities.

## BASIC ASSUMPTIONS REVISITED

The unconscious aspects of group life described by Bion (1959) are known as "basics assumptions." The group assumes one of three stances: (1) basic assumption of dependency; (2) basic assumption of fight–flight; and (3) basic assumption of pairing, all of which are emotional stances toward leadership. Later, Pierre Turquet added a fourth basic assumption, the basic-assumption "oneness" group, in which the group has an oceanic sense of oneness with the universe (1974). The basic assumptions are viewed as concurrent to the work group, which is connected to the primary task of the organization. While the group may be enhanced by the basic assumption if it is related to the primary task, such as dependency in a church, or fighting in an army, the basic assumptions have been seen more often as detrimental to or avoiding the work of groups and organizations. I wish to revisit each of the basic assumptions here, in order to look at them in their relation to issues of gender. One's gender and the group's perception of it make a difference in how the basic assumptions are experienced in groups.

Dependency, the first basic assumption, is the area of life that has often been relegated to women. Melanie Klein's work (1957) on infant dynamics profoundly influenced group relations theory. It is not a coincidence that a woman with understanding of preoedipal phenomena provided the key conceptualizations which enable the regressive aspects of groups to be understood. However, my impression is that the early interpretations of dependency phenomena overemphasized envy, rage, and destructiveness, and omitted experiences of fulfillment and gratitude. Thus, "bad breast" phenomena were generally interpreted, and "good breast'' phenomena were often ignored. This may be based on a stance in which nurturance was taken for granted or denigrated. Early writings on collaboration in groups (i.e., Gustafson & Cooper, 1985) did address this unbalanced focus, but the descriptions were based on a cognitive, mastery level, rather than on the affective dynamics which were the core of Kleinian interpretations.

The focus on deprivation, disappointments, and rage involves a denigration of nurturance, which represents an unconscious misogyny present in the early theory. Dependence was interpreted negatively, stressing the helplessness, impotency, and disowning of one's own abilities and projecting them onto someone else. With the cultural glorification of independence, this negative bias toward dependency continues to be rife today. To enter a group or organization as a member is to encounter the realm of dependency and nonmastery and to project one's own powers onto the consultant or other figure of authority. Jean Baker Miller (1976) was one of the first authors to analyze the American myth of independence, and she stressed interdependence in a way that is reflective of a greater acceptance of dependency needs.

In conference work, I consult to groups about the positive aspects of nurturance and holding when this appears to be occurring, as well as about the fragmentation and destructive elements of dependency. This interpretative stance relates to a female comfort with nurturance and sees the potential for empowerment engendered by initial willingness to enter into feelings of vulnerability and dependence.

The next basic assumption to be reviewed here is fight-flight. Stereotypically, men are most often pictured as fighting for work, or as fighting or competing among themselves for women. Women are pictured as more passive or indirect in their fighting stances. In conferences, fight–flight dynamics are just as feisty, aggressive, and destructive in women, although women's style may be perceived differently. Anne Campbell (1993) wrote a book titled *Men, Woman, and Aggression,* describing cultural differences in the expression of anger by gender in street violence, in marriages, and in work. She describes men as viewing anger as instrumental, and aggression as a means to power. Women in general view anger as expressive, but also often see it as embarrassing and to be avoided. Her studies and formulations from naturalistic settings concur with my own impressions from early group relations conferences, in which men were most often prominent in the fighting, while women more often were witnesses, or instigators, or in flight. Tavris (1992), on the other hand, describes data showing that men and women are not opposites in issues of aggression, but behave in a variety of manners depending on context and how the behavior is defined and measured. During the past 20 years in group relations conferences, fight leaders of both genders emerge in roles previously associated with the opposite gender. The conferences provide opportunities to become aware of the projection of violence or aggression onto others, whether they be members of particular ethnic groups, or a particular gender. The conferences allow women as well as men to own their own aggressive impulses, and to express them in ways that may be empowering, as well as destructive. What has often emerged is that women have learned to fight in indirect ways, with women having experienced direct fighting as either noneffective or subject to severe punishment. The positive aspects of fighting, and what makes fighting "fair," are only beginning to be explicated by women for women.

Current images in literature of woman as warrior are relevant to women's roles in fight–flight dynamics in groups. These images often emphasize a woman claiming her power. An example is in *The Woman Warrior* by Maxine Hong Kingston (1976), a novel which presents a Chinese American woman using fantasy in her struggle for sanity and power. In *Women Who Run with the Wolves* (1992) Estes notes that a woman's ability to fight may be regained through ancient myths which legitimize her fighting nature in ways which do not masculinize it. These images involve a reconceptualization of anger and fight dynamics as empowering for women.

On the negative side, competition among women can be quite ferocious, resulting in either their being eliminated or their fleeing from the task. In addition, the lack of competition by both women or men can stifle a group and lead to an absence of leadership. While Horner (1972) presented research showing that women have a greater fear of success than men, later research suggested that fear of success and problems with competition are also prevalent among men, with no replicable differences by gender (Canavan-Gumpert, Garner, & Gumpert, 1978). Tavris (1992) writes about how gender differences faded quickly with changing times, as was the fate of "finger dexterity" when males got hold of computers and "fear of success" when females were admitted into law schools. My own work with men's groups in a Veteran's Administration Hospital has provided much clinical material showing that men's fears of success and failure are similar to women's.

Aries's (1976) research showed that women who are verbal in all-female groups become silent in mixed groups. However, her later research (1982), revealed that women initiated more interaction than men in mixed groups, a finding that marked a change from her past research. She stated that a content analysis of the interaction showed traditional sex differences along task-oriented versus social–emotional lines. Thus, there appears to be an increase in the visibility of women entering the public arena and fighting for their beliefs, but the content or the values that are being fought for may be different for women than for men. In brief, the fight–flight dynamics are present in both men and women, but their style and meaning may be different for each gender, and thus a woman may have a different impact as a warrior than a man as a warrior.

Gender issues can also be examined in the pairing basic assumption. The pairing of members of the group, with its hope for rebirth, creativity, and messianic renewal, can occur whether the pairs involve a man and a woman, two men, or two women. However, when issues of homosexual and heterosexual pairings are fully explored in conferences, traditional assumptions about gender and authority are challenged. Often in the past the leader who emerged in a pairing basic assumption was male, and the woman was chosen, or chose herself, to complement him in his leadership role. This tended to produce a comfortable familiarity in the group, with hopes for a productive future. Traditionally, women have often entered leadership roles through being paired with a powerful male. In contrast, when women assume the leadership role in a pair, they are often seen as frightening. There may be fears of women as the dominant member of the pair, with castrating images resulting in feelings of vulnerability and shame projected onto the male consort, making pairing fantasies frightening for both genders. On the other hand, the pairing coming from the women as relational rather than dominating, can create illusions of fertility and productivity that are comforting.

Perhaps the most disquieting images for many participants emerge in groups when the pairing is homosexual. Much of our basic social structure revolves around gender assumptions which are connected to heterosexual pairing. Homosexual pairing creates images and metaphors which jar many people's vision of their own gender identity. This is connected deeply to cultural prohibitions within the Judeo-Christian traditions, which link a woman's identity and place in society with a "proper" pairing with a man, and tremendous fears and negative reactions to her sexuality when she is not in a heterosexual pair. Likewise, male pairing evokes images of male vulnerability to attacks of sexual aggression, a vulnerability heretofore seen as limited to women. This accounts for the occurrence of phobic reactions to homosexual pairings. In group relations conferences, fantasies about various kinds of pairing can be explored and demystified, making various linking more conceivable as a basis for fertile, collaborative work.

I will touch only briefly on the fourth basic assumption, the oceanic feelings of oneness raised by Pierre Turquet. This oceanic feeling of utopia in a group can be viewed as a splitting of experience into "good breast" phenomena, in which all the world is good. The opposite feeling, one of panic or terror of annihilation in groups, can be viewed as the other side of this basic assumption. This may be linked to experiences in groups of death and rebirth, which will be metaphors raised later.

In addition to providing a different, feminist perspective on the basic assumptions, women entering the organization or group with their own voice may create a change in the value ascribed to work, as opposed to other aspects of group life. The traditional or masculine view is to place the importance of work above the basic assumption life of the group. Basic assumptions are seen as possibly aiding the group, but as more likely to get in the way of the work. A feminist model suggests placing unconscious phenomena and basic assumptions side by side in relation to consciousness and tasks. This challenges some of the major cultural assumptions, in which doing and productivity are more highly valued than nurturing and procreating, which are seen as more irrational. "Doing" is valued over "being." In our culture, the rational is valued over the terrifying and dangerous irrational.

It is possible that unconscious phenomena become more terrifying as they are split off and repressed. In a Jungian perspective, consciousness itself has been linked to the masculine and unconsciousness to the feminine. I disagree with this formulation, which I attribute to the prevailing, cultural views of reality as being written by men. It makes the feminine more unknown, and therefore more frightening and terrifying, if also more idealized and intriguing. The images of the terrifying Medusas and Circes who cause men to lose themselves can be heard echoing in the images raised in the groups of male veterans that I work with daily, images of seduction and abuse often used as excuses for the outbreaks of violence that are seen by the men as a reaction to women's power. Also, a denial of one's perhaps unconscious prejudice and stereotypes, often leads to an even greater oppression of the other. If unconscious group processes are more known, studied, and experienced as legitimate, they will command more respect and at the same time be less frightening and demonized.

Certainly analysis and group relations work are attempts to dive deeply into unconscious material, and to become aware of how it impinges on group life. I am suggesting a different way of framing the relationship between these aspects of group life, the basic assumptions, and the work on tasks. This is a perspective which values basic assumption phenomena as highly as work, and places them side by side, rather than in a vertical, hierarchical relationship to one another. It would lead to valuing interrelations of people in organizations as highly as the product of the organizations. It is my contention that this approach would lead to increased productivity in meeting human needs, rather than increased productivity in alienated work, in which the majority of the people feel out of control, whether as workers or consumers. It would require reexamination of the priorities of what work is important.

## MENTORING

Group relations work, which previously was a predominantly male field, in many aspects parallels male–female relationships in the larger society. A common factor in the early history of group relations work concerns the selection of the women to work in conferences. Women had traditionally been paired with male mentors who invited them onto the staff. In the late 1960s and early 1970s, I perceived that many of the women chosen to work on staff were involved in personal relationships with male consultants. It was only after the women's movement entered the awareness of leaders within AKRI that women were sought based on criteria other than pairing or tokenism. Women were increasingly sought out as issues of gender and authority began to be more consciously explored.

The women's movement created a profound change in how conference staff were chosen. The demand for female staff increased enormously. As the movement encouraged women to define their own lives and visions, the authorization of women became an issue in group relations work during the 1970s and 1980s. For example, there were special workshops on women and authority on both the East and West coasts, initiated by Zeborah Schactel, a senior A. K. Rice consultant, and others. There were separate group relations conferences studying gender at Yale University, Columbia Teacher's College, the City University of New York, and Northwestern in Chicago, summarized by Cytrynbaum and Hallberg (1993). The staffing of conferences changed, with a more equal gender representation.

Some of the early work on gender issues involved men appointing women to positions of authority and using them to study the effects of gender. However, for women to enter fully into the work and effect change, it was not sufficient that they be involved because men chose them as the correct thing to do.

At times, during a transition period as more women entered
the work, the pairing dynamic was replaced by an angry,
fight–flight dynamic. Some women were concerned about the
political relationships in the organization; for example, who was
being appointed to direct at a national level, and how women
were treated within the organization. This reactive, fight–flight
dynamic no more allowed women consultants to consult from
their own experiences than the previous pairing had done. As
an example, in my own experience, I found myself taking an
argumentative stance, which was heartfelt and based on real work
experience. I began to question some of the premises of the work
itself, and while I found each consulting and managing experience within the organization rife with learning for myself and
others, I developed a deep ambivalence about the work in which
there was a danger of throwing out the baby with the bath water.
I questioned the focus on authority issues as it was traditionally
presented. At the time, I was often unable to clearly explicate
issues while maintaining the creative core of the work. This angry
stance was no more productive of the freedom to develop my own
thinking, formulated from conference experience, than pairing
would have been. However, it was an important part of my own
process of differentiation, during which these ideas were perco-
lating.

Experiences in Israel enabled me to witness the development
of the work, authorization and mentoring, another time around
(Gold, 1993). It is not surprising that similar dynamics of mentoring occurred in Israel in the 1980s, especially since conference
dynamics present a microcosm of the larger society, and Israel is
very patriarchal. In an Israeli sponsoring board of five men and
four women, I was the only woman not married to another board
member. There were three couples; it was clear that the member
of the pair originally chosen was the man, although the women
were competent professionals in their own right. My own ability
to remain within the group was linked to a bond with Eric Miller
of the Tavistock Institute. It took me several years to feel that I
had entered into effective work ties with my Israeli colleagues.

There is another sponsoring group in Israel, in which the
early leadership was composed of four women, whose meeting at

a conference in Zagreb, Yugoslavia with two senior men led to its creation. The gender experiences here were different from those within my organization, but the linkages with male mentors and succession issues were also important.

I have chosen to focus on a particular aspect of mentoring here—that of men mentoring women. I am not including such issues as who chose and mentored the men. The writing of Levinson, Darrow, Klein, Levinson, and McKee (1978), is illustrative of the importance of mentoring on the male experience of adult career development.

There have been a number of articles written about how women are mentored. In particular, Rosabeth Moss Kanter, in *Men and Women of the Corporation* (1977) illustrates how women function in corporate authority structures. Kanter indicates that there are differences between the ways in which women, in contrast to men, are authorized in corporations. These differences are not only in how the women are chosen and perceived, but in how the internal perceptions and experiences of the women affect the ways in which they perceive and execute their authority. Kanter indicates that the three variables which relate to leadership positions in the corporation are opportunity, power, and tokenism. Those women working in the corporation often perceive themselves as having less opportunities, see themselves as less powerful, and find themselves having to devise coping strategies to deal with their token status.

Early research on gender emphasized the role incongruity of women in authority in a withholding, nonnurturant stance, and the dread and difficulty experienced by both men and women with females in the unaccustomed authoritative role (Cytrynbaum, Lee, & Wadner, 1981). They report that women need to be aware of covert processes which undermine women in authority, such as providing responsibility with little authority, appointing women to positions for which they lack skills, and perceptions of women in a distorted fashion. Despite women's difficulties in positions of authority, a study by Correa et al. (1988) found that women consultants produce more member learning than do more experienced male consultants, with male members learning the most. A further article summarizing gender research by Cytrynbaum (1995) emphasized contextual issues of women in authority accounting for variability in research results.

The context elaborated on here is that the majority of the people creating the work in conferences, as well as in the outside world, were men, despite a gradually increasing participation by women. Most often, in the beginning, the women were being mentored by men. Hennig and Jardim, in *The Managerial Woman* (1977), noted how the first wave of successful women had identified and obtained permission for success from their fathers rather than their mothers. This correlates with the traditional pathway in Western culture of women receiving men's blessing in order to work. These women may be seen in mythological, Jungian terms as "Athena" women, springing from the head of Zeus, their father in the workplace. It is necessary for women not to work "out of the head of Zeus," but rather to be wise in their own right. They need to remember Metis, the often forgotten mother of Athena, goddess of wisdom, who was swallowed up by Zeus. Women have their own source of wisdom, and it does not need to be discounted or usurped by men.

In AKRI, women disgruntled and/or intrigued by the roles that they had played in conferences and institutional work, have organized as a separate constituency. Gradually, more women have played major roles in the creation and development of the work. With a female president of AKRI recently elected, we will have the new experience of women in authority being a significant factor in the organization, and should be able to explore the effects of this shift in organizational development.

In a 1993 international meeting in Australia of organizations sponsoring Tavistock group relations work, women described how they generally wait for suggestions from men or from the organization before embarking on a project, rather than initiating major projects themselves. Women organizing themselves to share this information has led to women encouraging other women to initiate work as they actively seek institutional authorization for work they deem worthwhile.

The ways in which women enter the workforce are authorized by the organization, and are mentored, profoundly affect how their work is experienced by both themselves and by others.

## BALANCE BETWEEN CONSCIOUS AND UNCONSCIOUS PROCESSES

This section addresses how the balance between conscious and unconscious processes has been studied at recent conferences in California where I have been the Director or Associate Director. I will focus on the effects of two shifts: (1) the emphasizing of the unconscious, basic assumption process equally with the conscious, cognitive work task, and (2) the valuing of the administrative elements of the conference, which are nurturing in a material sense, along with the cognitive, interpretative input which is embodied in consultation.

Until recently, this reconceptualizing of conference dynamics which values unconscious on a par with conscious processes was only theoretical, although the Tavistock approach of focusing on unconscious dynamics has been a consistent, defining part of the work from its inception. The conferences which involved a shift in conceiving the relationship between conscious and unconscious material were very difficult and challenging. They led to the staff doing considerable soul searching while retaining the tasks of studying the complexities of group, intergroup, and institutional phenomena. As painful as this learning was, the willingness to delve into the unconscious material and to value it as highly as structural and institutional phenomena enriched the learning experience.

In one conference I was the Associate Director. An important dynamic was the dominance of male psychiatrists in the sponsoring institution. One psychiatrist was the Conference Administrator, who appeared in a dream of the Director as the Associate Director. The dream was brought into the preconference staff work, and it foreshadowed the ambivalence by which I had been authorized by the Director, and my difficulty in taking up the managerial aspect of the Associate Director role.

A striking aspect of this conference was the difference in how I experienced the large-group work, in which I felt fully authorized as a consultant, and the role constraints of being the Associate Director. In writing this paper, I present myself as a confident advocate of self-authorization in women. In the conference, however, I found my ability to remain in a self-authorized stance very difficult. This is an illusion of the complexity of maintaining a self-authorized stance in the midst of organizational dynamics with many stresses and projections upon the person in role.

I began the conference feeling cooperative and pleased to be there. As the conference progressed, with its demands for the maintenance of organizational structure being balanced by demands to delve into unconscious dynamics, there was much more role strain. There were times in which I felt like a steel rod, holding together a focus on the time boundaries, unable to see the forest for the trees, feeling I was carrying too much rationality. This sense of loss of self I likened to a type of dying, being present but not fully myself. Only when the staff and members began to own their own projections, was I able to return to feeling like my usual self. The process of feeling split off, containing too much of the structural, rational elements, was painful for a woman who emphasizes irrational aspects. The struggle to be re-born in the service of the work required a diminishing of myself, remaining in a receptive mode, allowing staff and members to work through their projections, and regain both instrumental and affective aspects of themselves. This in turn enabled me to return to a more integrated sense of myself. I was aware that my containment of the rational focus at the expense of the emotional was due in part to the Director's willingness to go with the irrational and emotional materials. I believe this enabled members to explore depths of feelings and fantasies which can only occur when the unconscious elements of the work are fully honored and worked with to the best of staff and member abilities.

These events were followed by conferences that I directed with an equal valuation on basic assumptions and work, on unconscious and conscious phenomena. I became aware of the ebb and flow of my own abilities to be self-authorized, especially when the authorization from the system appears to be unclear. Not only was I struggling with my own issues of self-authorization, but I was, as systems theory would predict, involved in larger systems issues of the sponsoring organization. The issues involved struggling with whether the "innovations" of attempting to balance the conscious and unconscious materials were so radical that the "traditional" approaches to Tavistock work were being trampled. Fortunately, I was able to see this struggle in a humorous perspective, thanks to my long-term associates within Tavistock work who would question being characterized as representing "tradition" rather than "innovation." Miller (1985) described the process of projection in political processes of organizational change, in his work on the politics of involvement. Thus, the shifts of emphasis which may be related to gender issues—such as balancing the valuation of conscious and unconscious processes—are enacted within the political dynamics of the organizations in which they take place. This is illustrative of the complex interaction between self-authorization and institutional authorization which is always at play within social systems.

Another area of study is the role of administration in recent group relations conferences, and the pressures carried by this aspect of organizations (Gold, Hayward, & Lee, 1995). The negative projections about dependency often are acted out or displaced toward the conference administrators, who provide the material containment and nurturing that occur. The longing for creature comforts, recognition, and feeding are often accompanied by feelings of shame and humiliation when one's needs are unmet. Having a woman in authority intensifies the confrontation with unmet fulfillment of expectations and "bad breast" phenomena. However, a shift in focus which allows us to see the many facets of the dependency issue brings a different emphasis to the physical work which provides the material basis to allow the enterprise to proceed. In this example, I have focused on the unconscious, gender-related projections onto a particular part of organizational systems, the administration, and not only on the gender of the persons in the role. By understanding and valuing gender-related unconscious dynamics, we are able to refine our understanding of the work itself.

My personal experiences in group relations conferences, as described above, have contributed to my adult development and have helped me to be more comfortable with issues of self-authorization. I find myself more capable of negotiating institutional authority and more comfortable dealing with projected dependency, competition, and envy. I will now describe some applications of these ideas to the workplace.

## APPLICATIONS TO ORGANIZATIONAL WORK

The power of defining the primary task of an organization, and of understanding how unconscious dynamics influence the performance of the primary task, is central to the contributions of the Tavistock approach to organizational work. Insights from my own experiences in various conference roles have led me to reconsider how gender might affect the definitions of work within organizations rather than only who does what work. As women enter executive positions in organizations, they would be empowered to define work priorities.

The changes to which I am referring include the quality of personal and institutional authorization which need to be reconsidered to create a less alienated workplace. Studies of the changing workforce have often emphasized changing demographics, without considering whether the demographic change will also change the work structures which now exist. Tavris (1992) described how the changes of the industrial revolution which transformed the United States from an agrarian society in which both men and women worked in the home, brought about changes in appropriate role behavior differences for men and for women. In particular, she attributes the current stereotypes of men as less emotionally expressive than women, and women as less active and instrumental, as a result of the work demands in large industrial organizations where men predominate, especially at higher levels of the organization. I am suggesting that bringing more of oneself into work, the emotional and physical as well as the mental, will change work for both men and women.

Merely placing women in positions of authority does not change the manner in which the work is done. The examples of Margaret Thatcher in England, Golda Meir in Israel, or Indira Ghandi in India, did not lead to different governance. However, successful women leaders become precedents for others who may take up these roles in new ways. Women entering executive positions in more than token numbers, and men having to consider family as their own direct responsibility, may redefine the work day, how time is spent, the way childcare is handled, and how people balance their needs for work and relatedness. Also, women entering into top management in enough numbers may change the projections and fantasies of how top management needs to behave to be effective.

The resistance of organizations to allowing women to penetrate the "glass ceiling" may be explained by male fears that the definition of work will change if women break through barriers and are authorized in leadership roles. Naomi Wolf's book, *Fire with Fire* (1993), which describes women as having succeeded in winning the gender battles, may be premature. She is effective in elucidating the problems associated with women portraying themselves as victims, and the advantages of emphasizing the empowerment that women have already accomplished. However, to date, the processes necessary for women to become empowered in business have only just begun.

Kathleen Kelley Reardon, in *They Don't Get It, Do They?* (1995) describes ways in which women may learn to acquire more authority in the workplace, and to get beyond the "glass ceiling." She shows how the subtle communication patterns between men and women prevent women from exercising full effectiveness when they do enter management positions. However, in her description of the route to top levels of management, she does not suggest that women would contribute to different definitions or authorization of work in organizations if they were in positions of greater power.

It is not clear that women in positions of management in business organizations will be the women who will redefine ourselves and social reality. Much controversy surrounds the issues of whether women really are different from men or whether these supposed differences are merely social constructs, projections, and cultural definitions. Group relations conferences give deep, first-hand experiences into the creation of vivid, intergroup, social realities from fantasies, and the processes of transformation which can take place as people withdraw their projections and become aware of other viewpoints. Often, the most clarifying insights come from the "outsider," not the management of the conference. Likewise, some of the most interesting literary versions of effects of gender have come from women who are marginal to positions of power. Bell Hooks (1990), in *Yearning: Race, Gender, and Cultural Politics,* is an example of a woman using postmodern theory and her experiences being black and female to describe her visions of culture.

Another area of controversy involves associating women with nature, or the body. As stated previously, women have been connected with nature in a derogatory or an idealized manner in the past. Part of the women's movement of the 70s involved the attempt to sever that assumed connection so that women could more readily enter into fields of work previously the province of men. Griffin (1978, 1995) documented the historical male writing which had connected woman and nature in a derogatory way, and she juxtaposed this to women's connection with nature from both deep within and outside herself. It is my view that men also have potential for deep connections to their internal states, and to nature. However, often in creating a political and social reality that is divorced from the personal feelings from within and from nature without, men have not valued being in touch with these elements, and have often sacrificed these parts of self to "higher" tasks. It is from this feminist social view that I redefine a task of organizations to include applications of ecology and respect for the environment.

Another application of understanding the gender-related dynamics of groups would be to reevaluate various intergroup relations in organizations, taking into account a woman's point of view. The current health care crisis has affected the ways in which both doctors and nurses, as well as administrators, interact in health care systems. Administrators have gone from being in the service to the professionals who were in service to the patients, to being primarily in charge of managing our hospitals and even the practices within doctors' offices. There is an increase in the percentage of women doctors, and male nurses. However, the actual time spent with individual patients and the nurturance given to them when they are sick has been curtailed enormously, by both doctors and nurses. In order to transform the hospital setting, management would have to value the nurturing, "healing" elements of health care as highly as the time-management, production elements. This is parallel to valuing a "basic assumption" dependency in health care, while at the same time being cognizant of the potential destructiveness of regressive dependency. There would have to be some fight–flight behavior in hospitals in the struggle to make these changes possible. And there would have to be some collaboration among staff and between staff and patients, in a pairing sense, before these changes could be actualized.

## IMPLICATIONS OF WOMEN BEING FULLY AUTHORIZED

Self and institutional authorization of women will lead to structural and experiential changes, both in group relations conferences and in their applications. For this to occur, women must feel the work in their bones, at the deepest levels of their being. Only when this occurs are women free to fully engage in the work and be creative.

To value and to learn from one's bodily experiences and to relate these to group and institutional phenomena is a shift in cultural values. Since the Enlightenment, the norm has been to view experience rationally, which divorces experience from the passion and the intensity which bodily involvement represents. Passion did not disappear, but it is split off from legitimate work and family life, and reappears in street and media violence. Woman's association with the material, with "matter" versus "spirit" has often placed them in the position of denigrated other, with the material aspects of men being projected onto women. However, if women can bring the material and bodily focus into work, not as something split off, but integrated into decision-making processes, then the potential exists for a reintegration of self into work for both men and women.

The issues of feeling the work in one's bones, in one's body, is a phenomenon I have discussed with women. Whenever there is a profound involvement with the work, these experiences come up. We joke and laugh about it. I am convinced that men also experience these connections. The factor which makes a difference is how relevant the bodily sensations are considered, and whether this experience is viewed as central to the work. To be profoundly connected to the group's experience on a bodily level, without losing the ability to think about it at the same time, is a key indication of a person's self-authorization and connection to the work. This involves an integration of the mind–body split—not only conceptually, which is now accepted professionally—but in experiential learning. It is the ability to remain connected to one's own body, and to relate internal experiences, translated into ideas and images, to the group, that enables self-authorization in the work. Thus, the timing of headaches, belly aches, being turned on, turned off, and how this is connected to the group context are as important as dreams in providing the metaphorical understanding of collective life.

After using the metaphor of the work in one's bones, I discovered that others were using this as a metaphor for creative writing and using one's deep powers. Specifically, Natalie Goldberg's book *Writing Down the Bones* (1986), uses this metaphor for learning to write from the inside. Clarissa Pinkola Estes, the Jungian author of *Women Who Run with the Wolves* (1992), describes the storyteller "singing over the bones" as a description of returning to woman's wilder, more essential self and role as teller of her own myths. One needs to connect on a bodily, internal level to understand the deeper, unconscious dynamics of groups and organizations. These dynamics are embodied in members of organizations; thus organizations become the embodiment of social structures which permit or hinder work and creativity.

## CONCLUSIONS

What has been a central metaphor for me, both in group relations and institutional work, has been a sense of waxing and waning, somewhat like dying and being reborn again, going to hell and back. One is able to vividly witness wide ranges of human experience—engagement and disengagement, creation and destruction—which occur all the time in our social lives.

This metaphor of waxing and waning, of psychological death and rebirth, allows new understandings and insights into the self and collective phenomena which bring us to conference work again and again, despite the enormous amount of energy demanded. There is a sense of renewal and discovery when this connection between one's bones and the group is maintained. This type of awareness is very different from the notion of the isolated hero, who ventures alone on the perilous journey into the unconscious.

One of the loveliest descriptions of conference work was written by Margaret Rioch in her article entitled "Why I Work as a Consultant" (1985). I remembered this tale from the 1970s as a hero's journey, one metaphor for experience and individuation which occupies a profound place in Western thought. Now, re-reading the article in the 1990s and focusing on the introduction, I realize that Margaret Rioch used the metaphor of the hero to describe the journey of the consultant in the group, but that she was actually also addressing issues of death and rebirth within groups. She wrote, much to the consternation of some of the people present at the AKRI Scientific Meeting when she first presented the paper, that:

> The deepest secret and the deepest reason why we engage in this work and in similar pursuits is, I think, mystical and spiritual . . . and yet, what on earth is our 'systems theory' all about, if not the merging of the one in the all? . . . It is perhaps only in death that one finds a complete merging of the self with the other or others, but conferences give brief moments of insight into what that might be like, when the I of the consultant is really the same as the entity called the group. (p. 372, 373)
>
> Thus, Margaret Rioch, one of the most influential woman working in the group relations field, used the metaphors of birth, death, and rebirth for describing group life.

The Tavistock approach emphasizes the containment functions of the group and the conference, as much as the heroic efforts of individuals within the organization. By our concentration on clear boundaries and group as a whole phenomena, this approach focuses on the containment and holding within systems. However, like the surrounding culture, we often revert to emphasizing the heroic, individual model as the dominant issues. These heroics are often needed in order to do difficult aspects of work, but its predominance has often led to an unhealthy narcissism in work. There has already been a conscious shift from a heroic, individual model of work to one of team building and group functioning. This allows many perspectives about work and organizational life, some of which are gender-linked, to be explored in conferences, and to be applied to the institutions in which we work.

Understanding group dynamics comes from the heart, head, and bones of the consultant and group members who are deep-sea diving into the unconscious aspects of collective life. As people bring forth experiences from their very depths, the understanding of how we live and die within our groups, connect and relate in our organizations, becomes clearer. Precisely because women have only recently become "authors" of organizational behavior, women will have to self-authorize to work at the bodily, emotional, as well as intellectual level if gender is to make a difference in organizational structures. Otherwise, women become tokens in positions of authority with the assumption that gender and other characteristics do not make a difference.

Feeling connected to work and feeling fully authorized changes the way we see the roles we adopt and are assigned. This gives us more opportunities to consciously choose our roles, and to survive and to influence the roles we have not always consciously chosen.

Moreover, women self-authorizing from the depths not only changes women's roles, but also changes perspectives about group dynamics, social systems, and work. The relevance of these issues is striking in the context of the alienation in today's workforce. Ed Klein summarized this as follows:

> Major organizations are less safe containers for career and personal aspirations, so people withdraw. Since the psychological contract has been broken in the workplace, there is less trust. With

unclear boundaries, there is more alienation and violence at work, in the community and in politics. Hopefully, a more balanced view provided by women in senior leadership roles will address these concerns by stressing the connections between work and love. (Ed Klein, personal communication, 1996)

Being fully authorized in our work, feeling our work in our bones, is intimately and integrally connected to the self-authorization of women to work and to be instrumental in organizational change.

## REFERENCES

Aries, E. (1976). Interaction patterns and themes of male, female, and mixed groups. *Small Group Behavior, 7*(1), 7–18.

Aries, E. (1982). Verbal and nonverbal behavior in single-sex and mixed-sex groups: Are traditional sex roles changing? *Psychological Reports, 51,* 127–134.

Baker Miller, J. (1976). *Towards a new psychology of women.* Boston: Beacon.

Bion, W. R. (1959). *Experiences in groups.* New York: Basic.

Campbell, A. (1993). *Men, women, and aggression.* New York: Basic.

Canavan-Gumpert, D., Garner, K., & Gumpert, P. (1978). *The success–fearing personality.* Lexington, MA: Heath.

Correa, M. E., Klein, E. B., Stone, W. N., Astrachan, J. H., Kossek, E. E., & Komarrajo, M. A. (1988). Reactions to women in authority: The impact of gender on learning in group relations conferences. *Journal of Applied Behavioral Sciences, 24,* 219–233.

Cytrynbaum, S. (1995). Group relations research progress report: Contextual and methodological issues in the study of gender and authority in Tavistock group relations conferences or "It depends." In K. West, C. Hayden, and R. Sharrin (Eds.), *Chaos or community* (pp. 47–56). Proceedings of the Eleventh Scientific Meeting of the A. K. Rice Institute.

Cytrynbaum, S., & Hallberg, M. (1993). Gender and authority in group relations conferences: So what have we learned in fifteen years of research? In S. Cytrynbaum & S. Lee (Eds.), *Transformations in global and organizational systems: Changing boundaries in the 90's* (pp. 63–73). Proceedings of the Tenth Scientific Meeting of the A. K. Rice Institute.

Cytrynbaum, S., Lee, S., & Wadner, D. (1981). *Devaluation of professional and managerial women: Conceptual viewpoint and intervention strategies.* Unpublished manuscript, Northwestern University.

Estes, C. P. (1992). *Women who run with the wolves: Myths and stories of the wild woman archetype.* New York: Ballantine.

Gold, V. (1993). Intergroup issues in a center of global conflict: The development of Tavistock group relations work in Israel. In S. Cytrynbaum & S. Lee (Eds.), *Transformations in global and organizational systems: Changing boundaries in the 90's* (pp. 21–26). Proceedings of the Tenth Scientific Meeting of the A. K. Rice Institute.

Gold, V., Hayward, M., & Lee, E. (1995). Internal caring: The role of administration in Tavistock group relations conferences. In K. West, C. Hayden, & R. Sharrin (Eds.), *Chaos or community* (pp. 177–194). Proceedings of the Eleventh Scientific Meeting of the A. K. Rice Institute.

Goldberg, N. (1986). *Writing down the bones.* Boston: Shambala.

Griffin, S. (1978). *Woman and nature.* New York: Harper & Row.

Griffin, S. (1995). *The eros of everyday life.* New York: Doubleday.

Gustafson, N., & Cooper, L. (1985). Collaboration in small groups: Theory and technique for the study of small group processes. In A. Colman & M. Geller (Eds.), *Group relations reader* (Vol. 2, pp. 139–150). Washington, DC: A. K. Rice Institute.

Hennig, M., & Jardim, A. (1977). *The managerial woman.* New York: Doubleday.

Hooks, B. (1990). *Yearning: Race, gender, and cultural politics.* Boston: South End Press.

Horner, M. (1972). Toward an understanding of achievement-related conflicts in women. *Journal of Social Issues, 28,* 157–173.

Kanter, R. M. (1977). *Men and women of the corporation.* New York: Basic.

Kingston, M. H. (1976). *The woman warrior.* New York: Ballantine.

Klein, M. (1957). *Envy and gratitude.* London: Tavistock.

Levinson, D. J., Darrow, D., Klein, E. B., Levinson, M. H., & McKee, J. B. (1978). *The seasons of a man's life.* New York: Knopf.

Miller, E. J. (1985). The politics of involvement. In A. D. Colman & M. H. Geller (Eds.) *Group relations reader* (Vol. 2, pp. 383–397) Washington, D.C.: A. K. Rice Institute.

Reardon, K. K. (1995). *They don't get it, do they? Communication in the workplace—Closing the gap between women and men.* Boston: Little, Brown.

Rioch, M. (1985). Why I work as a consultant. In A. D. Colman & M. H. Geller (Eds.), *Group relations reader* (Vol. 2, pp. 365–381). Washington, DC: A. K. Rice Institute.

Tavris, C. (1992). *The mismeasure of women.* New York: Touchstone/ Simon & Schuster.

Turquet, P. (1974). Leadership: The individual and the group. In G. S. Gabbard, J. J. Hartman, & D. Mann (Eds.), *Analysis of groups* (pp. 337–371). San Francisco: Jossey-Bass.

Turquet, P. (1985). Leadership: The individual and the group. In A. Colman & M. Geller (Eds.), *Group relations reader* (Vol. 2, pp. 71–87). Washington, DC: A. K. Rice Institute.

Wolf, N. (1993). *Fire with fire: The new female power and how it will change the 21st century.* New York: Random House.

# 13

## The Myths We Lead By

### Faith Gabelnick, Ph.D.

Myths form the unconscious backbone for societal and organizational structures. Indeed, we learn about our social assumptions through stories which project our representational arrangements. This chapter will present and explore a variety of tales that presume different ideas about leadership and organizational structure. Some of the tales presented early in this paper point to heroic psychosocial assumptions that have informed educational and corporate arrangements and still form the underpinnings of how we think about leadership and authority. The later tales described herein offer other kinds of relational assumptions that are being expressed currently through "new" and futuristic literature on leadership. This paper hypothesizes that moving away from the heroic model and incorporating a more collaborative, gender-neutral, and process approach toward leading and learning is not a new concept but is embedded in our cultural psyches and is therefore available to us now. The so-called new leadership is actually a linking with forms other than the heroic, and the

323

voices for that new leadership are found with women and with peoples who have not yet occupied places in corporate board-rooms. It is important that we understand these mythic arrangements and the assumptions about authority, because if we are to change significantly the way we work and learn together, we must make conscious and examine openly these other frames.

In sum, this is a paper about the interrelationship of myth and organizational leadership. Jill Janov writes in *The Inventive Organization: Hope and Daring at Work* (1994):

> When we see ourselves and our organizations in the process of becoming, we can act with greater awareness about our process. We can better understand that how we go about change—how we make the journey—determines the outcome, the destination we reach. . . . To change the destination, we must change the process by which we make the journey. To do this, we have to be willing to examine and give up some of our entrenched assumptions. Many of these beliefs may be old friends—so old we cannot be sure when they originated. (p. 24)

## THE HEROIC JOURNEY

Once there was a young man; call him a prince; call him a manager. He wanted a prize; call her a princess; call her a promotion. He encountered a wise person who said: "In order to gain what you want, you have to travel over unknown territory, meet many strangers, climb three dangerous mountains, kill three fierce creatures, and bring back a snippet of their fur as proof of your victories. If you return, you will receive what you most desire." He followed this advice, he returned a hero, and he received what he most desired. For a while he lived happily but alas not forever after. During his fortysomethingth year he looked around and found that he yearned again; call it a midlife transition; call it a divorce. He felt as if he did not understand who he was; old urgings emerged to write, travel again, reexamine what he really wanted. Remembering his mentor's advice, he decided to take another journey and set off to climb another mountain, but because he was older and more experienced in traveling, he went with others and he gave himself a time frame, call it a sabbatical, to accomplish his task. Thus, he went to the Himalayas on a mountain climbing expedition. His goal was to get to the top and to remind himself of his virility, his corporate stamina, and retrieve that earlier ambition and energy. He prepared extensively for the trek for he feared altitude sickness, and he went with others because he needed the new technology for this higher mountain. Things were going pretty much as he expected when suddenly he and his group encountered a frail old man, a Tibetan, who seemed disoriented and suffering from exposure and altitude sickness. Other climbing groups who encountered this man tried to pass him off to the next group because they were anxious to proceed to the top. He, too, was made impatient by this distraction and somewhat angry that the man was so ill clad and undernourished. To bring him back to the camp would entail going down 1500 feet and delaying the completion of the journey in the allotted time frame. Instead the men decided to set him in a sunny, visible place with some food and hope that he would revive or that another group would take other action. When they reached the base camp near the top of the mountain, one of the climbers turned to our hero and asked, "How does it feel to murder a man?" Our hero was stunned. The end to this story was the beginning of another.

When he returned, he wrote an article about his experiences on the mountain that he called, "The Parable of the Sadhu," which was published in the *Harvard Business Review* in 1983. Bowen McCoy, the traveler in Tibet, realized that he had missed an important opportunity to change the way he understood power relationships. Although he was only able to ask questions and not ready to frame a different paradigm for understanding, there was a part of his psychic intelligence that was mobilized to search for other models for action. McCoy realized that the sadhu was operating on different assumptions, and he discovered dramatically that although he was attempting to take a sabbatical from corporate life and explore new territory, he brought to Tibet his heroic assumptions and enacted them on the mountain. Wrote McCoy:

> For each of us, the sadhu lives. Should we stop what we are doing and comfort him; or should we keep trudging up toward the high

pass? . . . What is the nature of our responsibility if we consider ourselves to be ethical persons? Perhaps it is to change the values of the group so that it can, with all its resources, take the other road. (p. 108)

Once there was a young woman, call her a princess; call her a manager. Like many women of her generation she lacked a good mother; call her a mentor; call her a friend. Instead she had a wicked stepmother who was intimidated by her good looks and potential and wished to destroy her. Both of these women spent a lot of time paying attention to how others saw them; the younger was content with adoration because she assumed that she would be preparing for her role as adorer and support to her partner, call him her husband; call him her boss. The older woman was less sanguine about the future, and she worried constantly about young women who could supplant her in her marriage, in her office. So, whenever she saw her stepdaughter, she also saw these other creatures who were potential competitors for the prizes she had won. When the tension became too much, she decided to destroy her. She tried many ways, poison apples, scorpionlike combs, as well as the more conventional ways such as nagging and undercutting. The young woman's self-image began to fade, but miraculously, the young woman met a charming person who saw her as the answer to his search and asked her to be with him forever after. She accepted gratefully. Yet like our hero, she, too, became restless after a while. She grew tired of being the object of everybody's searches and fears, and she determined to set off on her own. Like the stories she had read, she decided that she needed to slay a lot of dragons and climb many mountains. So she went to law school while she stayed married and raised her kids. She began to look at the many younger women who were entering law school as competitors; she urged her daughters to go to the right schools and to have fast track careers, and she prided herself on her mentoring of them. She joined an athletic club and developed an intense, pinched look. People called her successful. Sitting down in front of the mirror again, she saw her stepmother.

These two retellings of heroic journeys are very familiar and appear everywhere in Western culture. Men and women become partners in these journeys and persons of different cultures are often abandoned or killed in the quest for power. We have been taught to think of the heroic themes as reliable guideposts for an effective, satisfying life. "And they lived happily ever after" is the siren song for many of us even as the daily newspapers broadcast evidence to the contrary. We want to believe that heroes are good people who do those things that we want to be able to do. Heroes hold out hope that good will triumph and that disappointment is transitory; that effort is rewarded, and that we will eventually be recognized for the essentially good persons we know ourselves to be. The American ideal is a full-color version of this folktale. Success means triumph over external adversity; it means being contained and focused, intent on a goal; it means that we know our place and that we respect our elders until we are tapped to succeed them. Yet as we see in these tales, there are other less admirable elements in these stories. Heroes succeed by vanquishing or killing those who are different or who come from different cultures. To succeed as a hero, therefore, one must destroy. Wars are the most majestic platforms for creating heroes because the primary task of a war is to win by vanquishing. Our cities are filled with statues and other tributes to those who "served" their country by making sure that foreign invaders did not reach our shores. Interestingly, when soldiers came back from Vietnam and did not receive a hero's welcome, some elements of our society were signaling a change in the platform that was tolerable for creating heroes, not that heroes were not wanted. The heroes of the sixties were those who tried to vanquish the establishment, another alien group, and the newcomers, the women and persons of color, quickly created their own heroes who also tried to slay establishment dragons. Nothing changed in the paradigm of power.

Heroes who receive the most attention in our society have been male, and, since they have been the creators of most of the corporations and educational institutions, they have set up models that reflected their own vision of the world and its leadership. The patterns of the journey toward a higher office or goal are embedded in our tenure system in academia and in most organizational personnel structures. The value is that higher is better, and success means progress toward an upward goal. How frustrating, it is, then, to underrepresented groups in our society who see and to some extent buy into this system, but then are excluded from competing in it. Susan Faludi's study, *Backlash* (1991), provides fascinating data about how women framed their own paradoxical positions during the 1980s. Many women who had "successful" careers gave them up in favor of having children, and many who had children started fast track careers. Neither group seemed content because the paradigm had not shifted. Success from the hero's point of view was still seen as "moving up the ladder," but success from a heroine's point of view included "doing it all" or being a superwoman. Women were exhausted and angry, and many started to drop out of high level positions and rethink their priorities. Something was wrong with the picture that everyone was drawing.

## THE HEROIC SHIFT

If the heroic myth is comforting, even perversely so, then moving to change it can be terrifying. One of the reasons Faludi's book has been so popular is that she has noted the backlash associated with some women's challenge of the heroic model. Again, what looks like political rhetoric or social reconstruction harks back to more essential elements in psychodynamic relationships.

Maxine Hong Kingston's novel, *The Woman Warrior* (1989), is an autobiographical novel about a first generation Chinese American heroine. The novel is constructed through a lyric tapestry of myth and narrative and connects Kingston's own development with her relationship to her mother and her heritage. Like any heroic mentor, her mother told her tales "to grow up on" and thereby instructed her in how to live and succeed in their culture. The heroic shift occurs as Kingston begins to separate and individuate from her mother and to some extent from her culture. It is from this emerging stance that she writes her text and captures for us the complexity of this paradigm shift.

In the opening story, "No Name Woman," Maxine is warned by her mother not to relay this tale to anyone else. Thus she begins her heroic awakening by being instructed to be silent! Breaking the silence forms the motivation for writing the book. The tale concerns a village where the men leave to go on their heroic journeys; the women are, for the most part, left behind to be fetched when the men reach the golden mountain (also known as San Francisco) or some other lucrative destination. There is much poverty in the village and a sense of constraint while waiting for the men who have left to return and save the village. Inexplicably, Maxine's aunt becomes pregnant. Gradually her family notices and the villagers notice, too, because her pregnancy occurs well after the time when her husband left. As the time for delivery nears, the villagers, with painted faces and masks, invade her parents' house, slaughter the animals, empty the cupboards, and spread blood throughout. Their message is that she and therefore her family have broken the village mores, have cut open a hole in the circle of sameness, and have dared to step forth and claim a separate existence. Later the aunt goes outside in the pigsty to have her baby, and then she drowns both herself and her child in the family well. The author's retelling of this story weaves speculation about who this woman was and how she felt, and wonders about whether she was raped or instead had a wonderful lover who never came forward to claim his partnership with her. In other words, the author wonders whether her aunt is a different kind of hero or simply someone who was trapped, victimized by the system.

By presenting her own speculations about her aunt, Kingston captures psychodynamically the processes needed to create a shift in thinking about leadership and change. The first hypothesis Kingston presents is that her aunt was seduced or raped by another villager, whom presumably she knew. In this scenario, she would be doomed to secrecy because the assault was more shameful to her than to the man. Since the village maintained an overt culture of morality, her pregnancy would indicate a flaw in the community system that it was not willing to acknowledge and own. It would be easier to blame her for a lack of discretion than to acknowledge the existence of something uncontrollable among the villagers. This group denial and her silence would enable her to be targeted as the scapegoat for the intolerance of passion and spontaneity. Our Western understanding of the Garden of Eden and Eve's role as seductress is perhaps the most fundamental casting of woman as an object capable of destroying our idea of security and containment.

The second hypothesis is that instead of someone being acted upon, this aunt, this anonymous villager took a lover with full knowledge of the risks, that she looked at herself in a different way, that she reached for a new life, and created a different dream. Paradoxically, the village seemed to react as if it believed this second interpretation, even though in reality this interpretation was the more unlikely, given this young woman's culture. The severity of the punishment spoke to the presumption of audacity and a different kind of heroism. The community became enraged about difference and terrified that it might allow other forms to emerge. The woman's death, which Maxine Hong Kingston calls a "spite suicide," completes the destruction of the family household by poisoning the well. Both the family and the community will not be able to "swallow" what has happened.

It is not easy to forget this story. The strength of the community's feeling about deviance is so impressive that it is willing to turn on itself to preserve the illusion of security even as the world as the village has known it is about to change. At one level the village knows it will not be able to function as it has before because many of its men have left, and they have left for economic reasons. In other words, the economic conditions that upheld the safety of the community have so changed that the community must now export some pioneers who are willing to take new risks and learn new ways of being in the world. Yet one of the many myths that this village attempts to contain is that it is not changing and that in order to preserve this myth any deviance must be eradicated. Paradoxically, it continues to try to operate in the old ways even as it begins to change as a social and economic entity. Thus another interpretation emerges from a systemic level: the village hopes that change will not occur and that the pioneers who leave the village will somehow be able to create the same village in another place, and that social and cultural relationships will somehow stay the same. Anyone who challenges that assumption by implying that one or two individuals can take leadership in the village or can satisfy their own desires for love and companionship challenges in a most essential way the core heroic myth.

The villagers' act is a statement about the fear of chaos. Writes Ian Percival (1991):

> If you watch from a bridge as a leaf floats down a stream, you may see it trapped by a small whirlpool, circulate a few times, and escape, only to be trapped again further down the stream. Trying to guess what will happen to a leaf as it comes into view from under the bridge is an idle pursuit in more senses than one: the tiniest shift in the leaf's position can completely change its future course. Small changes lead to bigger changes later. This behavior is the signature of chaos. (p. 10)

The villagers are like the people on the bridge, trying to predict and control human behavior through a complex series of community customs. They fear a single act will lead to larger and uncontrollable events, and they try, by attacking the home, to eradicate the act and more importantly the existence and awareness of the act. Thus, the aunt's suicide and the events of the village must remain secret in order to preserve the illusion of order and predictability and ignorance. Maxine Hong Kingston's mother's breaking of the silence, while at the same time ordering its continuation marvelously describes the linear and nonlinear elements of her psychological—sociological universe. And then, at the end of the chapter, the author joins her aunt, hero or victim, by saying that although she had known this story for many years, she kept it silent and therefore kept the question of her aunt's act unexamined. In writing the novel, Maxine Hong Kingston breaks out of her own circle of victimization and learns through reflection and risk.

Looking outside the novel we can readily see other efforts to preserve the status quo. We observe immigrants coming to the United States, setting up their own enclaves, and establishing their trades or occupations from their country of origin. Assimilation is terrifying to some of the immigrants because it may annihilate the unconscious sense of order and stability that binds communities, and it is equally terrifying to the longer term residents because newcomers can introduce unpredictable elements in a community or organization. Those elements will inevitably produce changes that are not controllable. As our communities become more economically pressed, we huddle together to keep what we have, and we are as terrified as the villagers when corporate or academic leaders begin to use words like restructuring or reengineering. Suddenly our worlds seem more fragile than they were a moment ago, and we want to flee towards a secure space. The most intriguing aspect of this fear is that the unpredictable is ever with us, and that we only act as if we lived in a reasonably predictable world. What is predictable is that our lives will change unexpectedly.

## THE LEADER AS LEARNER

As we near the end of the 20th century, many books are being written about new frameworks for leadership and learning. One of the most intriguing perspectives has been put forth by Peter Senge, who is director of the Systems Thinking and Organizational Learning Program at MIT's Sloan School of Management. His 1990 book entitled *The Fifth Discipline* examines the processes of creating a learning organization based on a systems theory approach to leadership. Moving away from the idea of a single leader or a single solution, Senge and others urge us to think more complexly about issues and to take up the art of looking at both details and generalities, change and stability. Adapting to only one heroic paradigm closes off creativity and life. Senge writes:

> Real learning gets to the heart of what it means to be human. Through learning we re-create ourselves. Through learning we become able to do something we never were able to do. Through learning we reperceive the world and our relationship to it. Through learning we extend our capacity to create, to be part of the generative process of life." (p. 14)

Senge's complex book often refers to the myths by which we live, and he seems to assume a connection between our inner lives and the worlds we construct. The heroic myth, modernized and transformed by women and persons of color, still relies on the individual, the charismatic leader, to impel our society and speak to our futures. Senge and others realize that that model will not work in our future and has not worked in our past. We live and learn in context, and we enable ourselves and our children to see the world in different ways if we are willing to encounter loss and disappointment, if we are willing to make unusual connections, if we can suffer and love.

"The Tale of the Seal Maiden" is a story recounted in *Women Who Run with the Wolves,* by Clarissa Estes. It is a tale about connection and separation, about the joining of individuals who have different backgrounds, different identities, and different ages. It is a tale about a child of this union and the creation of poetry from loss and connection. There are no formal heroes in this story; there is no winner and loser; no one is conquered and no one is killed; yet there is a great deal of sorrow and a great deal of love. It is a different kind of "story to grow up on," another paradigm for learners and leaders.

Once there was a man who lives in the North. He is very lonely, and as he moves in his kayak across the water, his tears dry in the ridges of his face and he can read his words in the frozen breath of the air. One day as he paddles through the northern sea, he hears wonderful voices coming from a near-by rock in the water. As he nears the rock, he sees young maidens dancing nude over the rock. They are happy and innocent and very beautiful. As he moves nearer, the maidens sense his presence, and two of the maidens bend down to put on their sealskins. They again become seals and slip quietly into the water. Before the third maiden is able to put on her sealskin, the man grabs it and says, "I am so lonely. Marry me and be my wife." When the maiden protests, the man makes a bargain with her that if she lives with him for seven years, he will return the sealskin. She agrees, and they live together. Soon she has a child. Her husband teaches the child about the land animals, and the mother teaches the child about the creatures in the sea. The mother sings songs to him; the father teaches him about the trees and the landscape. But as the years pass, the sealwoman begins to lose weight, her skin begins to dry and her eyesight begins to fade. She realizes that it is time to return to the sea and to her seal family, and she asks her husband to return her sealskin. He is dismayed and says that if he returns it, she will leave. Then he runs out of the house. The child hearing this argument also runs out of the house, and as he runs towards the sea, he brushes against a rock and dislodges a package. He brings the package to his mother and, discovering that it is her sealskin, is filled with sadness. He asks her not to leave him. As she puts on the sealskin, her eyes grow brighter and her skin softens. She says that she will take her son with her for a while and breathes air into his lungs so that he may journey with her to the home of the seals. When she returns to her home under the sea, she is greeted with warmth and curiosity, and her son is made welcome. Soon, however, she tells him that he must return to land and he does. As the boy becomes a young man, the people in his culture recognize him for his understanding of the animals on the land and the creatures in the sea. And although they try to harpoon a seal who often swims in the nearby waters, she eludes the hunters and continues to return. The young man becomes a poet and teller of tales, and he is often seen sitting on a rock seemingly talking to a seal who swims nearby.

This story is not heroic but reveals a very different way of leading. There is no magical mountain to be climbed or a dragon to be slain. Instead there are the mundane tasks of raising a child and of the passing on of different heritages. The woman is beautiful but she is also complex and connected to her family. She agrees to marry, and learns to be a mother and a companion. The arrangement is not perfect, but it is not unlike many marriages. Still, the seal maiden's choice to go with this man and be his wife limits her options. She no longer has the freedom to dance on the rocks or to swim freely in the ocean. She takes up a more constrained role as a wife and mother. When it appears that her health is in jeopardy, she moves to claim her husband's part of the agreement, the return of her sealskin. This is a poignant moment in the tale, for her request will bring her vitality and could return him to a more lonely state. He cannot bear this prospect and runs away in despair. And so their child becomes the agent of change. He brings to his mother the material that will produce her transformation, her return to her inner identity, and her ability to live in the future. He acts out of love and loyalty but also out of innocence, for his act propels him into a different relationship with his parents and inaugurates a different level of separation and individuation.

This, too, is a "story to grow up on," but it not a bitter tale nor a superficial one. It is restrained, poignant, and somehow hopeful. Reading this story we are not caught up in wishing things were otherwise; there is a quiet acceptance that living moves in unexpected ways. Why has not this tale become the prominent paradigm for our leaders? Is it because the seal woman plays a different, more instrumental role and that a child is the agent of change? The connection here between mother and son is beautiful and mysterious. The people of the village perceive the young man as unusual as he sits on the rock, and although they have tried to kill the seal, she seems to elude their harpoons. Still, the village does not turn on this young man, nor, most likely, does the father ultimately abandon him. The mother separates herself in order to integrate all parts of herself and to do that she must return to her family of origin. She does not become a career woman who abandons her family to pursue a dream of conquering the corporate world. She instead retrieves her soulskin, that part of her that gives her life, and she breathes life into her son as she makes this transition. Her son learns to understand and accept this mother and to see her as she is—a seal/mother. He knows that he cannot physically follow her, but he can remain connected through his imagination and his creative spirit.

Looking for models in our world we overlook our folktales and the connection with our past. Someone created and told this story, and it has been repeated throughout the northern countries of the world. Its message helps us to understand a different psychological process of leadership and learning, a connected process that moves from one type of learning exhibited by the husband to another type exhibited by the son and his mother. The mother is both a leader and a follower; the child is a leader and a learner. Together they become a complex system and learn with each other.

Senge's idea of learning and its connection to being human is what permeates the sealwoman story. The man is not evil; he is lonely and he lives in a lonely, isolated land. Connections are hard won and prospects for survival, slim. The joy of the seal maidens who bridge the lower and upper worlds reminds him of a part of his inner self that has been frozen and unreachable. In reaching for the maiden's skin, he also reaches out for connection. His approach is clumsy and somewhat aggressive but perhaps he touches something in the maiden because for a while she is able to live with him and bear a son. This child is another occasion for learning. Although the mother pays a price for his birth, she also has an opportunity to create a new being with a more integrated consciousness than neither she nor her husband possesses. She continues her connection with the upper world, and with her husband, they produce a child who can translate and connect the spiritual and the real through song and poetry.

We who work in organizations often find versions of the seal maiden story. This story blends the old paradigm of the conquering hero with a newer negotiated model of relationship. It does not make a case for living on land or in the sea, for choosing one path over another; it offers instead through the product of these two models, a third position that combines aspects of each world into a more poetic framing of our work. The child becomes a different teller of tales, connected and distinct, a teacher and a learner, available to his parents, to his cultures and to himself.

## LEADERS IN THE TWENTY-FIRST CENTURY

The idea of leadership is changing dramatically and so is the idea of a leader. If leaders are not heroes, who are they and how do they arise? Most of our corporations are still organized around these traditional motifs, but more and more companies and educational institutions are working in teams in distributed environments. The work site is everywhere and leaders are multiple. Sharing competencies, working on one project in one place, and then moving to another work site perhaps in a different state or country will become the norm. Leaders are temporary and learning seems unending. The new leaders will have to be able to be followers, will have to be flexible and trustworthy. In the new work environment, skills and competencies will mean more than graduate degrees and pedigrees. And those who work in the organizations will no longer be represented by a single gender and race.

Stanley Herman, an organizational consultant and writer, has taken the work of Lao-tzu and written *The Tao at Work: On Leading and Following* (1994), which reflects in a contemporary style the 2,500-year-old tract on living with complexity. He takes each of the 81 verses and connects it to stories from the corporate world and to his own reflections. Writes Herman:

> It is not necessary to possess all the data to know your best course. Without exhaustive inspection of each and every factor, what feels right and good your spirit will announce. There are times when data are no use, when information distances, and learnedness obscures the heart of certainty. The keen-minded, without hurrying to meetings knows the crucial issues, without analysis recognizes the choices, without programs does what needs doing. The best of all action stems from the fact of being. (p. 79)

The story of Jumping Mouse is a Native American story of exploration and wonder; it is a journey of transformation and discovery; it is yet another "story to grow up on" and stems "from the fact of being." (Storm, 1972)

> Once there was a mouse. . . . He was a busy mouse, searching everywhere, touching his whiskers to the grass, and looking. He was busy as all mice are, busy with mice things. But once in a while he would hear an odd sound. He would lift his head, squinting hard to see, his whiskers wiggling in the air, and he would wonder.

When Jumping Mouse tries to find out what the roaring is all about, he is rebuffed by his fellow mice who are to busy keeping their noses to the ground. He wanders away from his small mice community and meets a raccoon who knows what the "odd

sound" is. He tells the mouse that the sound he hears is the
roaring of the river and invites the mouse to accompany him.
With some trepidation, the mouse goes with the raccoon to see
this thing called a river and then assumes that he can return to
his community and to his work of "examining and collecting."
When he sees the river, he is awestruck by its power and complexity, but when he peers into the river and sees his reflection, he
observes a frightened mouse. A frog who "has been given the
gift from birth to live both above and within the river" offers to
give the mouse some medicine power. The frog says, "crouch as
low as you can, and then jump as high as you are able. You will
have your medicine" (p. 73). When the mouse jumps, he beholds
the sacred mountains and is determined to go back to his community and share this new knowledge. However, when he returns,
his mouse community thinks he is crazy. Using the "data" of his
being wet, the mice conclude that he has had a close call with an
eagle or other animal who has attempted to eat him, and therefore they ignore him. However, the little mouse cannot forget his
vision and the possibility that his vision holds for him. He feels
drawn to move away from his community and the assumptions
about his identity which the community holds. He moves out into
the unknown as a learner and a leader of his destiny.

The mouse's journey brings him into contact with many
strange new animals, many of whom, he discovers, need his help.
When he meets the great buffalo who is sick and dying, the buffalo says that he has been told that only the "eye of a mouse can
heal me. But little brother, there is no such thing as a mouse"
(p. 78). When the mouse hears this, he is stunned and frightened,
but he decides to give one of his eyes to the buffalo. When he
does, the buffalo recovers and is able to walk across the prairie
and shield the mouse from the eagles who are looking to eat him.
When the buffalo leaves the mouse at the edge of the prairie, he
encounters another ailing animal, a wolf, who seems to be senile.
Realizing his power, the mouse offers to give him his second eye
and restore the wolf's memory. Then the wolf is able to lead the
blind mouse to the sacred mountains and the great medicine
lake. Because the mouse is blind, he knows he is at risk of being
eaten by the eagle. When he hears an eagle approaching, he

prepares himself. "And the eagle hit. Jumping mouse went to sleep. Then he woke up. The surprise of being alive was great, but now he could see!" Soon the familiar voice of the frog asks him again if he wants some medicine, and when he says yes, the same instructions are given: "Then crouch down as low as you can . . . and jump as high as you can." When jumping mouse obeyed, "The wind caught him and carried him higher." " 'Do not be afraid,' the voice called to him. 'Hang on to the wind and trust!' " And as he trusts and hangs on to the wind, his sight becomes clearer and he sees the frog below. The frog calls out to him, "You have a new name. . . . You are eagle!' " (pp. 84–85)

This tale recounts a different kind of encounter with change. It includes the community that wants to remain intact; it includes a lonely voyager who meets others along the way; it includes connection and contact with strangers and the unknown, but this Indian tale moves us to a different position in relation to change and transformation. This is a tale about a different kind of hero, an innocent, a journeyer who does not have a majestic goal in mind but does have a vision of where he wants to be. Most notably, his journey involves giving up or giving away part of his current vision and "losing" his sight so that he can see more clearly. He heals others by giving away a part of himself, not by killing off an enemy. In fact, he yields to a traditional predator and in so doing discovers even greater power and illumination.

What we learn from this tale is that if we stay in our communities of common heritage and knowledge, we can preserve the illusion of feeling safe and wise. Yet if we listen and dream, we notice that there are worlds beyond our imaginings. Those of us who choose a different organizational path may lose our jobs, our identities, even our lives, but the result may be a fuller, deeper, more inclusive experience which makes the old ways a memory of a former life. This tale teaches us that learners are leaders; that an innocent, a young journeyer, can affect her environment by not ignoring what she hears and feels, by being available to be thunderstruck, to go to sleep, to awaken with new perspectives. This is the stuff of organizational transformation. Leaders can enable others to follow their visions and tell a story that others can hear. Leaders as learners must enable, must give away some of their own version of authority in order to continue on their journey.

Although many of the transformational experts do not use these tales as bases for their writings, the language and imagery that we find in folktales is everywhere echoed in their more technical and philosophical tracts because the processes are embedded in our human consciousness. In Senge's chapters on mental models and shared visions, he writes:

> A goal limited to defeating an opponent is transitory. Once the vision is achieved, it can easily migrate into a defensive posture of "protecting what we have, of not losing our number-one position." Such defensive goals rarely call forth the creativity and excitement of building something new. . . . A shared vision . . . uplifts people's aspirations. . . . It fosters risk taking and experimentation. . . . Shared visions compel courage so naturally that people don't even realize the extent of their courage. Courage is simply doing whatever is needed in pursuit of the vision. (pp. 207–208)

The tale of the jumping mouse is about the pursuit of such a vision. The mouse literally shares his vision and transforms his identity. This tale is enacted throughout our histories when people of deep conviction confront oppression or injustice. This is a tale about integrity and humility, about risk and change, about the interconnectedness of all beings.

In creating our organizational world, we recreate our internal experiences. Many of these experiences are based upon our own fears of being abandoned by our caregivers and being thrust out into the world to fend for ourselves. Thus the organizations we create become defensive structures against annihilation, and competitive strategies enact the more primary processes of self-preservation and identification with those who could do us harm. These types of oedipal dramas have dominated our Western literature and our society. However, if we open our eyes to other types of configurations embedded in the folktales, we discover a variety of approaches to the same types of challenges, and we discover that heroes can be recognized in unexpected circumstances. The little mouse has an unidentified urge to move out of his confined mouse world. He experiences it as a strange noise that beckons him and makes him lift up his head. As soon as he begins to see that there are different kinds of mountains to seek, he cannot remain at home. Yet his journey is not one of slaughter but one of healing. When he realizes that he has some capacity to enable others to work, he offers what he has, his vision. He is an enabling leader, and although it appears as if he loses his vision by offering it to others, he gains a different kind of illumination and power. He does not seek anything for himself but rather allows himself to be a journeyer and encounter the magic mountains. He learns and teaches and becomes an eagle, a symbol of illumination, and as he becomes an eagle, he connects with all of the natural elements of the world.

Most of us aspire to be eagles, but because we have been raised on the more traditional folklore, we think that we must journey alone and slay dragons. This is the path that is designed through our educational and social systems: we value getting good grades regardless of what we learn, getting admitted to the most prestigious schools regardless of their suitability for our inner needs, choosing a profession more in terms of its economic viability than in terms of our inner vision, choosing our clothes, our partners in terms of their ability to move us forward. It is the old heroic journey. Recent writings from women like Sally Hegelson (*The Female Advantage: Women's Ways of Leadership* [1990]), or Carol Gilligan (*In a Different Voice* [1982]), offer a different image, that of a circular, nonlinear web of connection. The journeyer is not an isolate and does not proceed in a hierarchical fashion. Instead the journeyer moves in different complex spaces and creates different connections. Success is based more on affiliative sensitivity than on material reward. Although the goals to achieve are similar, the pathways that these writers describe are weblike. This web is woven both consciously and unconsciously; it embraces the hierarchical and the accidental. In the sealwoman story and more subtly in *The Woman Warrior*, we see women who are struggling to give voice to their visions. They encounter the type of resistance that new heroes with newer and more radical vision find. Maxine Hong Kingston's aunt is defeated by this opposing vision, but her niece finds a way to reclaim her story and use it as a teaching story for others. Her novel, after all, is about a woman warrior, and the chapters of the book uncover a consciousness that is complex and integrated. The shape of the novel is a series of stories weaving a web of relationship between a mother and a daughter and the intrapsychic journeys they take together. The novel moves from initially portraying the mother as a wicked stepmother to a gradual realization by the daughter of the mother's love and vision for her. When she looks in the mirror at the end of the novel, she sees a strong young woman.

## THE NEW LEADER'S PURPOSE STORY

What we have been providing are types of stories that guide leaders. Many of these stories are faintly grasped because we are not listening to the roaring in our ears that leads us to seek out and discover new stories. Yet we predict that the new leaders are those who listen, who feel, who test, and who are willing to trust the story that they carry within and jump up to perceive the sacred mountains. Writes Senge about leaders whom he has interviewed:

> Although the three leaders with whom I talked operate in completely different industries . . . and although the specifics of their views differed substantially, they each appear to draw their own inspiration from the same source. Each perceived a deep story and sense of purpose that lay behind his vision, what we have come to call the *purpose story*—a larger "pattern of becoming" that gives unique meaning to his personal aspirations and his hopes for their organization. . . . The leader's purpose story is both personal and universal. It defines his or her life work. It ennobles his efforts, yet leaves an abiding humility that keeps him from taking his own successes and failures too seriously. It brings a unique depth of meaning to his vision, a larger landscape upon which his personal dreams and goals stand out as landmarks on a longer journey. It places his organization's purpose, its reason for being, within a context of "where we've come from and where we're headed," and the "we" goes beyond the organization itself to humankind more broadly. In this sense, they naturally see their organization

as a vehicle for bringing learning and change to society. . . . But the stories are also incomplete. They are evolving as they are being told—in fact, they are "*as a result of being told.*" (pp. 346, 351)

The tale of the jumping mouse presents both heroic and nonlinear elements; it speaks to a view of the world which is circular and connected and which recognizes different types of leaders; the leaders do not have a specific gender nor a specific culture. They move in a community of creatures and work with each other to enable, produce and heal. The mouse as innocent moves through various processes that produce a kind of illumination akin to awe. It is this spiritual dimension that moves the conception of leadership into a different realm. The mouse creates her own story by being drawn to seek a vision, and in so doing, she *loses* her old vision and finds new ways of seeing the world. Yet we know, because this is an Indian tale, that the journey for the mouse/eagle is circular, that this mouse is simply on another aspect of his or her learning and that the purpose story finds life because it is being told to others.

When I think about my purpose story, I think of Dorothy in *The Wizard of Oz*, the first film I saw at the age of 4—it terrified me. Although I hid my face in my mother's arm when Dorothy encountered the wizard, the tale of that little girl entered me and guided me through my life. Princes slaying dragons always seemed a little silly to me while people helping others and wandering on their own version of a yellow brick road seemed wondrous and exciting. In the film, the yellow brick road unravels and turns in many ways, and the instructions to "follow the yellow brick road" are so compelling that other paths fall away. Externally, my own development has seemed to have taken a vertical path with my taking on more expanded leadership roles, but my own vision of who I am and what I can be has been shaped by working with others and being privileged to witness and minister to their learning. Dorothy is helped by a tin man, a lion, munchkins, fairy godmothers—all unlikely and unexpected teachers; I have always been helped by unexpected agents. I learned from those who were struggling to grow. They didn't know they were teaching me; I didn't know what I would learn from them.

As a child, my vision for myself far exceeded what my family could imagine, but I acceded to their vision and to the advice of others to remain within the small community. Still, like the little mouse, the world seemed ever to invite me out. When I encountered the magic of teaching, consulting, and writing, I was drawn beyond my family of origin's belief system. When I became afraid to fly in airplanes during my thirties, I understood that my parents' disapproval was, in part, motivating this fear. I imagined myself not being able to "fly," and my reaction was strong and unmistakable. Not flying was not living.

The stories I grew up on derived at first from my parents' view of the world. I was routinely taken to films such as *Snow White* and *Cinderella*. I watched the "Miss America" pageant, dreamily waiting to be chosen for stardom. When at 20, I read *The Feminine Mystique* (1963) and *The Second Sex* (1953), my vision clarified and the world looked different. I began to create my own journey and to leave behind elements that no longer fit. As an adult, I have been struck many times by the eagle of illumination and lost my way as I gained a new perspective. Remembering-forgetting-reremembering—these are the cycles of change within a chaotic learning system. My life, like most, is encompassed by all of these tales. They remind me that others have discovered, long ago, the patterns I retrace, forming a yellow brick road for the psyche. Dorothy's journey was a powerful dream, but she awoke and promised never to disobey again. Many of us stayed with the dream and do not apologize for our visions.

## REFERENCES

de Beauvoir, S. (1953). *The second sex* (H. M. Parshleg, Trans.). New York: Knopf.

Estes, C. P. (1992). *Women who run with the wolves: Myths and stories of the wild woman archetype.* New York: Ballantine.

Faludi, S. (1991). *Backlash.* New York: Crown.

Friedan, B. (1963). *The feminine mystique.* New York: Norton.

Gilligan, C. (1982). *In a different voice: Psychological theory and women's development.* Cambridge, MA: Harvard University Press.

Helgesen, S. (1990). *The female advantage: Women's ways of leadership.* New York: Doubleday.

Herman, S. M. (1994). *The Tao at work: On leading and following.* San Francisco, CA: Jossey-Bass.

Janov, J. (1994). *The inventive organization: Hope and daring at work.* San Francisco, CA: Jossey-Bass.

Kingston, M. H. (1989). *The Woman warrior.* New York: Random House.

McCoy, B. (1983). The parable of the Sadhu. *Harvard Business Review, 61*(5), 103–108.

Percival, I. (1991). Chaos: A science for the real world. In N. Hall (Ed.), *Explaining chaos: A guide to the science of disorder.* New York: Norton.

Senge, P. M. (1990). *The fifth discipline: The art and practice of the learning organization.* New York: Doubleday.

Storm, H. (1972). *Seven arrows.* New York: Ballantine.

# 14

# Future Directions

*Edward B. Klein, Ph.D., Faith Gabelnick, Ph.D.,
and Peter Herr, M.A.*

As the text of this book illustrates, leaders in the future will be required to adopt different approaches from those of the past because of profound societal changes. At the end of the 20th century, changes are occurring at a rate not experienced previously and leaders will need to manage in new ways—or be left behind. New organizations rise and fall in a matter of years rather than decades or centuries. The survival of the fittest is now based on the bottom line. Sound and flexible leadership has, therefore, never been more important.

In the past the dominant power structure made the rules, managed the conflict, and wrote the accepted history. Because of the information explosion and the inability of leaders to control its flow, leaders are now more likely to be challenged. Whether it is the faxed news of Tiananmen Square, leaked government reports, or bomb making on the Internet, information is more readily available. The most powerful executive can be

347

brought down with a well-placed e-mail or fax. Therefore leaders will have to deal with a culture based less on the old dominant–subordinate relationship.

In the future there will be as much concern about supermarkets as superpowers. This will be the case because of an increasing emphasis on service; whether in a specialty store or government agency, service will be the modus operandi. An organization that fails to properly handle transactions will be disadvantaged. If leaders fail to take into account what the market wants, the want will remain, but the institution may be replaced.

Attempts at transforming organizations often falter because of misperceptions of the level of unrecognized anxiety and resistance. In addition, managers called on to help their institutions function effectively in transitional and often turbulent environments need a dynamic systems perspective.

As current trends indicate, workers will be encouraged to manage themselves in their task roles with the requisite authority to effectively perform these roles. Systems will become more streamlined as hierarchical authority structures evolve into more collaborative models. In a global economy managers will have to respond to international marketplaces and work effectively across multiple cultural, ethnic, class, and gender boundaries. One illustration is that organizations are becoming increasingly "feminine." We see this in fields traditionally identified as male: medicine, engineering, the military, and sports. Time will tell whether the feminization of the workplace changes women or whether women change the workplace, as previously noted by Long.

These transformations will require a more sophisticated approach to the psychosocial and systems dynamics that shape modern institutions. The text has provided an understanding of the powerful, often covert processes involved as organizations strive to carry out their tasks. Clearly the structural dimensions of institutions need to be continually modified if leaders and organizations are to function effectively in the next century. This is the case because changes are occurring in the environment as well as within institutions. In the past, when the leader needed to deal with external challenges he could count on a stable and reliable internal structure based on traditional views and beliefs. Currently there is no guarantee that employees will unquestioningly follow the path that leadership dictates.

There are generational issues which also affect organizations. For example, leaders, particularly in the United States, find it difficult to establish their authority in a hierarchical manner. The Baby Boomers, because of their experience with Vietnam, Watergate, and other scandals, find it hard to follow anyone. Their own resistance to formal authority suggests that they will have difficulty managing their own authority. For instance, those who are now middle-aged managers have a hard time with their elders who are more accepting of authority as well as with younger, more questioning people whom they do not understand.

If we think critically about how new leadership patterns will affect executives, managers, and consultants in the 21st century, a number of additional factors need to be taken into account. First, with the demise of guaranteed lifetime employment, there is the changing, unspoken psychological contract. Leaders can no longer count on the uncritical support of their subordinates. Managers are only as good as the last quarter results. The end of the psychological contract makes employees feel like temporary hires, waiting for the next corporate buyout, business cycle downturn, or leadership transition. Employees may bond with the work task, but there is limited bonding to the leader since they no longer experience him as protecting them. Because of this contract violation, major institutions need to find ways to develop job security, career protection, and reduce the focus on excessively compensated executives in order to improve work relations and productivity.

Second, with the increasing number of mergers, acquisitions, and takeovers, executives, managers, and external consultants need to more effectively address the conflicts and anxieties involved in ending personal, community, and work relationships while managing a divestiture or merger. This issue is paramount in the industrial world now and will continue to be so for years to come.

Third, since the majority of Fortune 1000 companies started as family businesses, we need clear examples of how the use of the experience and insight of external consultants help them work effectively with executives in both current and future family businesses. That is, the consultants' own family histories and their reactions to the dynamics of the family business enhance the psychological effectiveness of their work. Such case studies need to be shared with social scientists and managers to help produce more effective adoptation in the future.

Fourth, given the stresses relating to changes in organizational boundaries, an increasing problem involved in long-term consultation will be countertransference, or the transferring of employee emotions and conflicts onto the consultant. This phenomenon occurs as the consultant becomes the vehicle for the expression of employee anger or frustrations. One way to effectively address this problem is for the consultant to work with a "shadow" consultant. This is an approach similar to that of a clinician using a supervisor in order to obtain a more objective perspective on the dynamic processes involved in the therapist–patient relationship.

If we had to predict where in society to look for new organizational developments, we suggest the health care industry. Health care represents one-seventh of the economy; many health related institutions are open to innovation and can therefore provide models for future leadership. This is the case because the health care industry deals with intense competition, rapidly advancing technology, highly educated professionals, and some of the most difficult social issues of the day.

There is little doubt that the transformations discussed in this book cause anxiety for both leaders and those they lead. How leaders manage these anxieties will determine their success in the workplace. It remains unclear whether the work team will be a satisfactory container of employee emotion. While a call for workers to creatively link together is an ideal, connectivity runs counter to individualism and self-reliance. As previously noted by Gabelnick, new visions will have to contend with the old heroic myth of leadership. Nevertheless it still remains a strong and active part of our unconscious as illustrated by the leadership role of the president against the aliens in the movie *Independence Day* and Bob Dole's strong endorsement of the film in the 1996 presidential campaign.

These complex current and predicted future developments suggest that it is a combination of psychodynamic and open systems theories which best helps managers understand the nature, quality, and structure of institutions and the roles of individuals within the organization. It is our hope that such an understanding will translate into more competent management, leadership, and organizational consultation as we move into the 21st century.

# Author Index

Acker, J., 254
Adreasen, N., 165
Agazarian, Y. M., xii, 129, 130, 154, 155, 158, 159n
Aker, S., 202
Alderfer, C. P., 47, 197, 280
Andrews, J., 200
Argyris, C., 23, 214
Aries, E., 302
Armstrong, D., 220
Astrachan, B. M., 178–179
Astrachan, J. H., xii, 281, 307–308

Bain, A., 95, 102–103
Bakan, D., 194, 280
Baker Miller, J., 194, 200, 202, 203, 205, 209, 210, 212, 258, 260, 263, 300
Balin, J., 250, 251
Bamforth, K. W., 70
Barham, P., 55, 170
Bartow, A., 250, 251
Bayes, M., 199, 201, 226, 255
Belenky, M., 194
Bell, G., 55
Bennis, W., 193, 214
Berg, D., 200
Bernauer, J., 169
Bertalanffy, L. von, 132, 175

Best, D. L., 280
Bion, W. R., 7, 61, 66–67, 92, 101, 164, 165, 171, 174, 175, 180, 186, 223–224, 241, 299
Bogdamoff, M., 261
Bohm, D., 69
Bond, J. T., 17
Borker, R., 225
Bowen, M., 172
Breggin, P., 165
Breisach, E., 168
Bridger, H., 86, 180
Brown, D., 261

Campbell, A., 300–301
Canavan-Gumpert, D., 302
Cargill, B., 237
Carpenter, W. T., 172
Carr, A., 77–78, 85
Carter, R. T., 270
Casemore, R., 65
Champy, J., 193
Chattopadhyay, G., 220
Chodorow, N., 225, 226, 235
Chomsky, N., 222–223
Clincy, B., 194
Cohen, A., 204
Comte, A., 166
Cooper, L., 300

353

# Subject Index

359